D1355897

Colonial Chaos in the Southern Red Sea

Today, the countries bordering the Red Sea are riven with instability. Why are the region's contemporary problems so persistent and interlinked? Through the stories of three compelling characters, *Colonial Chaos in the Southern Red Sea* sheds light on the unfurling of anarchy and violence during the colonial era. A noble Somali sultan, a cunning Yemeni militia leader and a Machiavellian French merchant ran amok in the southern Red Sea in the nineteenth and twentieth centuries. In response to colonial hostility and gunboat diplomacy, they attacked shipwrecks, launched piratical attacks and traded arms, slaves and drugs. Their actions contributed to the transformation of the region's international relations, redrew the political map, upended its diplomatic culture and remodelled its traditions of maritime law, sowing the seeds of future unrest. Colonisation created chaos in the southern Red Sea. This book offers an interdisciplinary approach to understanding the relationship between the region's colonial past and its contemporary instability.

NICHOLAS W. STEPHENSON SMITH received his PhD in African history from Northwestern University, Illinois, where his research won awards including an International Dissertation Research Fellowship from the SSRC. His research was funded by the UK Arts and Humanities Research Council and was nominated for the Royal Historical Society History Today Prize. He has written several articles, including for the *Journal of Eastern African Studies* and Routledge Series on Indian Ocean and Trans-Asia. He is currently qualifying as a maritime solicitor in the UK.

Colonial Chaos in the Southern Red Sea

A History of Violence from 1830 to the Twentieth Century

NICHOLAS W. STEPHENSON SMITH

CAMBRIDGE
UNIVERSITY PRESS

CAMBRIDGE
UNIVERSITY PRESS

University Printing House, Cambridge CB2 8BS, United Kingdom

One Liberty Plaza, 20th Floor, New York, NY 10006, USA

477 Williamstown Road, Port Melbourne, VIC 3207, Australia

314–321, 3rd Floor, Plot 3, Splendor Forum, Jasola District Centre,
New Delhi – 110025, India

103 Penang Road, #05–06/07, Visioncrest Commercial, Singapore 238467

Cambridge University Press is part of the University of Cambridge.

It furthers the University's mission by disseminating knowledge in the pursuit of
education, learning, and research at the highest international levels of excellence.

www.cambridge.org
Information on this title: www.cambridge.org/9781108845663
DOI: 10.1017/9781108990400

© Nicholas W. Stephenson Smith 2021

This publication is in copyright. Subject to statutory exception
and to the provisions of relevant collective licensing agreements,
no reproduction of any part may take place without the written
permission of Cambridge University Press.

First published 2021

A catalogue record for this publication is available from the British Library.

Library of Congress Cataloging-in-Publication Data
Names: Smith, Nicholas W. S., author.
Title: Colonial chaos in the southern Red Sea : a history of violence from 1830 to the
    twentieth century / Nicholas W. Stephenson Smith, Northwestern University, Illinois.
Description: New York : Cambridge University Press, 2021. | Includes bibliographical
    references and index.
Identifiers: LCCN 2021019458 (print) | LCCN 2021019459 (ebook) |
    ISBN 9781108845663 (hardback) | ISBN 9781108964777 (paperback) |
    ISBN 9781108990400 (epub)
Subjects: LCSH: Red Sea Region–History. | Red Sea Region–Politics and government. |
    Red Sea Region–Foreign relations. | Red Sea Region–Colonization. | Violence–Red Sea
    Region–History. | BISAC: HISTORY / Africa / General | HISTORY / Africa / General
Classification: LCC DT39 .S65 2021 (print) | LCC DT39 (ebook) | DDC 953/.04–dc23
LC record available at https://lccn.loc.gov/2021019458
LC ebook record available at https://lccn.loc.gov/2021019459

ISBN 978-1-108-84566-3 Hardback

Cambridge University Press has no responsibility for the persistence or accuracy
of URLs for external or third-party internet websites referred to in this publication
and does not guarantee that any content on such websites is, or will remain,
accurate or appropriate.

In Memory of David

Contents

Figures

Maps

Acknowledgements

This book began life almost a decade ago. It has been a long trip, encompassing many people and places. Among others at SOAS, I am especially grateful to Richard Reid, Wayne Dooling, James McDougall and Tom McCaskie. I truly appreciate the kindness and the confidence they showed in me. I am grateful to the UK Arts and Humanities Research Council Research Masters scholarship at the School of Oriental and African Studies (SOAS) for financial assistance.

The bulk of the research and development of this project was completed in the history department at Northwestern University. The dissertation project was supervised by Jon Glassman, to whom I am very grateful as a scholar and a friend. The Program of African Studies (PAS), Nicholas D. Chabraja Center for Historical Studies and the Buffet Institute for Global Affairs provided various forms of vital support for language learning, research visits and conference attendance. The Social Science Research Council allowed me to conduct a year of international research in Kenya, Ethiopia, France, Italy, Switzerland and the UK via their International Dissertation Research Funding scheme. I am grateful to the many archival staff and interviewees who have assisted me. Aliki Arkomani in the Asian and African Studies Reading Room went out of her way to help me track down various obscure and moth-eaten files.

Several others read drafts and provided valuable feedback at several stages. David Schoenbrun and Rajeev Kinra were generous dissertation committee members, guides and readers whose advice went beyond the call of duty and beyond my own graduation from Northwestern University. Henri Lauzière was generous with his time and erudition, reading sections of the draft and providing invaluable assistance on the aspects of this study that relate to the Arabian Peninsula. Will Reno was a wise, well-travelled and free-thinking guide to the world of politics and political science. His direct and indirect input enriched this study considerably.

Other faculty provided advice from which this project has benefited. Carl Petry and Deborah Cohen were particularly generous. I am grateful to Helen Tilley, Tessie Liu, Elzbieta Foeller-Pituch and Daniel Immerwahr for providing feedback on versions of this project in presentation or paper format. Thanks are due to Annerys Cano, who made day-to-day life in the department a pleasure. Several friends brightened life and took a generous interest in my research. I offer special thanks to Raevin, Alvaro, Brock and Melissa for their kindness and enthusiasm. Andy Rosengarten laboured through the entire manuscript at a critical moment, in record time, providing invaluable comments and encouragement just when I was flagging. I am grateful to her; she could have been out in the Namibian sun. Jayman has been an unwavering source of support and cheer. Abdeta Beyene was a font of knowledge and introductions in Ethiopia.

Several others beyond the sanctuary of Northwestern University have offered advice, hospitality and encouragement. I am grateful to the anonymous reviewers and editors at Cambridge University Press who provided careful and edifying criticism. Warm thanks to Christopher Chien, whose incisive and thorough edits helped improve these pages. In East Africa: Abdisaid, James Smith, Jay Bahadur, Ayan Mahamoud and Roger Middleton all provided excellent guidance. Shelagh Weir provided helpful advice on researching the history of the Tihama. Guillaume de Monfreid generously took the time to talk to me about his grandfather in Paris. In London, Agustin Blanco-Bazan read an early draft and provided valuable advice. David Anderson, Iza Hussin, Michael Walls, Ian Urbina, Lee Cassanelli and Simon Layton all provided valuable advice as well as thought-provoking conversation for which I am indebted. Sam Fury Childs Daly provided me with characteristically kind and smart comments and support throughout, as well as providing useful comments on a draft of this study. I am grateful to them all and several others. All shortcomings are my own.

Many more besides have offered cheer, wisdom, reassurance and hospitality. I am grateful to Ruth for her advice on the copy in the project's latter stages. Imo was the perfect guide to the world of shipping in London. Aileen is the wisest person I know. My Italian research was immeasurably enriched by Marlis, Manlio, Bettina,

Marzia, Daphne, Roberto, Daniele and Petra – who are friends and gracious hosts. Finally, I am deeply thankful to Oliver and Freya, to Mum and to Mairi. They are unwavering supporters. Without them, it really would have been impossible.

Note on the Text

Aban – Somali word connoting the English-language idea of 'broker', 'guide' or even 'protector'. Abans came from a ruler's retinue and lineage. Under the care of an aban, a foreigner became an honorary member of the ruler's lineage or subjects. Abans performed a simultaneously commercial, ceremonial and diplomatic role. An outsider's relationship with their aban was far from transactional; it involved the exchange of gifts and hospitality as well as payments of customs on purchased goods.

Abdali Sultanate – The Abdali Sultanate was a small independent kingdom ruling over the far southwestern corner of the Arabian Peninsula. The Abdali family was originally from Sanaa and served as representatives of the Imams of Sanaa (see Zaydi Imamate/Imams of Sanaa), guaranteeing the caravan routes between the Yemeni highlands and the seaport of Aden and collecting customs and duties on passing trade. In about 1740, the Abdali ceased paying dues to the Imams of Sanaa and governed independently for the next century. The Abdali Sultan's relations with the British East India Company (EIC) began in the 1830s, partly through trade, and partly because the EIC identified Aden as a potential coaling station on a proposed steam-shipping route between India and Egypt. After a series of disagreements over the EIC's rights to the port, the reigning Abdali Sultan, Sultan Muhsin, signed a truce with the EIC in 1843, though he did not surrender Abdali sovereignty. Thereafter, Aden remained a small Anglo-Abdali enclave, known to the British as the Aden Protectorate. The Abdalis' capital moved to Lahej, a fertile and slightly elevated region just north of Aden, on the road to the caravan town of Ta'izz, which in turn led to Sanaa. The sultans became the pre-eminent local rulers in the British Aden Protectorate. They took part in the imperial durbars in India in the late nineteenth century and were often referred to by British officials as the sultans of Lahej.

Abyssinia/Ethiopia – The term Abyssinia (derived from the Arabic Habesha) is used throughout the text to refer to the pre-twentieth-century empires and kingdoms of the northeast African highland zone, comprising contemporary Ethiopia and Eritrea. Ethiopia refers to the nation-state of Ethiopia (and is a toponym derived from the much more general Greek term 'Aethiop', meaning roughly 'sub-Saharan African', incorporated into Amharic and adopted as the national name by Emperor Haile Selassie in the 1930s). Thus, Abyssinia as used in the text indicates the region subject to the Kingdom of Aksum, the Zagwe dynasty, the Solomonic Empire, the Muslim Ifat Kingdom, and so on.

Aman – Arabic word which literally translates as 'security'. The Arabic term connotes the clemency offered by Muslims to non-Muslims, or even Muslim foreigners, for the sake of trade.

Dar al-'ahd – Arabic phrase meaning the 'territory of truce, treaties or agreements'. A concept that was introduced by early Islamic rulers and jurists to describe the middle lands that, while not non-Muslim, were also not fully recognised as part of the Islamic ecumene. In the view of some Muslim scholars, the dar al-'ahd was a standalone category of territory equal in status to those described by the terms "dar al-harb" and "dar al-Islam" (see the following two entries in this list). By contrast, other Muslim scholars considered it a subcategory within the dar al-Islam. None of the references in the text are intended as a comment on this debate or on the status of particular regions mentioned in the text. Rather, the term is used to highlight the important role and standing that treaties played in Islamic jurisprudence.

Dar al-harb – Arabic phrase literally meaning the 'territory of war', referring to non-Muslim lands. Generally interpreted as connoting confessional differences rather than a summons to fight. Note that the concept does not derive from the Qur'an but rather came into use by Muslim jurors and rulers in the eighth century.

Dar al-Islam – Arabic phrase literally meaning the 'territory of Islam', or in other words the lands under the spiritual and/or temporal control of the Caliph. As with dar al-harb, the concept does not derive from the Qur'an but rather came into use by Muslim jurors and rulers in the eighth century.

East India Company/British India – A trading company founded in London in the late 1500s. The Company became highly influential in the trade with South Asia in the 1600s. By the 1700s, it was a full-blown commercial and military organisation, more highly capitalised than the Bank of England. In the 1700s it won military victories over several South Asian kingdoms – and their European allies – securing even wider access to South Asia's markets. Notable EIC victories included those against the Nawab of Bengal at the Battle of Plassey in 1757 and the Sultan of Mysore at the Siege of Srirangapatna in 1799. By the nineteenth century, the EIC had provinces from Baluchistan to Burma, as well as satellite ports, for example in Aden on the Arabian Peninsula and Basra in the far north of the Persian Gulf. In response to accusations of corruption and misrule among its leadership, and also in reaction to the Company's outsized power, British Prime Minister William Pitt passed The India Act in 1784, which made the Company subject to parliamentary scrutiny. In 1813 and 1833, parliament stripped the Company of its monopoly over trade in South Asia and made the Company an instrument of the British Crown. In 1858, the Government of India Act transferred the Company's role to the British Crown, ushering in the period of direct British government rule in India known as the 'British Raj', which lasted until India's split from Pakistan and their independence in 1947.

Egyptian Empire – term used to describe the historical empires of Egypt, which spanned the Mediterranean in the north to Juba and the border with contemporary Uganda in the south. Nineteenth-century Egypt was a semi-autonomous province of the Ottoman Empire, ruled by descendants of the Mamluk Empire, a slave dynasty of Perso-Turkic administrators whose pre-eminence in the Middle East dated to the first Islamic Caliphates. A series of strong Ottoman-Egyptian governors, who used the Persian title 'khedive', expanded the empire south into what is today Sudan and contemporary Eritrea. A number of European administrators served in the Ottoman-Egyptian Empire's government, including Major General Charles Gordon, who served as Governor-General of Sudan. Protests against Gordon's rule – part of a widespread opposition to rising British interference in Egypt – culminated in a British invasion of the Sudanese region and the British occupation of Egypt from 1882 to 1956. Contemporary Egypt is far smaller than the historical empires that came before it.

Hadhramaut – the Hadhramaut consists of a series of river valleys, or wadis, which run down from the Yemeni highlands towards the Indian Ocean coast of the southern Arabian Peninsula. The Hadhramaut stretches east from Aden towards the border with the Omani sphere. The main port of the Hadhramaut is Mukalla, where the al-Kasadi sultans ruled until they were displaced by the Ku'ayti dynasty in the mid-to-late nineteenth century. At the same time as the Ku'ayti dynasty (who had served as officials and military personnel in the government of Hyderabad in South Asia) conquered the region, Britain increased its political contact with the region to the east of Aden, claiming the Hadhramaut region as part of the Aden Protectorate in 1888. The region became part of South Yemen in 1967.

Ifat Sultanate/Adal Sultanate/Afar Sultanates – the Afar are an ethno-linguistic group living in the region surrounding the Gulf of Tadjoura. Their influence once stretched well into the Abyssinian highlands, into the historical Abyssinian province of Shoa, now semi-contiguous with the Oromo population of Ethiopia. Afar-speaking peoples made up the majority of the population of the Ifat Kingdom, a large Muslim empire ruled by the Walashma dynasty which was centred around the western Somali port of Zeila and the Gulf of Tadjoura, and wielded influence up the Awash river valley and indeed across much of eastern Abyssinia between the thirteenth and fifteenth centuries. In the early fifteenth century, the Ifat Sultanate was conquered by the Solomonic rulers of highland Abyssinia. However, the Muslim state was partly resurrected by the Adal Sultanate, which expanded dramatically under the influence of Ahmad al-Ghazi in the 1520s and 1530s. After a battle with the Abyssinians and their Portuguese allies, al-Ghazi died and the Adal Sultanate went into retreat, splintering into a number of Afar Sultanates, including the Sultanate of Aussa; the Sultanate of Harar, reputedly the fourth most holy city in Islam in the Ifat-Adal era; the Sultanate of Tadjoura; and the Sultanate of Rohayto, which we will meet in Chapter 4.

Majerteen Sultanate – ruled the northeastern tip of the Horn of Africa, a region roughly contiguous with contemporary northern

Puntland, from the mid-eighteenth century. A Muslim polity and a successor to the Warsangeli Sultanate, which ruled contemporaneously with the Ifat and Adal Sultanates to the east. Like the Warsangeli, the Majerteen trace their origins to Darod, a foundational figure whom the origin story relates was a member of Prophet Muhammad's Quraysh lineage and came to Somalia by being wrecked on the coastline in the twelfth or thirteenth century CE. In the nineteenth century the Majerteen sultans entered a series of treaty agreements with the British in Aden, which initially focused on the protection of British ships. However, these agreements became increasingly detrimental to the Majerteen sultans' sovereignty as the century wore on, and stoked division between the sultan and other members of the Majerteen aristocracy. The Sultanate divided in the 1880s, when the ruler of Alula established a rival sultanate in Hobyo. Both Sultanates became Italian colonies in the 1890s.

Mughal Empire – the Mughal Empire was established by descendants of Ghengis Khan who by the 1400s had strong links to the Persianised Timurid Empire in central Asia. The first Mughal Emperor, Babur, conquered Samarkand, the Afghan polities and the Delhi Sultanate in the late 1400s and early 1500s. Babur's grandson, Emperor Akbar, conquered the wealthy coastal sultanate of Gujarat in the 1570s. By the seventeenth century, the Mughals dominated the Indo-Gangetic plain and Himalayan foothills, which stretch from what is today Pakistan and Afghanistan all the way to Bengal and contemporary Bangladesh. It was the rise of the Mughal Empire (and especially its powerful province in Gujarat), coinciding with the advent of the Cape route from Europe to Asia, which spurred the huge rise in Eurasian and global trade, particularly in South Asian textiles and spices, and paved the way for the success of the EIC. The rise of the Mughals and the attendant spike in international commerce prompted other regional and South Asian states, notably the Marathas and Persians, to expand. Regional rivalry weakened the Mughals and allowed the EIC to expand. In 1818 the Maratha Confederacy, which included wealthy Gujarat, collapsed following war with the EIC. The EIC deposed the last Mughal Emperor, Bahadur Shah, in 1857. Just under two decades later, Queen Victoria was crowned Empress of India.

Oman, Zanzibar and the Kingdom of Hormuz – much of the coast of contemporary Oman was part of the Kingdom of Hormuz, based on the island of Hormuz in the Strait of Hormuz in the Persian Gulf, in the sixteenth century. In the Arabian interior, the Imam of Oman was the most significant authority. The Portuguese conquered the Kingdom of Hormuz and many of the Kingdom's Omani coastal settlements in 1515. The arrival of the Portuguese spurred a process of counter-conquest and political consolidation by the Imam of Oman. The Imamate ultimately drove the Portuguese from the coast by 1650 and even wrested some of Portugal's East African settlements from Portuguese control, including several coastal enclaves and the East African island of Zanzibar. Internecine conflict, as well as tensions with the Ottoman and Safavid Empires, saw Omani power wane in East Africa. However, in 1749, the al-Bu Said dynasty, which still rules Oman, consolidated control in the southeast of the Arabian Peninsula. The al-Bu Saids also reinstated Omani control on the East African coast, including at Zanzibar. In 1798, the EIC signed treaties with Oman's rulers to prevent Oman from establishing diplomatic relations with other European powers, notably the French. A succession dispute within the dynasty precipitated the creation of two independent kingdoms in Oman and in Zanzibar/ East Africa in the 1850s. While Oman would remain independent, the Sultanate of Zanzibar lost many of its East African possessions and became a British protectorate in 1890. This lasted until 1963, when Sultan Jamshid bin Abdullah became the independent ruler of Zanzibar. However, in 1964, he was overthrown and Zanzibar was joined with Tanzania.

Ottoman Empire – a Middle East empire that originated among the Turkic polities that succeeded the Seljuk opponents to the Mongols on the Anatolian plateau in the early 1300s. Moving west, the Ottomans conquered Constantinople in 1453, and by the late 1400s had taken control of much of what is today considered eastern Europe and the Balkans. Thereafter, the Ottomans set their sights on the Middle East, increasingly conceiving of their empire as a Caliphate, as successors to the Umayyads and Abbasids. In 1517, they conquered much of what is today Syria and Iraq, as well as Egypt, Sudan, the Hejaz and Yemen. The Ottomans withdrew from the Yemeni provinces of the Arabian

Peninsula in 1635. In the early 1800s, the Porte – as the Ottoman
capital was known – instituted a series of modernising reforms
known as the Tanzimat. This included reform of government
administration and the military. At the same time, the Ottomans
embarked on a series of imperial adventures in the Arabian
Peninsula, expanding south of the Hejaz into the Tihamat 'Asir
and Yemen in 1849 and into highland Yemen in 1870.

Prize – from the early seventeenth century, in European Admiralty
law, a prize was an enemy ship captured during armed conflict.
The captain and crew of the capturing ship would normally be
entitled to claim part of the value of the captured ship's cargo and/
or hull. Note that while prize law in many countries still allows
navies to claim the value of ships seized during wartime, following
the end of World War I the funds were not normally retained by
the captain and crew, a change that removed the financial incen-
tive for a captain to capture enemy ships.

Salvage – a concept in both European and Islamic maritime law
whereby when a ship is wrecked or found in distress at sea, the
salvor may claim either (in Islamic maritime law) a reward for
assistance rendered or (in European maritime law) a part of value
of the ship's cargo. The amount that the salvor may claim (alongside other vested interests such as the ship and cargo owners) is
governed in Europe by the rules of general average and in the
Islamic world by provisions for rewards made by treaty between
seafaring governments.

Sanjak – an old Ottoman term for 'flag', denoting an administrative
district. Following the promulgation of the Vilayet Law of 1864 as
part of the Ottoman Tanzimat reforms, sanjaks became 'second
order' administrative districts, subordinate to larger vilayets, or
provinces. Some of the regions mentioned in this study, particularly those in the Arabian Peninsula, had been sanjaks after the
Ottoman-Egyptian conquests of the Arabian Peninsula in the early
sixteenth century. Following their reconquest in the mid-
nineteenth century, they became vilayets, subdivided into sanjaks.

Sayyid – an honorific title, used by both spiritual and temporal rulers
in the Islamic world, which connotes direct descent from one of
the lineages of the Prophet Muhammad. In the pre-Islamic period,
the title applied to chief of the tribe and was used somewhat
interchangeably with the title *Shaykh*.

Shafi'is and *Zaydis* – a school of Sunni Islamic law that is prevalent in the coastal regions of the southern Red Sea and across the Indian Ocean littoral. The Shafi'is simply subscribe to a particular school of Islamic law; their political leaders are diverse and their theological beliefs can be similar or identical to those of other Sunni Muslims in the Middle East. In the Yemeni context, the coastal Shafi'is are often contrasted with the highland Zaydis. Zaydis are described as sectarian because adherents are bound to follow the temporal and spiritual rule of the Imam of Yemen, whose ninth-century founder – Zayd ibn 'Ali – diverged from the rule of the Caliphs and gave the Zaydis their name. By contrast, Shafi'is followed an array of different rulers. While there are doctrinal differences, the ground-level reality was that the Zaydis and Shafi'is were often mixed, with followers of the Zaydi Imams practicing a Shafi'i form of Islam when they lived in the coastal regions of Yemen.

Shaykh – a pre-Islamic honorific title that connotes the idea of a patriarch of a kinship group such as a tribe, a clan or even simply a family. The title is also used by the heads of religious brotherhoods and other non-lineal groups and may even refer simply to certain virtuous qualities of leadership, including but not limited to religious knowledge.

Tihamat 'Asir – *Tihamat* means 'coastal plain' and *'Asir* refers to its 'difficult' geography, being composed of a steep escarpment and a narrow, arid, coastal plain between the Yemeni mountains and the sea. The plain is, in fact, part of the far northern ridge of the great Rift Valley, the prehistoric continental rift which runs all the way to southern Africa. The northern boundary lies around Kunfida, north of the Farasan Islands. The southern border was quite fluid, contested by different rulers from both 'Asir and Yemen. Sometimes referred to simply as "Asir'. The ruler most strongly associated with this region in this study was Sayyid Muhammad Ibn Ali al-Idrissi.

Tihamat al-Hejaz – most often referred to in Europe simply as 'the Hejaz' and encompassing the Muslim Holy cities of Mecca and Medina. Under the control of the Islamic Caliphates in the Middle Ages, and later in the Ottoman Empire, it was administered by the Sharifs of Mecca, who claimed lineal descent from the Prophet Muhammad (the most well-known of whom was Sharif Husayn

Ibn 'Ali, who entered a doomed alliance with the British during World War I). The Sharif's influence, and thus the extent of the Hejaz, extended north to the Sinai Peninsula and south to Kunfida. The coast includes the ports of Jiddah and Yan'bu. Their influence was challenged by Wahhabi rulers from the inland desert region of Nejd from the early nineteenth century; Ibn Saud ultimately displaced the Sharifs as rulers of the Hejaz in 1925.

Tihamat Yemen – a continuation of the western Arabian Peninsula's coastal plain, which runs roughly between Shaykh Said in the south and to somewhere north of Hodeida, but south of Jazan, in the north. The main port of the region is Mukha. The location of the northern border of the Tihamat Yemen changed over time as regional rulers took control of different ports and anchorages along the coast. For example, following World War I, Hodeida fell to the 'Asiri ruler Sayyid Muhammad Ibn Ali al-Idrissi, but was reclaimed for Yemen by Imam Yahya in 1934 (for details of both, see Dramatis Personae). The northern border of the Tihamat Yemen is shared with the Tihamat 'Asir.

Tihamiyin – a general-purpose noun derived from the root, referring to the people of the whole Tihamat Hejaz, Yemen and 'Asir.

Zaraniq – an ethno-military movement led by Shaykh Nasr Ambari. Based originally in the Shaykh Said peninsula in the far south of the Tihamat Yemen, British, Ottoman and later French military patronage helped the movement to expand in the 1880s. Under the rule of Ambari's lieutenant, Ahmad Fatini, the Zaraniq was briefly transformed into a fighting force numbering some 10,000 men and their families, whose control of the Tihamat Yemen stretched from Mukha almost as far north as Hodeida. Fatini briefly lobbied the international community for recognition of Zaraniq sovereignty along the coast in the 1920s but was subsumed by the conquests of Imam Yahya and Ibn Saud in 1928.

Zaydi Imamate/Imams of Sanaa – beginning in the ninth century, the Zaydi imams ruled over highland Yemen until 1962. Sometimes described as a branch of Shi'ism, Zaydism is a heterodox form of Islam peculiar to highland Yemen. The fourth Caliph and son-in-law of the Prophet, Caliph 'Ali, was the first to introduce Islam from the Yemeni highlands. 'Ali's descendant Zayd later rose against the Ummayad Caliphate in the ninth century CE. The Zaydis' belief in the spiritual supremacy of the Imams does have parallels with Shi'ism, and while Zaydism was and remains distinct, it has become increasingly mixed with Shi'ite Ismailism, as well as blending with some Shafi'i ideas.

Dramatis Personae

Majerteenia

Sultan Uthman Mahmud Yusuf – long-serving head of the Majerteen Sultanate in the northeast of contemporary Somalia, roughly contiguous with northern Puntland. Ruled between the late 1850s and the 1920s. Commonly abbreviated in this text to Sultan Uthman.

Nur Uthman – regent to the Majerteen ruler Sultan Uthman Mahmud Yusuf during his minority in the 1840s and 1850s.

Lt. Charles Cruttenden – a lieutenant in the Indian Navy in the 1840s who travelled and wrote widely about the north-western Indian Ocean region. Shipwrecked in Majerteenia in 1844.

Brigadier William Coghlan – Political Resident, or ruler, of the British settlement of Aden under East India Company rule. His Residency lasted between 1854 and 1863.

Sir Robert Lambert Playfair, KCMG – joined the Madras Artillery (a branch of the East India Company army) in 1846. In 1854, Playfair transferred from the Madras Artillery to become an Assistant Political Agent to the Resident in the East India Company port of Aden. He remained in Aden until the late 1860s, whereafter he entered British Foreign Office service in Zanzibar and North Africa until his retirement in the 1880s. While in Aden, he took part in a number of treaty negotiations in what would become British Somaliland and led several missions to Majerteenia, where he signed treaties with Sultan Uthman (see Sultan Uthman) in 1858 and 1866.

Major J. S. King – Assistant Resident in Aden in the mid-1880s who led a number of diplomatic missions to Majerteenia and the northern Somali coast. One of the first Europeans to attempt to create a system for transcribing Somali into Arabic.

Major Charles Goodfellow, VC – Assistant Resident in Aden in the late 1870s who led a diplomatic treaty and salvage mission to the Majerteen coast in the wake of a number of significant steamship wrecks in the east of the country in 1878–1879.

Georges Révoil – French explorer, diplomat and writer who led a number of missions to Majerteenia in 1878 and the early 1880s.

Yusuf 'Ali – a minor member of the Uthman lineage in Majerteenia and governor of the port of Alula in the 1870s and 1880s. Self-declared Sultan of Hobyo from 1885.

Count Paul von Hatzfeldt – German diplomat and Foreign Minister who served as the German Ambassador to London from 1885 to 1901.

Archibald Primrose, Earl of Roseberry – British Foreign Secretary in 1886 and between 1892–1894. Briefly Prime Minister of Britain between 1894 and 1895.

Vincenzo Filonardi – Italian naval captain and shipping-line owner based in Zanzibar who advocated for Italy's interests in Somalia in the 1880s and signed treaties with Yusuf 'Ali and Sultan Uthman.

Cavaliere Giulio Pestalozza – Italian diplomat and traveller who served as Italy's consul to Zanzibar in the 1890s and 1900s. Involved in negotiations for an Italian treaty with Sultan Uthman and Yusuf 'Ali.

Sayyid Barghash bin Said al-Bu Said – the second Sultan of Zanzibar who ruled between 1870 and 1888. His father, Said bin Sultan, was a ruler of Muscat and Oman and moved to Zanzibar in the 1840s (see 'Oman, Zanzibar and the Kingdom of Hormuz' in Note on the Text).

Muhammad Abdille Hassan – the Somali-born and Somali-speaking leader of anti-colonial jihad in what is today Ogaden, which lasted, on and off, between the late 1890s and 1920.

Tihamat Yemen

Shaykh Nasr Ambari – the leader of a clan of the Subahi based on the Shaykh Said peninsula to the west of Aden. Ambari became a powerful military leader of a group known collectively as the Zaraniq in the Tihamat Yemen, especially south of the port of

Hodeida, in the 1880s. Ambari remained leader of the Zaraniq until the 1910s.

Ahmad Fatini – a lieutenant to Shaykh Nasr Ambari; succeeded Ambari as de facto leader of the Zaraniq in the late 1910s or early 1920s.

Naqib of Mukalla – Naqib is an honorific abbreviating the Naqib al-ashraf, or the head of the ashraf, i.e. the descendants of the Prophet. Such groups formed into corporate organisations throughout the Muslim world. In Mukalla, the Naqib served as a sort of corporate ruler who wielded considerable influence over religious, legal and diplomatic affairs.

Sayyid Muhammad Ibn Ali al-Idrisi – ruler and spiritual leader in the coastal 'Asir region of the Arabian Peninsula between approximately 1905, when he was teaching in the Sudan, and his death in 1923. Allied with the British and French during World War I. The Sayyid was succeeded by his son, 'Ali, and later by 'Ali's uncle, Muhammad's brother, Hasan. The Idrisi state lasted until 1934.

Imam Yahya – elected Imam of Yemen in 1904. Imam Yahya ruled the Zaydi population of highland Yemen alongside the Ottomans from the highland city of Sanaa until 1918, when the Ottoman Empire collapsed, and the Imam became the independent leader of highland Yemen until his death in 1948. From the 1920s, Imam Yahya fought various wars of expansion, including a border war with the British in Aden in the 1920s, and including his (re) conquest of the coast, the Tihamat Yemen, to the Imamate in the 1920s.

Abdulaziz Ibn Muhammad al-Saud – conquered Riyadh from the Rashidis in 1902 and became the founder of the contemporary kingdom of Saudi Arabia. Conquered Nejd in the 1900s, the Hejaz from the Sharifian rulers in the 1920s, and as far south as Hodeida by 1934. Hodeida ultimately fell to Imam Yahya and the border between contemporary Saudi Arabia and Yemen lies just north of that port city. Referred to in this text as Ibn Saud.

French Somaliland/Gulf of Tadjoura

Governor Léonce Lagarde – the first governor of French Somaliland in the mid-1880s. Moved the capital of the French colony to Djibouti, a port he founded in 1888. Served until 1899.

Sultan of Tadjoura – ruler of the port of Tadjoura, a town in the west of the Gulf of Tadjoura. The Sultanate was established in the early 1600s, after the collapse of the Ifat Sultanate and its successor state based in Harar, under Ahmad Gran. In the nineteenth and early twentieth centuries the Sultanate was nominally subordinate to Abbysinia, after which it shifted allegiance to French Somaliland. Involved in the slave trade between Africa and the Arabian Peninsula.

Gabriel Guignuiony – French merchant and owner of an import and export firm that specialised in the trade in arms in Djibouti in the early 1900s. Employed and partnered with Henry de Monfreid in the 1910s.

Henry de Monfreid – French trader, writer and agent of the French empire in northeast Africa and the southwestern Arabian Peninsula. Career in the Red Sea spanning the years between 1911 and 1930, examined in Chapter 4.

Governor Adrien Bonhoure – Governor of French Somaliland between 1899 and 1915.

Gaston Doumergue – friend of de Monfreid's father. Elected as Deputy for one of France's Pyrenean regions in the 1910s. Minister responsible for the Colonies in France between 1914 and 1924. Became President of France in 1924, serving until 1931.

Joseph Kessel – Argentinian-born to parents of Russian heritage, but raised in France, and became a celebrated French author and journalist. Kessel was commissioned by *Le Matin* newspaper to write a series of articles about French Somaliland in 1928–1929.

Governor Pierre-Amable Chapon-Baissac – a veteran colonial official by the time he arrived as Governor of Djibouti in 1925. Prior to being posted to Djibouti, his most recent role had been the governorship of the Côte d'Ivoire.

Abbreviations

Archives

AD(P) (C)	Archives Diplomatiques, La Courneuve, France
AOM	Archives d'Outre Mer, Aix-en-Provence, France
AS	Archivio Centrale dello Stato, Rome, Italy
IOR	India Office Records, British Library, London, United Kingdom
LN	League of Nations Archives, Geneva, Switzerland
MAESS	Ministero degli Affari Esteri Servizio Storico e Documentazione, Rome, Italy
NA	National Archives, Kew, London, United Kingdom

Other Abbreviations

EIC	East India Company
FAR	First Assistant Resident (Aden)
GCC	Gulf Cooperation Council
GEAC	German East Africa Company
MT	Maria Theresa dollars
VOC	Dutch East Indies Company

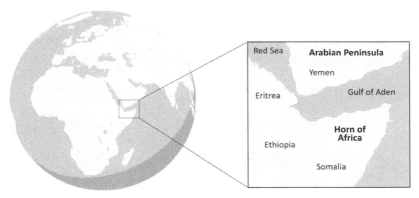

Map 1 The location of the southern Red Sea and Gulf of Aden region
(© 2021 Nicholas W. Stephenson Smith. All rights reserved)

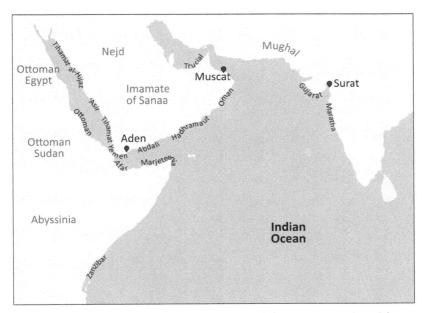

Map 2 Map indicating the location of some of the major precolonial kingdoms, empires and political entities mentioned in the text, circa 1820–1840
(© 2021 Nicholas W. Stephenson Smith. All rights reserved)

Introduction

In 1862, on a beach in what is today northeastern Somalia, a British colonial official told a Somali sultan that he faced a choice. It was a choice between personally beheading eight of his own subjects, or accepting the bombardment of his coastline by an armada of British gunboats looming in the distance offshore. Nine one-hundred-foot-long, fume-spewing steel-hulled frigates underlined the starkness of the decision confronting the Sultan. These ships were relatively new to the seas globally, and were a novel and menacing sight on this stretch of the Somali coast, which was more used to seeing elegantly-rigged wooden dhows. The combined cannons of the British and Indian Navies pointed threateningly towards the shoreline. In this particular coastal location, the Sultan and his people had witnessed the spectacle of cannon-fire only once before. On that occasion, the fire from three ships had destroyed a medium-sized town, resulting in numerous deaths. The Sultan attempted to reason with the British official, but he refused to listen. In the end, one after another, the Sultan beheaded eight of his own subjects before swearing allegiance to the British flag on the quarterdeck of one of the warships anchored off his coast.

The colonial history of the southern Red Sea region – contemporary Puntland, Djibouti and Yemen – is strewn with the bodies of victims of maritime violence. The whole culture of international relations in the region was transformed by colonial conquest. A permissive and cooperative system of diplomacy gave way to a violent and competitive regime. Incidents of maritime conflict proliferated. Focusing on three case studies from across the southern Red Sea region – Majerteen in northeast Africa, the Zaraniq coast in the Tihamat Yemen or Yemen coast, and the French enclave in the Gulf of Tadjoura (see Map I.1) – we see the unfurling of colonial chaos in the southern Red Sea. The late nineteenth century saw a steep rise in imperial competition, geopolitical jockeying and the proliferation of rival factions vying for recognition in the emerging colonial

1

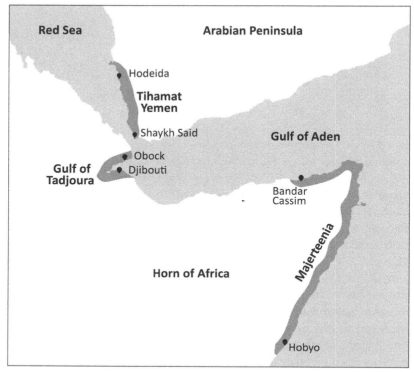

Map I.1 Majerteen north-east Somalia, Zaraniq Tihamat Yemen and the Gulf of Tadjoura
(© 2021 Nicholas W. Stephenson Smith. All rights reserved)

regime of sovereignty, scrambling for colonial military patronage to support their quasi-military insurgencies along the coast. By the mid-twentieth century, a historic network of coastal royals and a long-standing mode of diplomacy had given way to a tense, transactional style of international relations and lawmaking. Diplomacy was diminished in favour of colonial chaos.

Colonial officials normally described the protagonists of maritime violence as pirates, as self-serving criminals. This study takes a more expansive and historical look at peoples labelled as pirates by the international community. In three acts, focusing on three sets of characters from three corners of the southern Red Sea during the colonial era, we see that maritime violence served strategic ends.

By launching attacks against shipwrecked European steamers, taking hostages, negotiating salvage, seizing European-flagged ships on the sea, and trading arms and other colonially banned goods, upstarts and rulers from around the southern Red Sea littoral negotiated their inclusion into colonial treaty agreements. These agreements ultimately formed the basis of the modern map of regional and national power along the coast of northeast Africa and the southern Arabian Peninsula. Incidents of maritime violence and treaty making offer a porthole onto the culture of international law creation in the colonial period.

By making violence an entry-point to international relations, European colonialism created a zero-sum system we would today recognise as competitive geopolitics. Contemporary violence along the foreshores and reef-strewn coastline of the southern Red Sea originated in the colonial era, between about 1830 and the mid-twentieth century. During this time, European empires transformed the coastline into a crucible of international conflict. While we commonly think of the impact of colonial rule on the international sphere in terms of swashbuckling commonplaces such as 'divide and rule' and 'gunboat diplomacy', the true effect of colonial violence was profound. Europeans ran amok, transforming the very rules that governed the international system – and which purported to bring peace where there was conflict, and order where there was upheaval – into a violent competition for survival. Disputes over shipwrecks, treaties and maritime jurisdiction during the imperial period eroded customary forms of diplomacy, peaceful alliances between regional states and stable coastal monarchies.

Unravelling

Europeans did not introduce violence to a peaceful precolonial idyll. An extensive literature emphasises the cosmopolitan harmoniousness of the pre-colonial Indian Ocean, however this literature is now considered somewhat romantic.[1] There is in fact a long history of naval

---

[1] See, for example, Richard Hall, *Empires of The Monsoon: A History of the Indian Ocean and Its Invaders* (London: HarperCollins, 1996). For a critique of this literature, see Sugata Bose, *A Hundred Horizons: The Indian Ocean in the Age of Global Empire* (London and Cambridge, MA: Harvard University Press, 2006), esp. p. 44.

conflict, even imperial subjugation, by indigenous empires in the north-western Indian Ocean which long predates the arrival of nineteenth-century European colonists. Empires, port states, coastal kingdoms and island fiefdoms had long competed for control of the Red Sea and Gulf of Aden, which lie at the centre of East–West trade. When a world trade system first emerged with its centre in the Middle East five millennia before the present (BCE), the Red Sea became a site of commercial energy, the subject of political contestation and control. The Greeks, Romans, Phoenicians and Sabaeans all sought to some degree to control the Red Sea trade routes – notably by monopol-ising regional timber production and shipbuilding. The discovery of the monsoon wind patterns in about 300 BC – allowing for yearly sea-bound commercial voyages between Asia, Africa and Europe – increased traffic through and political interest in the Red Sea as a maritime thoroughfare.[2] The Fatimids, Mamluks, Rasulids, Ayyubids, and Ottomans all continued the tradition of shipbuilding and of using navies to protect merchant shipping in the Red Sea in the Middle Ages.[3] At the same time, a number of smaller regional ports such as Aden, Adulis, Dahlak, which straddled the Red Sea's choke-points, challenged the dominance of larger empires by building flotillas of smaller ships and using harassing tactics to overpower fairly large imperial navies in their quest to control shipping in the region, some-times for many decades at a stretch.[4]

---

[2] Markus Vink, 'Indian Ocean studies and the "New Thalassology"', *Journal of Global History* 2 (2007), p. 55. G. W. Bowersock Omerod, *The Throne of Adulis: Red Sea Wars on the Eve of Islam* (Oxford: Oxford University Press, 2013); Shlomo Goitien, 'Portrait of a medieval India trader: Three letters from the Cairo Geniza', *Bulletin of the School of Oriental and African Studies* 50 (1987), esp. p. 458.

[3] For example, Roxani Eleni Margariti, 'Mercantile networks, port cities, and "pirate" states: Conflict and competition in the Indian Ocean world of trade before the sixteenth century', *Journal of Economic and Social History of the Orient* 51 (2008), pp. 556–559; Giancarlo Casale, 'Global politics in the 1580s: One canal, twenty thousand cannibals, and an Ottoman plot to rule the world', *Journal of World History* 18(3) (2007), pp. 267–296; and Alexis Wick, 'Self-portrait of the Ottoman Red Sea, 20th of July 1777', *Journal of Ottoman Studies* XL (2012), pp. 399–434 and Rene Barendse, 'Trade and state in the Arabian Seas: A survey from the fifteenth to the eighteenth century', *Journal of World History* 11(2) (2000), pp. 173–225.

[4] Patricia Risso, 'Cross-cultural perceptions of piracy: Maritime violence in the western Indian Ocean and the Persian Gulf region during a long eighteenth century', *Journal of World History* 12(2) (2001), pp. 295–296.

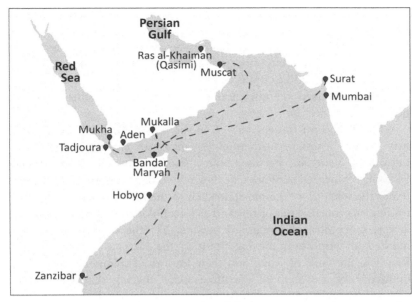

Map I.2 The precolonial commercial and diplomatic connections across the north-western Indian Ocean
(© 2021 Nicholas W. Stephenson Smith. All rights reserved)

Notwithstanding these tensions, there was an entrenched culture of diplomacy in the region. Commercial continuities and standards of behaviour in the international realm smoothed changes of political order in the region in the precolonial era. Conquest looked more like absorption than subjugation. The tenor of geopolitics was tolerant and permissive, rather than competitive and retaliatory. Maritime commerce carried on in a cooperative rather than a competitive fashion. Several ethno-cultural networks facilitated the movement of goods; at the same time, a culture of gift-giving and diplomacy between regional kingdoms, which treated one another as equals, oiled the wheels of commerce between different parts of the north-western Indian Ocean. Complementary commercial and diplomatic networks criss-crossed the northwestern Indian Ocean (see Map I.2). These regional networks bridged the far corners of the northwestern Indian Ocean, facilitating the exchange of goods from across the East, including coffee, incense, Chinese pottery and silk for staples such as rice and timber, as well as currencies in the form of cowrie shells and later silver in Maria Theresa dollars.[5] To borrow the anthropologist Alexander Lesser's analogy, precolonial international society was not a billiard table – a mass of collisions between discrete actors – but rather inextricably interconnected 'aggregates [interwoven] near and far, in web-like, netlike connections'.[6] Such networks were essentially cooperative, based on gift giving and reciprocity rather than on power and force.

When European traders arrived in the region in the sixteenth century, they insinuated themselves into pre-existing Hadhrami, Levantine, Venetian, Persian, South Asian, Armenian, Omani and Swahili commercial networks; or they nested their commercial interests under the wing of a regional state such as the Mughals and Gujaratis, trading as protected minorities and as leaseholders on the sufferance of larger, more powerful regional powers. Yet the nineteenth century marked an important turning point in the history of the southern Red Sea, the Gulf of Aden and their littorals. Diplomacy unravelled in favour of a system of maritime space sharing that was highly competitive, even adversarial. An environment in which trans-regional commercial and diplomatic dealings could be win-win, in which one person's power and fortune might strengthen another's, was replaced by a zero-sum logic. From the late nineteenth century onwards, one ruler's gain was another's loss – and the militarily, technologically and commercially powerful reaped the benefits while the weak were subordinated and marginalised.

The great commercial transformation driving this shift was the advent of the British East India Company (EIC). The EIC emerged from a series of internal crises and South Asian battles in the late eighteenth century as a new, imperial power; the EIC became financially secure, technologically proficient and militarily confident enough to force its way into new markets, and to seek to dominate those markets in which it was already involved. The EIC replaced the old

---

[5] Michael Pearson, *Before Colonialism: Theories on Asian-European Relations 1500–1750* (Delhi: Oxford University Press, 1988); Ashin Das Gupta, *Merchants of Maritime India, 1500–1800* (London: Routledge, 1994); Niels Steensgard, *Carracks, Caravans and Companies: The Structural Crisis in the European-Asian Trade in the Early Seventeenth Century* (Lund: Studentlitteratur, 1973); Barendse, 'Trade and state', pp. 173–225.

[6] Eric R. Wolf, *Europe and the People without History* (Berkley: University of California Press, 1997), p. 19.

South Asian empires, such as the Mughals and Marathas, with an array of local rulers and loyalist upstarts who used their association with the British to enhance their influence.[7] What emerged was an uneasy symbiosis between the East India Company and the surviving regional powers.[8] However, to describe the relationship between the colonial powers, regional rulers and merchants in the southern Red Sea in the nineteenth and twentieth centuries as an 'uneasy coexistence' is an understatement.

Europeans spent much of the nineteenth century disaggregating the cooperative and diplomatic bonds that knit the region together. Whereas the glue of international relations in the region had previously been exchange, gift giving, treaty making and mutual recognition, maritime powers increasingly turned to force, one-upmanship and violence to assert themselves in the international realm during the colonial period. Shipwreck and salvage, attacks against seaborne shipping, hostage-taking, slave trading and other trades to which the use of force was integral, all emerged as fundamental ingredients of the maritime political economy. The political scientists Patrick Chabal and Jean-Pascal Daloz argue that in the postcolonial period, African elites created and sold protection for disorder, violence and unrest to strengthen their authority in the domestic realm.[9]

---

[7] Kitri N. Chaudhuri, *The Trading World of Asia and the English East India Company* (Cambridge: Cambridge University Press, 1978), p. 47; on the reinvention of the East India Company as a political organisation in the late eighteenth century, see Nicholas B. Dirks, *The Scandal of Empire: India and the Creation of Imperial Britain* (Cambridge, MA: Harvard University Press, 2006); Bose, *A Hundred Horizons*, pp. 42–43; Kavalam M. Panikkar, *India and the Indian Ocean: An Essay on the Influence of Sea Power on Indian History* (London: George Allen and Unwin, 1946); Geoffrey Parker, *The Military Revolution: Military Innovation and the Rise of the West, 1500–1800* (Cambridge: Cambridge University Press, 1988); Elizabeth Mancke, 'Early modern expansion and the politicization of oceanic space', *Geographic Review*, 89(2) (1999), pp. 226–228; Jos Gommans, *Mughal Warfare: Indian Frontiers and High Roads to Empire, 1500–1700* (London: Routledge, 2002). More recently, see William Dalrymple, *The Anarchy: The Relentless Rise of the East India Company* (London: Bloomsbury, 2019). For a summary of this literature, see Markus Vink, 'From port-city to world-system: Spatial constructs of Dutch Indian Ocean studies, 1500–1800', *Itinerario*, 28(2) (2004), pp. 86–87.

[8] Christopher A. Bayly, *The New Cambridge History of India: Indian Society and the Making of the British Empire* (Cambridge: Cambridge University Press, 1988), esp. p. 69. See also Vink, 'From port-city to world-system', p. 86.

[9] Patrick Chabal and Jean-Pascal Daloz, *Africa Works: Disorder as Political Instrument* (Oxford: James Currey, 1999).

In this study, I argue that disorder-making as political strategy originated – or was at the very least prefigured – in the colonial era.
By instigating acts of aggression along the coast and at sea, actual
and aspiring rulers inflated their political stock, positioning themselves
as indispensable colonial proxies and military clients for
foreign powers.

The creation of a new international order in the region was not,
therefore, a top-down imposition on the region; on the contrary, it
emerged in the course of maritime conflicts between the colonial newcomers and coastal actors. Rather than approach international relations from the vantage point of the Colonial Ministries of European
capitals – or from the deck of a European steamship – I approach
conflict and violence from the level of the shoreline, from the point of
view of the coastal rulers, militias and mercenaries who tried their luck
in the international system. Each chapter follows the career of a
different protagonist of maritime violence. Each used violence to
compel – or attempt to compel – the colonial powers to share power
in the region, to nest their claims to sovereignty under the wing of the
imperialists. Positioning ourselves on the Red Sea's shoreline, each
chapter reveals another facet of the unfolding colonial chaos and
maritime violence in the region. Starting with a review of indigenous,
precolonial cultures of diplomacy, the story moves through the disrup-
tion of this system during incidents of shipwreck, salvage and treaty
making in the mid-to-late nineteenth century. We then see the unravelling of cooperative approaches to international relations when an
assortment of hitherto marginal social groups, including private individuals, upstart chiefs, traders and military commanders, became
embroiled in the work of international politics.

Told from the perspective of littoral populations, their stories are
discoverable in the colonial archives. Thus in one sense, this is an
imperial study, employing an archival methodology and backlit by
the kinds of grand geopolitical upheavals, new technologies and
epochal events, like the advent of colonialism in Africa, favoured by
imperial historians. The opening of the Suez Canal in 1869, which
imbued the region with a strategic and world economic significance
that it retains to this day, cuts the time frame of this study in two. After
the 1870s, what was once a six-month journey under sail via the Cape
route, or an arduous sea and land journey via Egypt, was transformed
by 1900 into a routine two-week steamship passage via the Red Sea

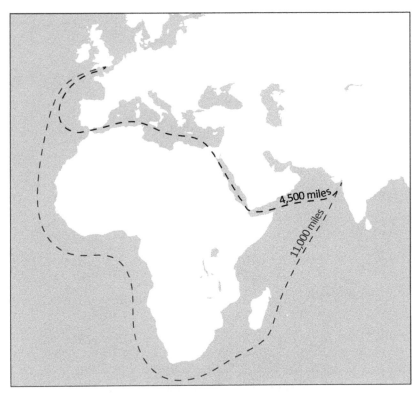

Map I.3 The Cape versus the Red Sea shipping routes between India and Europe
(© 2021 Nicholas W. Stephenson Smith. All rights reserved)

and Gulf of Aden.[10] The Red Sea shipping route to the East cut the journey between Europe and Asia by as much as a third (see Map I.3). As a result of the opening of the canal, the entire Red Sea region

---

[10] See Boyd Cable, *A Hundred Year History of the P & O: Peninsular and Oriental Steam Navigation Company, 1837–1937* (London: Ivor Nicholson and Watson Limited, 1937); Colette Dubois, 'The Red Sea ports during the revolution in transportation, 1800–1914', in Leila Tarazi Fawaz and C. A. Bayly (eds.), *Modernity and Culture: From the Mediterranean to the Indian Ocean* (New York: Columbia University Press, 2002), pp. 58–74; Robert J. Blyth, 'Aden, British India and the development of steam power in the Red Sea, 1825–1839', in David Killingray, Margarette Lincoln and Nigel Rigby (eds.), *Maritime Empires: Birtish Imperial Maritime Trade in the Nineteenth Century* (Woodbridge: The Boydell Press, 2004), pp. 68–83.

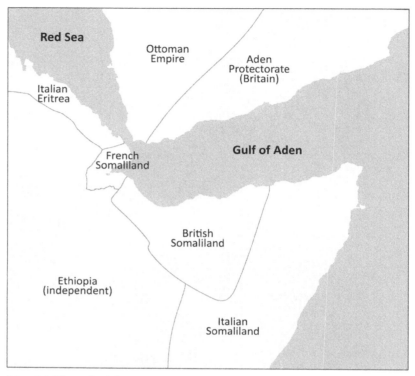

Map I.4 The colonial powers in the southern Red Sea, circa 1900
(© 2021 Nicholas W. Stephenson Smith. All rights reserved)

became crowded with rival imperial superpowers competing to advance their interests along the strategic route to the East with the advent of steam and large-scale commodity trading between Europe and Afro-Asia: Italy in Eritrea and northeastern Somalia, France in the Gulf of Tadjoura, Britain in Aden and Somaliland and the Ottoman Empire in the Tihamat 'Asir (see Map I.4). As we will see, even this steep rise in the region's importance as a trade route and the arrival of European empires jostling for influence does not capture the complexity of the geopolitical situation in the late nineteenth century. Added to these territorial players were several other meddling powers, notably Germany.

Yet while the surface of this study is colonial conquest, the real concern here is the new currents of international politics, law and diplomacy swirling beneath the large-scale political and technological advances. The twentieth-century colonial map of the region was just a superficial expression of rising geopolitical complexity. In the late nineteenth century an array of small-scale actors proliferated within colonial borders. Militias, secessionists and even private individuals intermingled with European and regional empires, pushing the boundaries of empire, championing their own ambitions, and new territorial arrangements. These coast-level actors played an equally important role in international relations as did the British, French and Italian governments in shaping and advancing the culture of colonial chaos, the new style of international relations. While the sources – and to some extent the subject matter – of this study are those of the imperial maritime historian, the sensibilities are those of the Africa- or Asia-specialist historian. Thus, in Chapters 1 and 2, the protagonists are Africans; in Chapter 3, they are Arab, from the Arabian Peninsula; Chapter 4 is about the machinations of a private French citizen. By putting the normally divergent fields of African and Imperial History into a single conceptual framework, the full impact of colonialism on the political, legal and international landscape swims more clearly into focus.

Colonial Chaos

In one sense, the story of colonial chaos is a straightforward narrative: a roster of colonial conquests and proliferating subaltern factions along the coast. But on another level, it involves reckoning with a new culture of international law, of maritime law and custom, of diplomacy and international relations. The subaltern and legal turn in maritime history in recent years has refocused historians' attention on the nature of maritime law and maritime economies in the Indian Ocean during the colonial era. These studies have focused on the impact of colonial rule on the maritime economy and on the development of new, hybrid legal cultures.[11] While studies of Africa's

---

[11] See Lauren Benton, *A Search for Sovereignty: Law and Geography in European Empires, 1400–1900* (Cambridge: Cambridge University Press, 2010), pp. 282–287; David Armitage, 'The elephant and the whale: Empires of land and sea', *Journal for Maritime Research*, 9(1) (2007), pp. 23–36; Tamson Pietsch, 'A British sea: Making sense of global space in the late nineteenth century', *Journal of Global History*, 5 (2010), pp. 423–446. On the Indian Ocean, see Simon Layton, 'Hydras and Leviathans in the Indian Ocean world',

international relations focus understandably on the postcolonial period,[12] treaty making has attracted more historical attention.[13] The older notion that colonial treaties established a 'pax colonia' has been thoroughly debunked.[14] But what is less well understood is the culture of international relations that colonial diplomacy left in its wake, the style rather than the form of hybrid international law and diplomacy.[15]

International Journal of Maritime History, 25(3) (2013), p. 213. See also Johan Mathew, *Margins of the Market: Trafficking and Capitalism across the Arabian Sea* (Berkley: University of California Press, 2016), *passim*; Renisa Mawani and Iza Hussin, 'The travels of law: Indian Ocean itineraries', *Law and History Review*, 32(4) (2014), pp. 733–747; Fahad Bishara, *A Sea of Debt: Law and Economic Life in the Western Indian Ocean, 1780–1950* (Cambridge: Cambridge University Press, 2017); Erik Gilbert, *Dhows and the Colonial Economy of Zanzibar, 1860–1970* (Oxford: James Currey, 2004).

[12] Kenneth Ingham (ed.), *The Foreign Relations of African States: Proceedings of the Twenty-Fifth Symposium of the Colston Research Society Held in the University of Bristol, 1973* (London: Butterworths, 1974); Gilbert M. Khadiagala and Terrence Lyons (eds.), *African Foreign Policies: Power and Process* (Boulder: Lynne Rienner, 2001); Christopher Clapham, *Africa and the International System: The Politics of State Survival* (Cambridge: Cambridge University Press, 2005); Kevin C. Dunn and Timothy M. Shaw, *Africa's Challenge to International Relations Theory* (Basingstoke: Palgrave Macmillan, 2001); Paul-Henri Bischoff, Kwesi Aning and Amitav Acharya, *Africa in Global International Relations: Emerging Approaches to Theory and Practice* (Abingdon: Routledge, 2016); Siba Grovogui, 'Regimes of sovereignty: International morality and the African condition', *European Journal of International Relations*, 8(3) (2002), pp. 315–338; Amr G. E. Sabet, 'The Islamic paradigm of nations: Toward a neoclassical approach', *Religion, State & Society*, 31(2) (2003), pp. 179–202; Surabhi Ranganathan, *Strategically Created Treaty Conflicts and the Politics of International Law* (Cambridge: Cambridge University Press, 2014).

[13] Compare C. H. Alexandrowicz, *An Introduction to the History of the Law of Nations in the East Indies: 16th, 17th and 18th Centuries* (Oxford: Clarendon Press, 1967).

[14] See more broadly, John Gallagher and Ronald Robinson, 'The imperialism of free trade', *The Economic History Review*, 6(1) (1953), p. 11; Antony Anghie, *Imperialism, Sovereignty and the Making of International Law* (Cambridge: Cambridge University Press), *passim*; Saadia Touval, 'Treaties, borders, and the partition of Africa', *The Journal of African History*, 7(2) (1966), pp. 279–293; Lauren Benton, 'Abolition and imperial law, 1790–1820', *The Journal of Imperial and Commonwealth History*, 39(3) (2011), pp. 355–374; Edward Keene, 'A case study of the construction of international hierarchy: British treaty-making against the slave trade in the early nineteenth century', *International Organization*, 61(2) (2007), pp. 311–339.

[15] Although interesting work has been done on the topic in other geographies and time periods, see for example Michael H. Fisher, 'Diplomacy in India, 1526–1858', in H. V. Bowen, Elizabeth Mancke and John G. Reid (eds.),

The creation of a colonial regime of sovereignty in the southern Red Sea did not simply involve the replacement of one set of documents with another, or the substitution of one constellation of international figureheads with a new cast of sovereigns. European colonial actors destroyed conventional habits of international coexistence and maritime space sharing in the region. They left in their wake a new, more violent, competitive and transactional culture of diplomacy.

The transformation of the culture of international law and international relations in the region under colonial rule stands to reason, given the worldview European conquerors brought with them. As Charles Tilly makes clear, the European state system was born of violence, emerging from the civil and religious wreckage of intra-European wars. Treaties such as the Peace of Westphalia in 1648 reconciled diverse, competing military powers who threatened to destroy one another over their confessional and regional differences. In the course of the 1600s the largest, most aggressive powers, namely central Europe's monarchies, signed various agreements with one another that gave them sovereign and territorial integrity, as well as freedom of religious conscience within their domains, setting aside their differences in exchange for self-preservation. However, the signatories of the Peace of Westphalia did not create an international treaty system based on the sovereignty of the state – on the state's monopoly over violence and law in a territory – solely to prevent bloodshed. Rather, Europe's states sought a practical alternative to the logical conclusion of total war, which was the destruction of the enemy. Peace treaties between European monarchies allowed contracting parties to preserve their power relative to other large entities with significant military capabilities like the Hanseatic League and the Papacy.[16]

Britain's Oceanic Empire: Atlantic and Indian Ocean Worlds, c. 1550–1850 (Cambridge: Cambridge University Press, 2012), esp. pp. 254–266 and elsewhere; Henning Trüper, 'Save their souls: Historical telelogy goes to sea in nineteenth-century Europe', in Henning Trüper, Dipesh Chakrabarty and Sanjay Subrahmanyam (eds.), *Historical Teleologies in The Modern World* (London: Bloomsbury, 2015), pp. 117–141; Ian Hurd, 'Law and the practice of diplomacy', *International Journal*, 66(3) (2011), pp. 581–596.

[16] Charles Tilly, 'War making and state making as organised crime', in Peter Evans, Dietrich Rueschemeyer and Theda Skocpol (eds.), *Bringing the State Back In* (Cambridge: Cambridge University Press, 1985), pp. 172–175. See also, Hendrick Spruyt, *The Sovereign State and Its Competitors* (Princeton: Princeton University Press, 1994), esp. pp. 3–33.

When European colonists began formalising their relations with Africans and Asians in the eighteenth and nineteenth centuries, they likewise started on a war footing, signing treaties of peace where possible and expedient. Treaties in the European view were contractual capitulations, a way of enforcing the outcome of battles, or agreements that forestalled the likelihood of defeat. Writing a little more than four decades before the Peace of Westphalia, Hugo Grotius completed his *Commentary on the Law of Prize and Booty* in 1608 in the defence of a United Dutch East India Company (VOC) ship's attack and seizure of the Portuguese merchant brig *Santa Catarina* in the Strait of Malacca in 1603. The value of the *Santa Catarina*, laden with a cargo of spices, was enormous, and the case attracted considerable public attention. In defence of the Captain's actions, and the Company's right to retain the spoils, Grotius subverted European law's focus on the state's duty to prevent the perpetration of wrongs, transforming the state's role into one that empowered its citizens to seek private retribution. 'It is wrong', Grotius wrote, 'to inflict injury, but it is also wrong to endure injury.' 'Regard for others', Grotius continued, 'is usually held up [by] us [the Dutch] with excessive zeal, the implication being that we are by nature sufficiently inclined to care for ourselves.'[17]

Grotius laid down two concrete principles of law which flowed from his observations about the justness of maritime aggression. The first was that all seizures of prize or booty are just if they result from a just war.[18] This was not a novel proposition: the ancient Greeks had established the principle that states could declare legal wars and legally sanction privateering and prize-taking in war. Grotius' second principle was more striking. It flowed from the natural rights of citizens to trade freely and to seek profit, that private companies could be agents of war, and therefore in certain conditions, justly claim their enemies' possessions as prizes. The first condition in which private companies could justly claim enemy ships as prizes was when the company's country of origin had publicly declared war on the country under whose flag the prize was sailing. Thus, a Dutch East Indiaman could justly seize Spanish or Portuguese ships during the Dutch–Iberian wars, as occurred in the case in the seizure of the Portuguese merchant ship *Santa Catarina*.

[17] Hugo Grotius, Gwladys L. Williams (trans.), *Commentary on the Law of Prize and Booty* (Oxford: Clarendon Press, 1950, first published 1608), p. 12.
[18] Ibid., pp. 68–88.

Grotius' second and more radical idea was that a trading company could engage in a private war against other merchants or the agents of another sovereign state. This, he claimed, was to 'enforce natural law, which mandated freedom of trade and navigation'.[19] The Dutch captain's right to war reparations from the *Santa Catarina* could be established by the fact that the Dutch and the Portuguese were embroiled in a trade war and that the Portuguese had been known to hinder freedom of commerce. Moreover, the private party seizing the prize would, according to Grotius, be entitled to take the prize as his own as repayment of the losses he incurred in the course of war and also to award himself compensation for general war losses and damages.[20]

This element of Grotius' thinking about the strong rights of private persons in international maritime law to attack other ships did not gain widespread acceptance, although Dutch domestic jurists accepted his case. Section 39 of the UK Naval Prize Act of 1864, for example, made it clear that only enemy combatant ships in a time of war could be taken as a prize (this was further limited by the Prize Act of 1939). Today, various bodies, notably the EU and the IMO, now coordinate internationally binding legislation and treaties governing maritime actors. Nevertheless, Grotius' radicalism endured in the spirit of maritime interactions witnessed throughout the maritime world, most visibly when the colonial era led to the spread of his legal approach to maritime space. The core Grotian ideas – freedom of trade and freedom of navigation; the rights of merchants to seek restitution for losses and reward for salvage; and the principle that all nations should be treated alike and not be divested of private or public rights of ownership on grounds of conquest, discovery or sovereign grant – all also became important features of international maritime law.[21] The sanctioned and widespread use of private security aboard commercial ships to tackle piracy, legal sanction for the payment of ransoms, international acquiescence in aggressive and even lawless competition for fishing stocks, and the limited duty owed by merchant vessels to others

---

[19] Ibid., pp. 89–91, 300–390.   [20] Ibid., pp. 195–196.
[21] Ibid., esp. pp. 300–390. See also the United Nations Convention on the Law of the Sea (1982), esp. Articles 89, 90 and 98–106. Available at: www.un.org/Depts/los/convention_agreements/texts/unclos/unclos_e.pdf. Last accessed 18 February 2020.

in distress are a few examples of the persistence in some quarters of the adversarial, even chaotic, culture of the seas.[22]

On one level, sanction for the defensive use of force by private merchants in the maritime arena makes sense. It was a jurisprudential defence of a principle that was of general utility to seafarers. The scarcity of assistance for ships in distress at sea, the importance of a ship's positive rights to take proactive steps to defend its free movement in ungoverned space, the inherent riskiness of seaborne enterprise and the downright loneliness of ships venturing to far-flung locations demanded that seafarers be allowed to take their own decisive actions in perilous situations. Crew should, moreover, not be discouraged from taking risks for other ships in distress, and rewarded for aid they provided to one another at their own expense. Such ideas have proven particularly important in areas such as the law of salvage, in which the rewards for salvors can be considerable and strong.[23]

However, the colonial case study outlined here points to the ways that European ideas about freedom and geopolitics created a fractious maritime realm. As well as establishing a foundation of rules and principles to which international maritime contact should conform, Grotius' approach unleashed a torrent of self-assertion among European seafarers and traders who journeyed to Africa and Asia. To adapt a phrase from Groitus' contemporary Thomas Hobbes, all men acquired an interest in all things.[24] Indeed, if Grotius' conception of the international maritime realm was more structured and rule-oriented than Hobbes', it was hardly more cooperative.[25] Notwithstanding the British government's efforts to regulate the practice via Admiralty Courts, and legislation such as the British Naval Prize Act of 1864, prize-taking and

---

[22] A fascinating first-hand account of the persistence of adversarial undercurrents among sections of various maritime industries can be found in Ian Urbina, *The Outlaw Ocean: Crime and Survival in the Last Untamed Frontier* (London: Vintage, 2019). Authority for the legality of ransom payments in the UK can be found in *Masefield AG v. Amlin Corporate Member Ltd* [2011], 1 Lloyd's Rep 630, para 66.

[23] See the judgments in *The 'William Beckford'* [1800] 165 E.R. 492 (Adm) and *Owners of the Glengyle v. Neptune Salvage Co Ltd* [1898] A.C. 519 (HL).

[24] Thomas Hobbes, J. C. A. Gaskin (ed.), *Leviathan, or The Matter, Forme, & Power of a Common-Wealth Ecclesiasticall and Civill* (Oxford: Oxford University Press, 1996; first edition, 1651), p. 83.

[25] See analysis in Hedley Bull, *The Anarchical Society of States: A Study of Order in World Politics Fourth Edition* (London: Palgrave Macmillan, 2011), pp. 95–193. See also Tuck, *The Rights of War*, esp. pp. 78–108.

coercive salvage practices became part and parcel of European seafaring. Indeed, generous awards of prize and salvage kept the British Navy's wage bill down from the seventeenth century through until the nineteenth century, allowing sailors to be paid without financial support from the British state.[26]

In short, there were several – political, military, cultural, juridical and environmental – aspects to colonial conquest. The commonplace characterisation of violence as an unsolicited interference with the integrity of a person, a state or their property is therefore a solid but insufficient starting point for a working definition of violence in this study. Violence is not an absolute category of behaviour: it is a field of action which 'moral imaginar[ies] ... legitimized, criminalized, or criticized'.[27] European colonists forcibly reordered international norms in the Red Sea region, reorganising the relationships between regional rulers along more hierarchic, chaotic and competitive lines.[28] Colonialism thus created systemic chaos in the region, it institutionalised international instability and conflict, it expanded the parameters for when aggression was permissible. Systemic chaos increased violent conflict between regional rulers. But colonialism also impelled the region's political leaders to expand their definition of legitimate behaviour in the international and maritime realm to include practices such as gunboat diplomacy, countervailing and power politics.

Precolonial Indian Ocean Diplomacy

The anarchic approach to maritime life was not mirrored in the Islamic ecumene of which the Red Sea forms a part. As we see in Chapter 1, regional, Islamic notions of international and maritime law were rooted in mutual gift giving, common faith, recognition and tribute between rulers and the protection of strangers. Bold assertions of individuals' or states' natural rights and military might were foreign to the rich, ceremonial and diplomatic texture of regional inter-ruler relations. The difference is evident, for example, in the contrast between Islamic and

---

[26] Gilbert, *Dhows*, p. 64. See also, E. S. Roscoe, *Reports of Prize Cases Determined in the High Court of Admiralty from 1745 to 1859, Vol. 1* (London: Stevens and Sons, 1905).

[27] David Schoenbrun, 'Violence and vulnerability in East Africa before 1800 CE: An agenda for research', *History Compass*, 4(5) (2006), p. 746.

[28] Grovogui, 'Regimes of sovereignty', esp. p. 323.

European approaches to salvage, an important theme in the narrative that follows. In Grotius' view, outlined in the previous section, the fortunate and the powerful had the right to extract salvage awards from the weak and unfortunate on their own – favourable – terms. The stronger, rescuing party received part of the weaker, rescued party's property. In Islamic maritime law, however, regional rulers in maritime trading zones such as the southern Red Sea agreed among themselves to pay rewards to salvors who protected and offered assistance to their ships floundering at sea. Systems of mutual aid between neighbouring empires were concretised by treaties – not by the natural rights of the strong to claim part of the property of the weak as a prize. As historian and legal scholar Hassan Khalileh writes, 'Latin law allowed a salvager to claim a certain percentage of salvaged goods. Islamic law ... did not'.[29]

The more cooperative and cordial approach to maritime safety was deep-rooted in the region. As early as the twelfth century, an Egyptian ship is recorded as having foundered in the southern Red Sea, resulting in the coastal African salvors taking from the cargo only an amount commensurate with their wages for the rescue operation; the rest of the property remained that of the ship or cargo-owner. Moreover, there is good evidence that Islamic rulers in the region inclined towards establishing treaty contracts with Latin rulers to safeguard their merchants' property rights in case of disaster. Thus, the Egyptian Mamluk Sultan Qalawun signed a treaty with Lady Margaret of Tyre in 1285 to the effect that the Sultan retained all rights over his subjects' ships and their cargoes whenever they were wrecked on Levantine or Cypriot shores. This in turn allowed the Mamluk Sultan to hold the property in its entirety on behalf of its owners.[30] Yet such Eurasian relations were the exception prior to the eighteenth century: the commercial centre of gravity for the southern Red Sea region was the eastern Arabian Peninsula, the Persian Gulf, northwestern south Asia and other, predominantly Islamic, coastal regions further afield.

---

[29] Hassan S. Khalileh, *Islamic Maritime Law: An Introduction* (Leiden: Koninklijke Brill, 1998), p. 109.

[30] Khalileh, *Islamic Maritime Law*, pp. 112–113. See also Majid Khadduri, *The Islamic Law of Nations* (Baltimore: The Johns Hopkins Press, 1966) and Majid Khadduri, *War and Peace in the Law of Islam* (Baltimore: The Johns Hopkins Press, 1955).

This is not to suggest that 'Europe' and 'Afro-Asia' constituted discrete and coherent zones of law or international relations prior to colonisation. To argue that the entire *dar al-Islam* approached the international and maritime sphere in a unified way would be as outlandish as suggesting that every European official carried with them a copy of Grotius' *Commentary* in their travelling trunks. In speaking of European and Islamic 'systems' of international relations and maritime law in the nineteenth century, I indicate simply that Europeans and the people of the southern Red Sea were not in regular or intensive contact prior to the colonial episode, and did not, as a consequence, share 'common interests and values', or even common notions of diplomacy.[31] As can be seen from this brief comparison, both Europeans and regional actors approached the international sphere in a coherent, rational way; both adopted observable and enforceable rules. But there was a disjuncture – a misalignment – in the way Europeans and Africans approached sharing maritime space in the southern Red Sea. Europe's expansion into the region put the two approaches into competition.

As we will see, these differences played out in the course of negotiations over treaties relating to maritime law and coastal sovereignty. Indigenous regional rulers sought to incorporate foreign trading partners and neighbouring sovereigns into a cooperative and reciprocal web of shelter. In contrast, European colonial officials reduced their relations to miserly, self-interested contractual agreements. Colonial actors forged ahead with contracts heedless of regional rulers' efforts to involve them in a system of regional diplomacy. Rather than be incorporated into a regional network of Islam and diplomacy, colonists threatened war, and foisted peace agreements onto local rulers with the spectre of gunboats looming in the background. Indeed, the bulk of diplomacy in the region was also truce-making, conditional offers of peace, against the backdrop of violence.

The impact of the warlike spirit of colonial treaties is difficult to overstate. Practically the entire colonial map of the region was created as protectorates, colonies by treaty rather than by effective

---

[31] This language is from Bull, *The Anarchical Society*, pp. 12–16. Bull himself draws on the work of the Göttingen school historian Arnold Heeren; see Arnold Hermann Ludwig Heeren, *Handbuch der Geschichte des europäischen Staatensystems und seiner Kolonien* (Göttingen: Johann Friedrich Bower, 1830).

occupation.[32] The only way to fully understand the complex and contingent ways these agreements unfolded is not simply to study these agreements' terms, but also their context. This context is in part that of Europe's ascendancy. Europeans became technologically, commercially and politically powerful enough to enforce their anarchic vision of maritime space sharing in the earlier period. But power relations is not the only lens through which to understand the encounter. Rather, the emergence of a regional system of international relations in the colonial period must be understood against the backdrop of the events that precipitated colonial agreements: shipwrecks and increasingly violent confrontations over the safety of international shipping.

Paying close attention to the circumstances surrounding the creation of Euro-African and Euro-Arab colonial agreements in the southern Red Sea region offers a new vantage on the nature of international relations that colonial rule created in the region. What emerges defies straightforward characterisation. But the new logic of international space in the region was shaped by colonial opportunists who used violence for their own benefit, by various actors who instrumentalised violence to compete with and partake in the new gunboat regime of diplomatic order. As Martin Wight puts it, treaties were often but 'empty professions of peaceful purpose and common interest' that belied a 'general preference for going down to defeat fighting rather than consenting to unresisted subjugation.' In the blunter words of Carl von Clausewitz, international law was little more than a fig leaf, a collection of 'self-imposed restrictions' which, compared to the imperatives of geostrategy and realpolitik, were 'hardly worth mentioning'.[33] But treaty negotiations did not simply paper over conflicts, they were also themselves a source of considerable tension, even bloodshed. To

---

[32] Some of these treaties can be found in the appendix to this study. The numerous volumes of Sir Edward Hertslet (see Sir Edward Hertslet, *The Map of Africa by Treaty Vols I–III* (London: Harrison and Sons, 1909)) are a useful continental guide to many of the colonial treaties which helped form the contemporary map of Africa. This study only deals with the Majerteen treaties in Somalia; on the colonial treaties with Somalia more generally, see D. C. S. Healy, 'British perceptions of treaties with the Somalis, 1884–1897', in Hussein M. Adam and Charles L. Geshekter, *Proceedings of the First International Conference of Somali Studies* (Atlanta: Scholars Press, 1992), pp. 167–168, 175.

[33] Carl von Clausewitz, J. J. Graham (trans.), *On War* (Ware, Herts: Wordsworth Editions, 1997), p. 5 and Martin Wight, 'Why is there no international relations theory?', *International Relations*, 2(1) (1960), p. 43.

borrow historian David Kennedy's phrase, war was legalised and the law was weaponised.[34]

Ironically, Europeans tended to blame the chaos which ensued colonial rule on the 'primitive' character of local groups. But as I highlight throughout this study, chaos and competition in the maritime realm was a colonial creation, not evidence of some imaginary, pre-civilised past. But nor was colonial chaos in the international realm simply an imposition, a great tsunami whose origins lay in a European earthquake. This study paints a messier picture. There were undoubtedly winners and losers; the whole system of colonial international relations was premised on strategic gains and concessions, advances and retreats. The winners in one sense were the colonial powers, who had gone from being mere guests to wresting control over the international system in the region. In the process, they gained control of the shipping lanes and adjacent littorals, reinscribed the rules of diplomacy, maritime law and international politics on their own terms – terms over which they could prevail. At the same time, established ruling aristocracies toppled; local coastal peoples became collateral damage in episodes of gunboat diplomacy and civilian casualties in contests for military patronage. Yet in another sense, there were no 'winners' or 'victims', at least not at the level of leadership on which this study is focused. In fact, chaos was cocreated by the regional rulers, upstarts, agents and insurgents who recognised the opportunities for personal advancement which a more competitive international arena offered. As we will see, no one enjoyed any permanent success in an inherently unstable environment; everyone was a victim of rising instability.

An Itinerary

The shift in the culture of international law and international relations can be best understood by considering the careers of various characters from the Red Sea's coastline. We meet a colourful sweep of characters, all of whom helped shape a chaotic, competitive and even cut-throat international environment in the southern Red Sea in the colonial era. Beginning in northeastern Somalia, in Chapter 1 we see Sultan Uthman Mahmud Yusuf, ruler of the Majerteen sultanate, used the

---

[34] David Kennedy, *Of War and Law* (Princeton: Princeton University Press, 2007), p. 12.

management of shipwrecks as a pretext to negotiate treaties and codify his rights as a coastal sovereign. Uthman initially approached the British in the same way he approached other regional rulers, as sovereign equals who could be incorporated into an existing regime of treaties and diplomacy. However, in Chapter 2 we see Uthman's early hopes for Anglo-Majerteen accommodation dashed. In part, this was the result of British colonial actors' differing approach to international relations and maritime law. On the other hand, we will see that imperial vanity and local intrigue was also at play – the British were easily exploited by Sultan Uthman's ambitious regional rivals. In the 1870s and '80s, Uthman's cousin, Yusuf 'Ali, promoted himself as a more attractive diplomatic partner, encouraging the British to renege on their agreement with Uthman. A diplomatic precedent began to emerge, leaving in its wake a culture of brinkmanship, countervailing, leveraging, realpolitik and competition. By the late 1870s, treaty making had become a fraught and divisive process, fundamentally different to the more cordial statements of coexistence signed between regional rulers, and between regional rulers and the colonial newcomers, until the mid-1800s.

By the early twentieth century, the whole tone of international relations in the region had begun to change. In Chapter 3, we move to another part of this emerging geostrategic circulation system, to adapt a phrase of the scholar of Oman, John Wilkinson.[35] On the opposite shore of the Red Sea, along the coast of the western Arabian Peninsula, the Tihamat Yemen runs from about the Bab al-Mandab straits in the south to just above the port of Hodeida in the north (Map I.1). This coastline played host to an important maritime uprising, the conditions for which were created by colonial chaos in the international sphere. The uprising was led by Shaykh Nasr Ambari, who was followed by his lieutenant Ahmad Fatini, and it spanned the late nineteenth and early twentieth centuries. Their followers were known by the British and Italians as the 'Zaraniq'.

After the collapse of the Ottoman Empire at the end of World War I, Ambari and Fatini perpetrated attacks against ships and other forms of maritime violence in the seas near Hodeida to try to lure the British into supporting their campaign for independence against their regional

---

[35] John Wilkinson, *Arabia's Frontiers: The Story of Britain's Boundary Drawing in the Desert* (London: I. B. Tauris, 1991), p. 33.

rivals, Ibn Saud and the Imam Yahya. In the late nineteenth and early twentieth centuries the British in Aden, the Ottomans in Hodeida, the French in the Gulf of Tadjoura and the Italians in Eritrea all began to cast around for local military allies along the coast of the Arabian Peninsula. The process set in motion the creation of a market for colonial proxies which proved perilous to its participants. Coastal sovereignty had previously focused on controlling shipping lanes and protecting the region from the disruptive influence of outsiders. After 1900, this venerable system of coastal governance collapsed, leaving in its wake a much more competitive struggle between coastal rulers for territorial influence and international recognition.

In the 1910s and 1920s, the doors to the international system – and sovereignty of the coast – had been thrown wide open to a whole host of ambitious traders and mercenaries. In Chapter 4, we meet Henry de Monfreid who was simultaneously a private citizen, an entrepreneur of violence, and an agent of French imperialism in the region. Following the demise of royalty in the diplomatic sphere, characters such as de Monfreid were free to insinuate themselves as delegates of the colonial state. The brittle, fickle temper of international affairs blurred the distinction between maritime mercenary and navy. In reality, the distinction between 'legitimate' state-sponsored violence and 'illegitimate' private violence was one mediated by the courts and by officials in colonial governments. So-called outlaws, pirates, privateers and maritime mercenaries always stood 'in dialogue with' rather than in simple opposition to power.[36] Although many colonial governments lasted

---

[36] See Sebastian R. Prange, 'The contested sea: Regimes of maritime violence in the pre-modern Indian Ocean', *Journal of Early Modern History*, 17(1) (2013), p. 33; Sebastian R. Prange, 'A trade of no dishonor: Piracy, commerce, and community in the western Indian Ocean, twelfth to sixteenth century', *The American Historical Review*, 116 (5) (2011), pp. 1269–1272; Michael Kempe, '"Even in the remotest corners of the world": Globalized piracy and international law, 1500–1900', *Journal of Global History*, 5(3) (2010), pp. 353–372; Anne Pérotin-Dumon, 'The pirate and the emperor: Power and the law on the seas, 1450–1850', in C. Richard Pennell (ed.), *Bandits at Sea: A Pirates Reader* (London: New York University Press, 2001), pp. 25–54; Janice E. Thomson, *Mercenaries, Pirates and Sovereigns: State Building and Extra-Territorial Violence in Europe* (Princeton: Princeton University Press, 1994); Molly Green, *Catholic Pirates and Greek Merchants: A Maritime History of the Mediterranean* (Princeton: Princeton University Press, 2010); Simon Layton, 'Discourses of piracy in an age of revolutions', *Itinerario*, 35(2) (2011), pp. 81–97.

for over a century, they depended for their survival on their ability to marshal force to their cause, to win by violence and imposition what might otherwise be achieved by diplomacy, consensus-building and cooperation.

As Yusuf 'Ali's, Shaykh Nasr Ambari's, Ahmad Fatini's and de Monfreid's stories show, local strongmen adopted the new rule of force enthusiastically. The new colonial international environment liberated men like Yusuf 'Ali, Ambari, Fatini and de Monfreid from the constraints of traditional diplomacy in the region, which involved a complex mix of factors, including birth and aristocracy, networks of contacts, and intricate, learned customs and ceremonials. The colonial modus operandi, by contrast, was crude: the threat or application of force, harsh bargaining, and written contracts were its critical elements. Being largely devoid of nuance, the colonial system also empowered upstarts such as de Monfreid, Yusuf 'Ali and Ahmad Fatini to burst onto the international scene, and to help transform the international situation into one of colonial chaos.

Hazards

Putting colonial officials, colonial subjects, indigenous royal rulers, upstarts, Europeans, Arabs and Africans in the same story reflects the reality of political life in the region. The increasing differentiation of historical sub-disciplines has pushed African and Imperial History further apart in the last few decades. Without in any way wishing to detract from the importance of understanding African history in its own right, this book seeks to blur the boundaries, at least a little, in order to reflect the multi-ethnic, multicultural and multi-governmental reality of life. De Monfreid, Uthman, Fatini and others were simultaneously architects of the system and its victims. The patron–client relationship was a two-way street.[37] It would be false to exclude these characters from the story of international relations, even though – apart from Uthman – they were not traditional, high-born members of Yemeni or Somali society, or just because they were not associated with one of the major regional powers. The characters at the centre of

---

[37] See for example, Clapham, *Africa and the International System*; Chabal and Daloz, *Africa Works*, esp. pp. 85–87, 155–163; Colin Newbury, *Patrons, Clients and Empire: Chieftaincy and Over-Rule in Asia, Africa and the Pacific* (Oxford: Oxford University Press, 2003).

this study were both the architects and the subjects of colonial chaos in the international, maritime realm.

The motley social make-up of the southern Red Sea in the nineteenth century is mirrored by the somewhat erratic geography of this study. Rather than remain safely in one place, we start south, strike north and finally head west, dotting from the Somali coast, to Yemen and on to the Gulf of Tadjoura, or contemporary Djibouti. Nevertheless, there are hazards associated with the blurring of geographical boundaries and mixing of sub-disciplines. One important danger is that telling the story from both sides of the Red Sea coast involves integrating the independently rich, and largely divergent, historiographies of northeast Africa and the Arabian Peninsula. These two regions are normally considered culturally, linguistically and historically distinct and are studied by highly separated, highly specialised groups of scholars. Historians of the Arabian Peninsula do not often venture to Africa; historians of northeast Africa tend to remain on the continent.

In many respects, the Afro–Middle Eastern continental divide in Red Sea studies remains strong. However, compelling arguments have been made about the connectedness, coherence or otherwise of the southern Red Sea region over the historical longue durée.[38] In this study I suggest an alternative basis for considering the region in a single composition: in the minds of regional rulers, colonial officials and various international actors, the southern Red Sea region was a single strategic theatre. By imposing on the southern Red Sea a geostrategic coherence different in nature and more limited in scope than the commercial and diplomatic connections that entangled the area before colonial rule, colonialism divided the region in a myriad of ways. Following the conquest of Aden in the nineteenth century, the entire

---

[38] See Ali A. Mazrui, 'Towards abolishing the Red Sea and re-Africanizing the Arabian Peninsula', in Jeffrey Stone (ed.), *Africa and the Sea* (Aberdeen: Aberdeen University African Studies Group, 1985) and Alexis Wick, *The Red Sea: In Search of Lost Space* (Berkley: University of California Press, 2016), pp. 97–103; Mostafa Manawi, *The Ottoman Scramble for Africa: Empire and Diplomacy in the Sahara and the Hijaz* (Stanford: Stanford University Press, 2016); Jonathan Miran, *Red Sea Citizens: Cosmopolitan Society and Cultural Change in Massawa* (Indianapolis: Indiana University Press, 2009); Roxani Eleni Margariti, *Aden and the Indian Ocean Trade: 150 Years in the Life of a Medieval Arabian Port* (Chapel Hill: University of North Carolina Press, 2007). An older review of the state of this literature can be found in Jonathan Miran, 'Mapping space and mobility in the Red Sea region, c. 1500–1950', *History Compass*, 12(2) (2014), pp. 197–216.

region became deeply embroiled in a cycle of change which culminated in a more chaotic, competitive, real-political international realm. Thus reading the region through the colonial archives allows us to observe connectedness in its absence, to reckon with the colonial impact in terms of what was destroyed, and to form an estimate of how the fabric of international relations and regional connectedness changed.

Piecing together their stories involved navigating a tangle of incomplete administrative records strewn across disparate locations. Much of the research took place in the India Office Records (IOR), now housed in the British Library in London, England. The IOR host the bulk of the records of the East India Company and its successor, the British government in India based in London and South Asia. The records are thus voluminous, but also impressively diverse. They touch on the history of the whole of the EIC's sphere – including South Asia, the Persian Gulf and Aden, but also Southeast Asia. For the period from 1600 to about 1800 they are a commercial company's records, but they are concerned with issues far wider than balance sheets, including ethnography, languages, local history and military operations. The British government took over, gradually, from the EIC beginning with the East India Company Act of 1784 – which placed the administrative aspects of the EIC's activities under British government control – and culminating in the Government of India Act of 1858, which nationalised the EIC. While the archive becomes increasingly governmental in form thereafter, it remained eclectic throughout the nineteenth and twentieth centuries.

A similar kind of heterogeneity characterises the records of France and Italy in the region, particularly those of their foreign and colonial offices. Research also encompassed the French diplomatic archival records and the French Colonial Ministry records in Paris and Aix-en-Provence respectively, as well as the Italian Foreign and Africa Ministry records in Rome. The nature of these records was similar to the British India Office Records – a mixture of military memoranda, diplomatic correspondence, local intelligence gathering, regional histories, treaties in local languages, translations of treaties into European languages, court records and administrative memoranda. Within are several points of view: colonial official, local agents interpreting colonial strategy and regional royalties asserting their own standpoints against colonial interests. Read over time, however, the shape of the archive points to the way in which the tone of regional relationships changed, as well as discernible developments in the kinds of regional people who appear in the records. Local royalties were sidelined in favour of upstarts and local military leaders, the content of official-local interactions became more concerned with local geopolitics than with historical rights. The form of the paper trail of colonial rule is thus sometimes as revealing as its content, notably of the governmental cultures.[39]

I sought to embrace the material diversity and geographic scatter of the records in other ways. Research for this study also involved stints in several smaller archives, as well as interviews with officials in the region, NGO workers, lawyers, journalists writing on Somalia during the piracy crisis and the descendants of some of the characters in this study in Europe and in East Africa. All of this work contributed to the study; direct links are cited, but other more indirect influences are omitted, mindful that this is already a densely footnoted study. Further archival research took place at the League of Nations archives in Geneva, Switzerland, and in libraries and interviews in Nairobi, Kenya and Addis Ababa, Ethiopia, as well as in the British Colonial, Admiralty and War Offices, all housed in the National Archives in Kew. I have pieced together a narrative which I hope is consistent but which, perhaps more importantly, evokes the deep shifts in the culture of law, politics and international relations that took place in the region in the course of the nineteenth and twentieth centuries.

The extensive geographical scope and diverse empirical substrate of this study presents some more practical hazards, mapping high among them. All the regions discussed in this book – Majerteenia, French Somaliland and the Tihamat Yemen – were malleable political zones rather than sharply demarcated administrative units in the nineteenth and early twentieth centuries. As we will see, the Ottomans and Europeans attempted to delimit the southern Red Sea littoral in the second half of the nineteenth and the early twentieth centuries, but even today the region's administrative borders are contested in prac-tice, in spite of the lines drawn around them. Maps are therefore no substitute for political narratives in understanding the region's geopol-itical history. And there is no good way to draw fluidity on a map. The

---

[39] Ann L. Stoler, 'Colonial archives and the arts of governance: On the content in the form', in Carolyn Hamilton, V. Harris, M. Pickover, G. Reid, R. Saleh and J. Taylor (eds.), *Refiguring the Archive* (Cape Town: David Philip, 2002), pp. 83–102.

maps placed throughout this study should be approached with this caveat in mind. I trust that the narrative that accompanies these geographical abstractions will do the work of unravelling the impression that the southern Red Sea can be 'mapped'.

There are other difficulties around complexity, notably in nomenclature. I have in general favoured simplicity and accessibility wherever possible. For example, my approach to the transliteration of Arabic and Somali words relies on common English or Latinate usages, wherever this does not distort their meaning too much. For example, I refer to Ibn Saud in the conventional Latinate way, rather than using his actual Arabic name – Abdulaziz ibn Abdul Rahman ibn Faisal ibn Turki ibn Abdullah ibn Muhammad al Saud. Similarly, in the transliteration of Arabic and Somali words I have mostly retained the Arabic 'ayn in the conventional way, using an apostrophe – as in 'a. But where modern standard spellings of people and places are available, notably as they appear in online maps and resources, I have used these simpler transcriptions because this makes them easier to look up. For example, I refer to Yemen rather than Yaman, Hodeida rather than Hudayda. Simplicity and accessibility is not always possible. With some place names, translation to the modern form would result in anachronism. I have therefore used the historic name – such as Bandar Maryah or Bandar Cassim – rather than the contemporary equivalent – Bossaso. In general, Somali first names are used more often than is common in Latin and Arabic cultures, as is conventional in the region. Dollar amounts are Maria Theresa dollars, unless otherwise stated.

More broadly, I have of necessity and by design removed historical and local detail from the story. The study makes reference to various entities and historical processes along the western coast of the Arabian Peninsula, the Hadhramaut, Oman, Zanzibar, northwestern South Asia, the East African coast, the Horn of Africa and the Egyptian ecumene. I have sought to include only as much detail in the body of the text itself as is necessary for the sake of understanding the international, geostrategic narrative. Instead, I have also included a Note on the Text, which contains a number of general notes on the history of many of the regions and political entities mentioned in this study. It is not necessary to read the glossary in order to understand the story, but it provides important context about the way these different imperial powers fit into the history of international relations in the southern Red Sea. The Note on the Text also provides guidance on the way in which certain terms, which have become overburdened with meaning, are used in the text, especially the many overused synonyms that occur in the wider literature, such as Ethiopia and Abyssinia, Djibouti and French Somaliland, or the Persian Gulf and the Arabian Gulf, to name a few. Such elisions sometimes conflate time periods – such as the precolonial, colonial and postcolonial histories of the Gulf of Tadjoura – and others elide political detail, such as the competing politico-ethnic claims to control the gulf region between contemporary Iran and the Emirates. The Note on the Text provides some explanation and guidance; so too, the Dramatis Personae offers a shorthand guide to some of the main characters in the story. There is clearly a cost to taking such an expansive approach, but it is hoped that placing several regions in the same analytical frame offers the advantage of a different perspective and a deeper understanding of the origins of the region's febrile international climate. In Chapter 1, we explore the older political culture of diplomacy in the Red Sea – before exploring in the subsequent chapters how it unravelled during the better part of a century of colonial conquest that lasted from 1839 until well into the twentieth century.

1 | *Sultan Uthman's Salvage Agreements*

I much doubt if a vessel were wrecked on any other coast ... whether the crew would have fared as well as those of the steam [f]rigate *Memnon*.[1]
— Charles Cruttenden

Cape Guardafui is the easternmost point of continental Africa, jutting impressively into the Indian Ocean. For much of the thirteenth to the eighteenth century, the coastline formed part of the Warsangeli Sultanate; to the east lay the Ifat-Adal Sultanates, and beyond this, the Abyssinian highlands. To the south of the Warsangeli Sultanate lay the empires of the Mogadishu and Ajuran Sultanates, part of the Swahili zone. In earlier times, the ancient Egyptians and Phoenicians knew the coastline as Punt, where a powerful local ruler protected shipwrecked sailors. Indeed, Punt appears to have confronted the Egyptian Middle Kingdom as a diplomatic equal: when the Egyptians offered the ruler of Punt 'laudanum and malabathrum, terebinth and balsam, and the incense of the temple estates with which every God is content' as well as to 'slaughter bulls for you as a burnt offering', the ruler of Punt is said to have replied: 'I am the ruler of Punt; myrrh is mine; that malabathrum you speak of bringing is this island's plenty'. The pharaohs made the shipwrecked sailor an envoy to the coast of Punt, and endowed him with a staff of two hundred men.[2] In this chapter, we trace the deep history of international relations, including the diplomatic, political and commercial history of north-eastern Africa from

---

[1] Charles J. Cruttenden, 'Report on the Mijjertheyn Tribe of Somallies, inhabiting the district forming the North-east point of Africa', *Transactions of the Bombay Geographical Society*, 7 (1844–1846), p. 412.

[2] R. B. Parkinson (ed. and trans.), *The Tale of Sinuhe and Other Ancient Egyptian Poems, 1940–1640 BC* (Oxford: Oxford University Press, 1997), pp. 89–101, esp. p. 96. On the story's rediscovery in the early twentieth century, see Alan H. Gardiner, 'New literary works from ancient Egypt', *Journal of Egyptian Archaeology*, 1(1) (1914), pp. 20–21.

approximately 1,000 BCE until the nineteenth century, before exploring how this system of trade and diplomacy dealt with the arrival of the
British in Aden in the mid-nineteenth century, and the steep increase in
maritime steam traffic after the opening of the Suez Canal in 1869.

Ancient International Relations

Close diplomatic relations between Punt and the Egyptian Middle
Kingdom are confirmed by various wall paintings in the temples of
Thebes, including in Deir-el-Bahari, where the archaeologists
Dumisten and Mariette discovered mural paintings depicting the
exchange of gifts.[3] Moreover, the connection was enduring. Punt
remained a trading partner of Egypt during the Persian Achaemenid
period, and the early Hellenistic/Ptolemaic periods. During the late
Ptolemaic and Roman periods in Egypt, the anonymous navigator
and author of the *Periplus of the Erythraen Sea* tells us that at least
three of the ports of what became Majerteenia – Bandar Cassim, Alula
and Ras Hafun – existed in ancient times. During late Ptolemaic times,
the *Periplus* states, the whole region was known as the Spice Coast,
named after its aromatic and medicinal resins exports, notably frankincense from the indigenous *Boswella sacra* tree, myrrh from the
related Commiphora myrrha tree and other spices imported from
South Asia via Egypt, such as cinnamon, from the bark of a of a laurel,
as well as aloes.

But Punt's ancient trade was not restricted to spices and aloes. It was
also a source of precious metals, including the distinctive copper min-
eral malachite and the gold and silver compound electrum, alongside
some wheat, an alcohol described as wine, tortoiseshell, ivory, a
cooking fat rendered from the skins of lizards and plumage from
indigenous birds such as the ostrich.[4] As well as with Egypt, Punt
traded with the opposite coasts of Southern Arabia, including what is
today Hadhramaut and Tihamat Yemen, in ancient times.[5] The

---

[3] Élisée Reclus, A. H. Keane (ed.), *Earth and Its Inhabitants: Africa, Vol. IV: South and East Africa* (New York: D. Appleton and Company, 1890), pp. 390–391.

[4] See Wilfred H. Schoff (trans.), *The Periplus Erythraen Sea: Travel and Trade in the Indian Ocean by a Merchant of the First Century* (New York: Longmans, Green, and Co., 1912), pp. 32–33.

[5] Radolfo Fattovich, 'The contacts between southern Arabia and the Horn of Africa in Late Prehistoric and Early Historical Times: A view from Africa', in A. Avanzini (ed.), *Profumi d'Arabia* (Rome: 'L'Erma' di Bretschneider, 1997), pp. 273–286.

Periplus informs us that the Spice Coast was ruled over by an independent king and lay to the east of Adulis, the ancient port of the Aksumite kingdom, which was located approximately in the location of today's Zeila.[6]

In the late-Roman and early Islamic periods, Punt continued to trade, though less with Egypt to the north, and increasingly towards the east, with the Arabian Peninsula, Persian Empire and South Asia. Punt is not part of what we typically think of as the Swahili coast – the region spanning the northern coast of Mozambique, Tanzania, Kenya and the far south of Somalia, which became an important part of the western Indian Ocean trading world from about the middle of the first millennium CE. From roughly 500 CE, the Swahili coast developed the distinct language from which it takes its name, as well as a characteristic political culture and architecture. By contrast, north-eastern Somalia was never Swahili-speaking, but its maritime character – as evidenced in the *Periplus* – suggests its seafaring roots stretch back to perhaps 1,000 years before those of the rest of eastern Africa.[7]

The longevity of Punt's international connections helps explain the durability of its distinct regional culture, and its stable position in the area's international politics. The people of the region of Punt spoke Somali, an Eastern Cushitic language that originated in the Red Sea hills of contemporary Sudan and Eritrea during the seventh millennium BCE.[8] But Cushitic-speaking Punt was nevertheless subject to many of the same forces as the Swahili coast. While Punt remained under the control of kingdoms that were the heirs to the ancient ruling structures, notably the Warsangeli Sultanate, the style of rule and of trade and architecture increasingly reflected its mixing with Arab influences from the Arabian Peninsula and elsewhere around the Indian Ocean. Thus, local littoral peoples converted to Islam between the ninth and twelfth centuries CE; they traded goods from as far afield as Gujarat, to Ming China and Iran, including Shiraz from around the turn of the second millennium CE. Around the same time, a distinctive coastal architecture evolved, reminiscent of both the Swahili coral-stone architecture and the Hadhrami style. Bandar Cassim – contemporary Bosaso – as

---

[6] Stuart Munro-Hays, 'The foreign trade of the Aksumite Port of Adulis', *Azania*, 17 (1982), pp. 107–125.

[7] Jeffrey Fleisher, Paul J. Lane, Adria LaViolette et al., 'When did the Swahili become maritime?', *American Anthropologist*, 117(1) (2015), pp. 100–115.

[8] Christopher Ehret, *History and the Testimony of Language* (Berkley: University of California Press, 2011), pp. 170–184.

well as Alula and Ras Hafun all continued to trade in many of the same goods throughout this period.[9]

Trade was significant but seasonal along the coast of northeast African peninsula; its place names provide a guide to its international commercial history. The south-west monsoon between October and December brought traders to Somalia from across the Arabian Peninsula, the Persian Gulf, South Asia and even as far afield as Mauritius; the north-eastern monsoon between July and September took them back.[10] Trading centres in northeastern Somalia proliferated during this time, generally clustering around the several creeks and ravines that intersected the shoreline and brought inland mountain rains – and commercial caravans – to provide fresh water and interior goods for consumption in coastal settlements. These natural features gave rise to the region's Arab–Somali toponymy. For example, the headland at the far tip of the Horn was known to Arabic speakers as Ras 'Asir, meaning 'the end of the coast'. Another of the region's names, Yard-Hafun, or Yardaf, blends Arabic and Somali, and translates loosely as 'the point followed by the surrounded', referring to the natural tombolo-like peninsula – Hafun – which lies about a hundred miles south of the tip of Africa.[11]

However, in translation to European languages, the cape's name took on a more sinister valence, coming to connote danger rather than nautical advice. The Arabic name 'Yardaf' gave the region its Somali name, 'girdifo', which made its way into European languages as 'Guardafui'. Reading the history of the word backwards, later

---

[9] Matthew C. Smith and Henry T. Wright, 'The ceramics from Ras Hafun in Somalia: Notes on a Classical Maritime Site', *Azania*, 23 (1988), pp. 15–41; Kenneth A. Kitchen, 'The elusive land of Punt revisited', in Paul Lunde and Alexandra Porter (eds.), *Trade and Travel in the Red Sea Region: Proceedings of Red Sea Project I 2002* (Oxford: British Archaeological Report International, 2004), pp. 25–31. See also, on the region further west, Alfredo González-Ruibal, de Torres, Jorge, Manuel Antonio Franco et al., 'Exploring long distance trade in Somaliland (AD 1000–1900): Preliminary results from the 2015–2016 field seasons', *Azania*, 52(2) (2017), pp. 135–172.

[10] Charles J. Cruttenden, 'Memoir of the Western or Edoor tribes, inhabiting the Somali coast of N.-E. Africa, with the southern branches of the family of Darrood, resident on the banks of the Webbe Shebeyli, commonly called the River Webbe', *The Journal of the Royal Geographical Society of London*, 19 (1849), pp. 75–76.

[11] Captain S. B. Miles, 'On the neighbourhood of Bunder Marayah', *Journal of the Royal Geographical Society of London*, 42 (1872), p. 72; Reclus, *Earth and Its Inhabitants*, p. 382. See also Cruttenden, 'Memoir of the Western or Edoor tribes', p. 74.

European scholars hypothesised that the peninsula's name came from the Levantine lingua franca 'guarda', meaning 'beware'.[12] That the later European translation stuck, and the region became inherently associated with maritime danger, is on one view unsurprising. The cape itself is formed of a headland rising six hundred to nine hundred feet out of the sea. Although the water is deep at the base of the cliffs, local weather systems create a host of dangers for sailors. In summer in the northern hemisphere, the south-west monsoon agitates the seas along the coast, creating cyclones and provoking great sea fogs, which impair visibility. The currents in the vicinity of the cape are strong and changeable. But it is important to recall that another, less prejudicial set of naming practices existed; even the British traveller and East India Company lieutenant Charles Cruttenden suggested that certain Somali words for the region meant 'beloved'.[13]

Commercial Continuity

In many ways, the advent of the EIC and the settlement of the Arabian Peninsula port of Aden by EIC men from South Asia continued this regional tradition of Indian Ocean trade in north-eastern Somalia. In the 1530s, the Abyssinian–Adal conflict instigated by Ahmad al-Ghazi precipitated the collapse of the Adal Sultanate to the west of the Punt region; it also led the Warsangeli Sultanate to contract. In the following two centuries, the Majerteen Sultans – likely a breakaway group of the Warsangeli – emerged as the pre-eminent regional power along the north-eastern Somali coast historically known as Punt (see Map 1.1). Trading increasingly with South Asian traders and the southern Arabian Peninsula, the Majerteen traded ever larger cargoes of food staples from the subcontinent for regional products, still including incense and gums, as well as catering to even further-flung tastes, such as shark fins for East Asia.[14] So too the increase in South Asian pilgrims taking the Hajj as the EIC expanded into South Asia led to a

---

[12] Reclus, *Earth and Its Inhabitants*, p. 382.

[13] Cruttenden, 'Report on the Mijjertheyn', p. 111.

[14] Charles Guillain, *Documents sur l'histoire, géographie et le commerce de l'Afrique Orientale, Deuxième Partie* (Paris: Arthus Bertrand, 1849), pp. 454–460; Charles-Xavier Rocher d'Héricourt, *Second Voyage sur les deux Rives de la Mer Rouge dans le pays des Adels et le royaume de Choa* (Paris: Arthus Bertrand, 1846), p. 293.

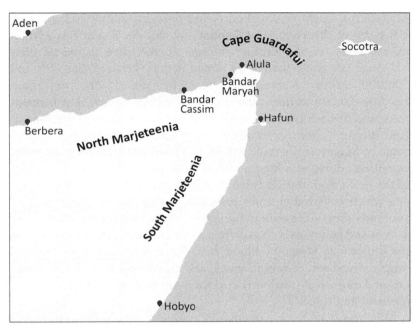

Map 1.1 North and south Majerteenia, circa 1900
(© 2021 Nicholas W. Stephenson Smith. All rights reserved)

rise in passing traffic. The settlement of the EIC outpost in Aden in 1839 created increased demand for Somali staples – coffee, hides, incenses, livestock, pearls, shark fins and spices.[15] Indeed, by the middle of the nineteenth century, the number of sheep exported from the Majerteen coast to Aden and onto other ports in the Arabian Peninsula reached some 15,000 per year, alongside exports of at least a thousand tons of gum per year to the Arabian Peninsula and India.[16]

Much of this trade was in the hands of EIC and South Asian merchants, but much was also undertaken by Majerteen merchants. By the mid-nineteenth century, local merchants owned some forty large merchant sailboats between them, each capable of carrying one hundred tons or more. The boats were spread across owners in

---

[15] Richard Pankhurst, 'Indian trade with Ethiopia, the Gulf of Aden and the Horn of Africa in the nineteenth and early twentieth centuries', *Cahiers d'Études Africaines*, 14(55) (1974), pp. 454–455, 460.

[16] Cruttenden, 'Report on the Mijjertheyn', pp. 120–122.

Majerteenia's eight principal ports, five ports in addition to the historical ports of the Periplus at Bandar Cassim, Alula and Ras Hafun. In monetary terms, British officials at the time estimated that Majerteenia's trade with Aden amounted to between 250,000 and 500,000 British Rupees per year by the 1870s, or about £25,000–50,000 sterling (about £30–60 million today) and between three and five per cent of Aden's total imports, including from mainland Britain.[17] British officials likely underestimated the volume and value of Majerteenia's trade, which also encompassed much unofficial commerce, notably in firearms, as we will see in later chapters. Much of the profit from this trade would have accrued directly to the sultanate, which collected customs dues and monopolised – perhaps since very early times – the right to harvest certain popular trade goods, such as bees and honey, as well as certain gums and resins from trees such as the indigenous Dragon's Blood tree. Spices including turmeric and saffron, livestock, certain incenses, and marine goods such as ambergris and mother-of-pearl were free for non-royals to cultivate, harvest, husband and trade.[18]

Majerteenia on the eve of colonial conquest was, in short, busy and prosperous – perhaps busier than it had ever been, given the rapid expansion in freight capacity and the intensification of trade in staple goods under the influence of the EIC and demand from Aden port. This stimulus was not, it should be noted, an unalloyed positive for the region. The use of land for export commodities rather than food production created ecological stress, animal diseases and, ultimately, precipitated an increase in the frequency of seasonal famines in Eastern Africa and the Arabian Peninsula.[19] One historian even argued that

---

[17] On Majerteen trade values, see Captain F. M. Hunter, *An Account of the British Settlement of Aden in Arabia* (London: Trübner, 1877), pp. 75, 90, 106, 116–120. See also Richard Pankhurst, 'The trade of the Gulf of Aden ports of Africa in the nineteenth and early twentieth centuries', *Journal of Ethiopian Studies*, 3 (1965), p. 62, and Georges Malécot, 'Quelques aspects de la vie maritime en Mer Rouge dans la premiere moitié du XIXe siècle', *L'Afrique et l'Asie Modernes*, Vol. 164 (1990), pp. 22–43.

[18] Giulio Baldacci, 'The promontory of Cape Guardafui', *African Affairs*, 9(33) (1909), p. 71, and Ferrand, *Les Çomalis* (Paris: Ernest Leroux, 1902), p. 136.

[19] Steven Feierman, 'A century of ironies in East Africa, 1780–1890', in Philip Curtin, Steven Feierman, Leonard Thompson, et al., *African History: From Earliest Times to Independence* (New York: Longmann, 1995), p. 405, and Richard Waller, 'Ecology, migration, and expansion in East Africa', *African Affairs*, 84(336) (1985), esp. pp. 352–355.

Somalia's integration into the world economy in the nineteenth century created 'atrocious misery' among the littoral's inhabitants, forcing proud pastoralists to breach long-held taboos about consuming fish in the region, and to turn to the sea as pirates.[20] Likewise, increased seaborne trade added impetus to the slave and arms trades, and triggered a spike in slave raiding in some parts of east and northeast Africa.[21] But northern Somalia appears to have suffered much less acutely than some parts of east Africa as a result of increased commercial interaction with the global economy in the nineteenth century. There were famines in northern Somalia in the nineteenth century, but contemporary reports suggested they tended to be fairly limited in impact, depleting livestock herds for only a year or two and making little difference to coastal communities whose livelihoods depended on trade rather than agriculture.[22]

In fact, the influence of Europe was probably slight until quite late in the nineteenth century, when steamships gave Europeans a commercial edge. However, steamships plying the Red Sea route to India were forced to carry so much coal that they regularly ran out of fuel at sea in the north-western Indian Ocean; only in the 1870s did technological advances allow steamships to sail the length of the Red Sea without the need to refuel.[23] Even when fuel ceased to pose such an acute obstacle to navigation, European traders' hydrographic knowledge of the region made steam ships unusually vulnerable to the vicissitudes of the weather and the vagaries of the seascape. The Indian Navy (then called the 'Bombay Marine') made the earliest hydrographic chart of the Red Sea in 1829, prompted by their failed attempts to run a steamship from India to Suez. The early steamship was stranded because it ran out of fuel, and the coal ship sent to refuel it was

---

[20] Wayne K. Durrill, 'Atrocious misery: The African origins of famine in northern Somalia, 1839–1884', *American Historical Review*, 91(2) (1986), pp. 292, 301–302.

[21] See Mordichai Abir, 'The Ethiopian slave trade and its relation to the Islamic world', in John R. Willis (ed.), *Slaves and Slavery in Muslim Africa* (London: Frank Cass, 1985), esp. p. 132; Abdussamad H. Ahmad, 'Ethiopian slave exports at Matamma, Massawa and Tajura, c. 1830–1885', in William Gervase Clarence-Smith (ed.), *The Economics of the Indian Ocean Slave Trade* (London: Frank Cass, 1989), pp. 93–102; Janet Ewald, 'The Nile Valley system and the Red Sea slave trade, 1820–1880', in Clarence-Smith, *The Economics*, pp. 71–91.

[22] See Miles, 'On the neighbourhood', pp. 61–76.

[23] Blyth, 'Aden, British India', pp. 70, 83.

wrecked on a reef. The incident also resulted in Captain Moresby's *Sailing Directions for the Red Sea*,[24] swiftly followed by Captain Owen's survey of the early 1830s and Captain Haines' chart in 1839.[25]

However, the level of detail offered in the chart, particularly in coastal waters, represented only a marginal advantage to mariners over guesswork. Territorial maps added little more than the Ancients had known about northeastern Somalia. For example, a London map dating only slightly earlier to 1804 mentions only a handful of ports along the whole of the southern Red Sea coast, and none whatsoever along the coast of northeast Africa (see Map 1.2). The challenge of creating an accurate hydrographic map, indicating ocean depth, anchorages, and coastal features was entirely beyond the scope of the EIC or any other European agency at the time. Although European mariners acquired more knowledge in the course of the 1800s, the situation was not much different by the turn of the twentieth century. As the marine biologist Cyril Crossland wrote in 1912, Admiralty charts mapping the southern Red Sea – the first Red Sea and Gulf of Aden Pilot appeared in about 1880 – were mostly useless 'monuments to the greatness of the Admiralty's conception of taking the whole world for its province'.[26] Local sailors therefore possessed the advantage of superior nautical knowledge of the region; they understood from experience the Red Sea's cyclonic wind patterns the dangers of its shallow reefs and the perils of high cliffs. Indeed, to this day the British Admiralty acknowledges the difficulties of accurately charting the region.[27]

Rather than transforming the whole economy and politics of the region, the initial nineteenth-century uptick in commerce amplified pre-existing patterns, routes and habits of commercial contact. Alongside intensifying contact with South Asia, Majerteenia in the nineteenth century developed even closer links with the Arabian

---

[24] See Sarah Searight, 'The charting of the Red Sea', *History Today*, 53(3) (2003), p. 44.

[25] W. F. W. Owen, *Narrative of Voyages to Explore the Shores of Africa, Arabia, and Madagascar, Vol. 1* (New York: J. & J. Harper, 1833); Captain S. B. Haines, 'Memoir to accompany a chart of the south coast of Arabia, from the entrance of the Red Sea to Misenat', *Journal of the Royal Geographical Society*, 9 (1839), pp. 125–156.

[26] Cyril Crossland, *Desert and Water Gardens of the Red Sea: Being an Account of the Natives and the Shore Formations of the Coast* (Cambridge: Cambridge University Press, 1913), p. vii.

[27] See Anon, *The Red Sea and Gulf of Aden Pilot: Eighteenth Edition* (London: The Hydrographic Department, Admiralty, 2015), esp. pp. 13–18.

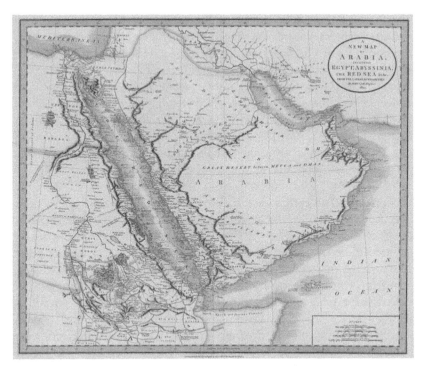

Map 1.2 Map of Red Sea region produced in London in 1804. Note northern Somalia is labelled simply as 'Myrrh and Incense Country'.[28]
(Courtesy of Qatar National Library)

Peninsula, especially Hadhramaut. Majerteen aristocrats imported a range of markers of social distinction such as horses, cavalry warfare, forts and multi-storey houses built in the style of the Hadhramaut.[29] They likewise worshipped Islamic saints from the Arabian Peninsula,

[28] A New Map of Arabia, Including Egypt, Abyssinia, the Red Sea, from the Latest Authorities [F-1–1] (1/1), Qatar National Library, 12886, in Qatar Digital Library <www.qdl.qa/archive/qnlhc/12886.1> [accessed 29 July 2020].

[29] C. P. Rigby, 'On the origin of the Somali Race, which inhabits the north-eastern portion of Africa', *Transactions of the Ethnological Society of London*, 5 (1867)', p. 91; Georges Révoil, *La vallée du Darror: Voyage au pays Çomalis* (Paris: Challamel Aîné, 1882), p. 381; Miles, 'On the neighbourhood', pp. 61–62; James Bird, 'Observations on the manners of the inhabitants who occupy the southern coast of Arabia and shores of the Red Sea; with remarks on the ancient and modern geography of that quarter, and the route, through the desert, from Kosir to Keneh', *Journal of the Royal Geographical Society*, 4 (1834), pp. 192–194.

intermarried, and sometimes used the Arabic script, since Somali Cushitic remained oral. As one nineteenth-century observer put it, the north-eastern Somali were 'Arabised' while their southern cousins swore 'by the rocks and worship[ed] large trees'. The existence of the Ajuran and Mogadishu sultanates hopefully dispels this racialised conceit, a snobbery that has proven incendiary in Somalia under the post-colonial Barre regime, which was widely perceived as north-eastern Somali Darod. However, the importance of the influence of the Arabian Peninsula and the Indian Ocean at large, including Islam, on northeastern Somalia, should not be underestimated.

While densely connected to the rest of the Indian Ocean, Majerteenia was distinct. The earliest written record of the Majerteen origin story was recorded in the 1840s, told by members of the sultan's family to the British visitor Charles Cruttenden. At that time, all Majerteen claimed descent from Mahmud, an ancestral ruler whose reign spanned the mid-eighteenth century. Mahmud, in turn, claimed descent from Darod. Darod's origins are normally traced to a shaykh, or elite Muslim from the Quraysh of the Hejaz – the Prophet's family – who is said to have been wrecked on north-eastern Somali shores around the turn of the first millennium CE. The Majerteen were connected via the Darod lineage to the Warsangeli. But early European visitors observed that the Majerteen formed a divergent 'branch' of the Darod under an ancestral figure known as Uthman Mahmud, whose rule dated to the late seventeenth century. Indeed, all Majerteen traced their origin to one of Uthman Mahmud's three sons – Uthman, Issa and Omar. Mahmud is said to have given different parts of his northern Somali dominion to each son. He gave Issa and Omar the hinterland for pasturage, and the coast to Uthman. In turn, Uthman Mahmud, the son of Mahmud, had seventeen sons. Each son and his heirs inherited a geographically described segment of the north-eastern Somali coastline, thus apportioning a form of collective, lineage-based ownership over beaches, harbours and anchorages.[30]

Although this lineage story suggests a relatively flat social structure, the Majerteen Sultanate, perhaps even more than the

---

[30] Compare Cruttenden, 'Report on the Mijjertheyn', pp. 116–118; Guillain, *Documents sur l'histoire*, pp. 399–400, 440; Georges Révoil, *Voyages au Cap des Aromâtes (Afrique Orientale)* (Paris: Librarie de la société des gens de lettres, 1880), p. 126 and Ferrand, *Les Çomalis*, p. 134. See also Francesco Battera, *Della tribù allo Stato nella Somalia nord-orientale: il caso dei Sultani di Hobiyo e Majerteen, 1880–1930* (Trieste: University of Trieste, 2004).

Warsangeli, Adal and Ifat Sultanates, was steeply hierarchical. The Sultanate had its capital in the port of Bandar Maryah.[31] As Cruttenden wrote in the 1840s, the Majerteen were the only Somali-speaking people 'who acknowledge the name of the sultan ... [whose position] descended in the direct line of the eldest son'.[32] Likewise, at the turn of the twentieth century the French traveller Gabriel Ferrand noted that the 'Majerteen alone give to their chief the name of sultan who passes the title in a direct line to the oldest male heir in the royal family'.[33] Indeed, Majerteen titular and lineage-claims reflected both the Arabic-speaking tradition of claiming descent through pre-Islamic prophets, but also a more straightforward assertion of power. Many Indian Ocean dynasties exalted their lineages by emphasising their longevity. A eulogy for the Mughal emperor Akbar, for example, traced the Mughal back to the biblical Adam. As historian J. F. Richards has observed, such an emphasis on the longevity of a royal lineage creates the aura of 'a calmly controlled energy', a sort of steadily beating royal heart of a place, which engendered 'harmony in the confusing mass of human action'.[34]

Majerteen Diplomacy

Commerce and diplomacy run deep in northeast Africa's history, and were densely interwoven into the fabric of Majerteenia's political culture. A culture and network of regional diplomacy emerged for the purposes of managing shipwrecks and facilitating trade during the Egyptian Middle Kingdom. The shape of the international regime changed over the years, notably with the decline of the Mediterranean world and the influence of Egypt in the post-Ptolemaic era. The spread of Islam and the rise of Persia in the Indian Ocean world created new webs of trade, pulling northeast Africa's focus eastwards. But the region remained resolutely outward-looking. Like regional rulers

[31] G. W. Kempthorne, 'Narrative of a hasty trip to the frankincense country', in George Buist (ed.), *Proceedings of the Bombay Geographical Society* (Bombay: The Times Press, 1844), p. 403.

[32] Cruttenden, 'Report on the Mijjertheyn', p. 117.

[33] Ferrand, *Les Çomalis*, p. 134.

[34] J. F. Richards, 'The formulation of imperial authority under Akbar and Jahangir', in Muzaffar Alam and Sanjay Subrahmanyam (eds.), *The Mughal State, 1526–1750* (Delhi: Oxford University Press, 1998), p. 143.

before them, the Majerteen Sultans played a critical role in the region's foreign affairs.

The Majerteen Sultans' role in conducting foreign relations can be somewhat artificially divided into its high-level, international relationships on the one hand, and its influence over the everyday management of foreign traders and visitors on the other. On a day-to-day basis, all foreign traders, travellers and shipwrecked sailors were obliged to engage an *aban*, or mediator, who took responsibility for a visitor's security, acted as broker for business transactions, made introductions, and played the role of host and interpreter.[35] In exchange, the *aban* levied a fee on all purchases made by the person under their protection, often in addition to presents and gifts which reflected the more-than-transactional nature of the relationship. The relationship between *aban* and client was less one of commercial convenience and more one of mutual recognition, mirroring the mutual recognition Majerteen rulers afforded to other regional coastal royalties. Certainly, some Europeans saw the *abans* as mercenary tax-collectors, as stooges furthering the Majerteen rulers' antipathy to free European trade.[36] But such a crude interpretation of their role does not capture their historical, religious and diplomatic importance.

In fact, *abans* were diplomats, guides, translators, merchants, and intermediaries. On the one hand, the *aban* made local introductions to outsiders, pointed the way to markets for particular goods which their guests sought; helped negotiate prices; served as translators; and even acted as hosts to their assignee. In exchange, the guest offered gifts as well as paying a proportion of the value of their transactions to the *aban*. While these charges became increasingly regular over time, amounting to what looked to Europeans like a customs charge, reckoned in percentage terms, such an impersonal interpretation of their role misses much of the deeper symbolic significance of the *aban*–guest relationship. In the Majerteen worldview, *abans* integrated guests into a local lineage for the duration of their stay. Specifically, *abans* came from the sultan's lineage, the house of Uthman Mahmud.[37] The majority of commercial visitors were thus incorporated directly into the Uthman Mahmud lineage, rather than to one of

---

[35] Rigby, 'On the Origin', p. 94. See also, Owen, *Narrative of Voyages*, p. 358.
[36] Ferrand, *Les Çomalis*, p. 137; Baldacci, 'The promontory', p. 63.
[37] Rigby, 'On the Origin', p. 94.

the more numerous regional lineage families. To focus on the purely commercial, mundane, and practical elements of the *abans*' role – to see them from the standpoint of the visitor – is to overlook this significant diplomatic element to their identities.

There are echoes of the Muslim practice of assigning different legal status to internal and external believers and unbelievers in the Somali concept of *aban*. Forms of non-Muslim protected minority status date as far back as the Arab conquests of the first caliphates and were a necessity in a rapidly-expanding theocracy to rationalise the place of unconverted subjects. It is a commonplace that Islamic jurists divided the world of conquest into the *dar al-harb* and the *dar al-Islam* – territories that did not acknowledge Islam and those which kept the faith. However, such a schematic view of the world was complicated by subdivisions. For example, the *dar al-Islam* included internal categories such as the *dhimma* and *himaya* – protected resident non-Muslims as well as traders, towards whom Muslim rulers had a duty of protection – as well as foreign enemies, normally militaries and crusaders whose intentions were clearly hostile. Similarly, in their relations with foreigners, non-Muslim "otherness" existed in degrees. Thus, within the *dar al-harb*, the *dar al-aman* was a land of security, wherein agreements existed with other Muslim rulers for the purpose of trade. Similarly, the *dar al-'ahd* was an abode of treaties with non-Muslims, wherein Muslims could expect protection for the purposes of trade and travel.[38]

However, Somali Islam was both internally complex and diverse in its approach to foreigners. The Majerteen Sultanate professed Sunni Islam and adherence to the Shafi'i branch of Sunni Islamic law. They sponsored madrasas, built mosques, encouraged prayer and pilgrimage, and undertook many of the other obligations of Muslim rulers. However, amongst pastoralists and some coastal populations, Shafi'i Islam was mixed with other practices and beliefs such as *Zar*, spirit possession, and saint worship. Similarly, a number of Sufi brotherhoods – including the *Ahmadiyya*, *Qadiriyyah* and

---

[38] See Note on the Text. See also Claude Cahen, 'Himaya', in *The Encyclopaedia of Islam*, vol. 3 (Leiden: Brill, 1971), p. 394 and Claude Cahen, 'Himaya: Notes pour l'histoire de la himaya', in Louis Massignon (ed.), *Mélanges Louis Massignon*, vol. 1 (Damascus: Institut Français, 1961), pp. 287–303.

Salihiyyah – infiltrated Majerteen society at various points.[39] Other local idiosyncracies – heretical from a strict Shafi'i standpoint – further complicated the picture. For example, the Majerteen rulers claimed that the fact they were descended from Hejazi shaykhs gave them special powers, or *baraka*, a view antithetical to the beliefs of most Sunni Muslims.[40] Majerteenia was thus simultaneously part of the *dar al-Islam* and the *dar al-'ahd*;[41] it was concomitantly Indian Ocean in its observation of Shafi'i Sunnism, and regional in its veneration of the sultan's status and other lineage saints. The quasi-Islamic concept of *aban* and Somalia's unique approach to foreign visitors was a manifestation of these particularities of place and history. Thus, while vestiges of the concept of *aban* persist in Puntland to this day in the form of hostage-taking, present practices of entrapment and ransom are notably devoid of ceremony and mutual recognition, although they are still an important area in which to conduct international relations.[42] Moreover, as we will see, *aban* and the right of lineages other than that of Uthman Mahmud to provide *aban* became increasingly contested as the nineteenth century progressed.

Nevertheless, before the arrival of Europeans, the *aban* system mediated everyday interactions between foreigners and the Majerteen lineage system. It also afforded foreign commoners the recognition which the sultan himself offered to Majerteenia's regional, and mainly coastal, ruling peers, such as the Ottoman-Egyptian Khedives, the Sultans of Tadjoura, the Naqibs of Mukalla, the Omani Sultans and the Mughal Sultans. The high, royal system of diplomacy was one equally shaped by permissiveness, mutual recognition, gift giving and relative independence.

---

[39] See B. G. Martin, *Muslim Brotherhoods in Nineteenth Century Africa* (Cambridge: Cambridge University Press, 1976), pp. 177–201; Said S. Samatar, *Oral Poetry and Somali Nationalism: The Case of Sayyid Mahammad 'Abdille Hasan* (Cambridge: Cambridge University Press, 1982), *passim*; Abdi Sheikh-Abdi, *Divine Madness: Mohamed Abdulle Hassan (1856–1920)* (London: Zed Books, 1993); Scott Reese, *Renewers of the Age: Holy Men and Social Discourses in Colonial Benaadir* (Leiden: Brill, 2008).

[40] Ioan Lewis, *Saints and Somalis: Popular Islam in a Clan-Based Society* (Lawrenceville, NJ: The Red Sea Press, 1998), pp. 33–58.

[41] Cruttenden, 'Report on the Mijjertheyn', p. 118.

[42] Jatin Dua, 'A sea of trade and a sea of fish: Piracy and protection in the western Indian Ocean', *Journal of Eastern African Studies*, 7(2) (2013), pp. 358–366.

One such high-level international relationship was between the Majerteen Sultans and the Omani Sultans, later the Sultanate of Zanzibar. The French diplomat and traveller Charles Guillain, who visited Majerteenia in the 1840s, recorded that the Majerteen had treaty relations and sent presents to Muscat. 'The Majerteen chiefs consider Sayyid Said [the ruler of Oman] as a great prince and are always keen to satisfy his wishes', wrote Guillain. But the Majerteen Sultans were not beholden: they conformed to the Sayyid's wishes in commercial, maritime and diplomatic matters only so 'long as they also conform to their own interests ... [and] there is no idea of subjection or inferiority'.[43] The Majerteen Sultans' liberty to opt in or out of new clauses in their treaty relations was in evidence when an Omani request to construct a lighthouse at the tip of Cape Guardafui, was rejected by the Majerteen Sultan, since this would lead to the loss of revenues he derived directly for the crown in the form of wrecks strewn on his shores.[44]

The Majerteen Sultans' relations were closer still with the Hadhrami rulers of Mukalla, on the opposite coast of the Arabian Peninsula. The French traveller Georges Révoil visited Majerteenia in the late 1870s and recorded a treaty between the Majerteen Sultan and the ruler of Mukalla, one of the major ports in the Hadhramaut, for the purposes of trade. However, treaties covered far more than just commerce, including criminal matters. For example, in 1875 a Majerteen Somali was killed by local residents in Mukalla, triggering blood-reprisals against Mukalla merchants in Majerteen ports. In an effort to prevent an escalation of the violence, the two rulers concluded a treaty which stated that the two peoples' 'condition should be one, and their port cities should be as one'. By the terms of the treaty both rulers retained authority in their own ports over their own subjects and others and agreed that 'whenever a Somali brings a complaint to the sultans', or when a Hadhrami brought a complaint against a Majerteen, the rulers

---

[43] AOM FM SG Océan Indien OIND/ 22, dossier 117, 'Note sur Abd-al-Gouri et la presqu'ile de Raz-Khafoun', 22/3/1848. See also Guillain, *Documents sur l'histoire*, p. 440.

[44] AOM FM SG OIND/10, dossier 43, Mission confiée à M. Guillain commandant de la Corvette 'la Dordogne' – 1839–41. See also G. Douin, *L'Histoire du règne du Khédive Ismaïl: L'Empire Africain, Vol. III, Deuxième Partie: 1869–1873* (Cairo: L'Imprimerie de l'Institut Française d'Archéologie Orientale de Caire, 1938), p. 186.

would refer the issue to one another for resolution. The two rulers also covenanted to enter an alliance whereby they would mutually prohibit the sale of land in their spheres to persons that either one of them deemed their adversaries.[45]

Both the Majerteen-Omani-Zanzibari and Majerteen-Hadhrami treaties facilitated trade and reinforced the regional rulers' respective sovereignty, as well as bridging any religious divisions between the different parts of the western Indian Ocean Islamic zone. The Majerteen Sultans' sovereignty in the maritime sphere was powerful, even intrusive by nineteenth-century Western standards, affording far fewer rights to individual merchants than did Western maritime law based on the Grotian model. But as the *aban* system and the Majerteen Sultans' treaty with rulers such as the Naqib of Mukalla show, civil rules and royal sovereignty were both more pervasive, but also more permissive and consensual. They were part of a shared 'galaxy' of codes and customs, government and rights that spanned the wider Indian Ocean region. As the historian Sugata Bose argued, precolonial empires 'envisioned incorporation, not subordination' in their approach to sovereignty and international diplomacy.[46] The same was true among the smaller polities of the Indian Ocean rim such as the Majerteen Sultanate, and Mukalla. Indeed, the culture of diplomatic recognition, gift giving and incorporation was pervasive.

In short, treaties strengthened and enhanced the Majerteen sultans' position as rulers. By contrast, as we now see, the European tradition of treaty making and of freedom of commerce stood in stark contrast. While the Majerteen treaties took a permissive, win-win view of political power and international relations in the region, the European view was far more transactional and contested. Indeed, even where the Majerteen informally entered relations with regional states that were manifestly larger and more powerful, there was little idea of subordination. For example, the Majerteen Sultanate flew the Ottoman and Egyptian Khedival flag in its ports – but only, the sultans insisted, to signify their affiliation in religious matters.[47] This more generous

---

[45] A copy of the treaty may be found in the Appendix to this study.

[46] Sugata Bose, *A Hundred Horizons: The Indian Ocean in the Age of Global Empire* (Cambridge, MA: Harvard University Press, 2006), p. 70.

[47] All archival abbreviations are explained in the 'Abbreviations' section in the front matter. All archival records are referred to by their record number followed by a brief description of the document in question, such as letter, its

approach to sovereignty and international relations chimes with other historians' views of precolonial African sovereignty elsewhere on the continent.[48] As Sugata Bose noted, he borrows the concept of a 'galactic' form of empire from Stanley Tambiah's book about the relationship between Buddhism and monarchical authority in Thailand.[49] Moreover, there are echoes of the approach to international space among non-Western civilisations around the globe, including the precolonial Americas.[50] While the royal aspects, contractual forms and some of the ceremonials of gift giving involved in international diplomacy in the Majerteen region would have been familiar to European colonists, its cooperative substance was not. On the contrary, European international relations were governed by force, strategy and transactional negotiations. It is to the forced reconciliation of the two which we now turn.

A Wreck

On the eve of colonial rule, therefore, the Majerteen Sultans were primed to approach foreigners in a cooperative, inclusive way – either by incorporation via *aban* or by treaty. As for Asian rulers in the Indian Ocean more broadly, so for the Majerteen, the rulers of northeastern Somalia were 'accustomed to using diplomacy'.[51] The historians Jeremy Jones and Nicholas Ridout identified several historic

parties and its date. The full file names of the cited records may be found in the 'Unpublished Primary Sources' section of the references. Where the file name is necessary to help identify the document, for example in very large records consisting of multiple files, the file name is included in the footnotes. IOR R/20/A/1171, Printed Papers Relating to the Red Sea and Somali Coasts. Red Sea and Somali Coast – Confidential – [section 288] & German Proceedings on the Somali (Mijjerteyn) Coast, Letter dated 31st March 1886.

48 James McDougall, 'The British and French empires in the Arab world: Some problems of colonial state-formation and its legacy', in Sally Cummings and Raymond Hinnebusch (ed.), *Sovereignty after Empire: Comparing the Middle East and Central Asia* (Edinburgh: Edinburgh University Press, 2011), pp. 45–46; Achille Mbembe, 'At the edge of the world: Boundaries, territoriality, and sovereignty in Africa', *Public Culture*, 12(1) (2000), pp. 259–284.

49 Stanley Tambiah, *World Conqueror and World Renouncer* (Cambridge: Cambridge University Press, 1976).

50 Lewis Hyde, *The Gift: Imagination and the Erotic Life of Property* (New York: Random House, 1979), pp. 3–39.

51 Lauren Benton, 'Legal spaces of empire: Piracy and the origins of ocean regionalism', *Comparative Studies in Society and History*, 47(4) (2005), p. 714.

principles of Omani diplomacy, which might equally be applied to the Omani's Majerteen partners: discretion and humility; favouring long-term geo-political stability and alliance-building over taking belligerent positions on topical issues; abstaining from sectarian and ideological conflicts; seeking consensus rather competing for influence; and respecting religious and customary differences.[52]

The British, by contrast, approached the region with their adversarial, competitive ideas about maritime trade and international relations. They arrived in the Gulf of Aden on the heels of a protracted maritime war in the Persian Gulf, which saw the creation of alliances with the rulers of Oman and war with the Qawasim rulers of the Trucial States, or the contemporary Emirates.[53] The stage was set for misunderstanding.

In July 1843, when the settlement of Aden still consisted of a garrison of a few hundred soldiers, an Indian Navy steamer named the *Memnon* bound for Suez was shipwrecked on Majerteen shores. Only a few days into its journey from Aden, a high southeasterly monsoon wind caused the ship to drift towards the rocky shores of Cape Guardafui. By nightfall, the ship was far off course and the coast of northeastern Somalia lay just over the horizon. During the night a heavy swell sent the ship onto a reef, rupturing the hull. Seawater soon inundated the ship's engines and rendered them useless. At daybreak, the passengers and crew found themselves on a deserted stretch of coastline, with only hurricane shelters and twelve days of rations.

After a few days exploring the area, a local chief from the port of Alula met the survivors at their camp. The chief requested eight hundred British Rupees (about £6,000 in today's money) as a payment of tribute and agreed to sail the survivors to Aden. The crew accepted the chief's offer. The chief loaded the passengers and crew into 'an array of large and small boats like sardines in a barrel'. But after only a few hours' sailing, the chief demanded his salvor's fee upfront. When the crew refused to pay until their safe delivery in Aden, the chief abandoned them. Alone in an unknown and sparsely inhabited part of the coast, the group purchased a small boat from an Arab trader and ventured up the coast in the hope of finding help. After a few days

---

[52] Jeremy Jones and Nicholas Ridout, *Oman, Culture and Diplomacy* (Edinburgh: Edinburgh University Press, 2012), pp. 3–4.

[53] See Jeremy Jones and Nicholas Ridout, *A History of Modern Oman* (Cambridge: Cambridge University Press, 2015), esp. pp. 35–98.

sailing searchingly up the coast, they ran across another wreck – a steamer named the *Captain Cook* – which a number of Majerteen were in the process of salvaging. Talking to the salvage party, the men from the *Memnon* discovered that the crew of the *Captain Cook* had been rescued and were *en route* to Aden. Realising that a British salvage operation would soon return to the spot, the passengers of the *Memnon* tarred a message about the location of their wreck on the *Captain Cook*'s mast and returned to Alula to wait for rescue.[54] After a few more days languishing in Alula, the Majerteen Sultan's camp learned of the shipwreck, and sent for the crew to be transported to Bandar Maryah, the Majerteen's main trading port and the Sultan's base on the coast.

Shortly after their arrival in Bandar Maryah, the Sultan called a meeting of chiefs to discuss the event. By this point, a newly commissioned lieutenant in the Indian Navy named Charles Cruttenden had found an interpreter and had begun recording the negotiations in detail. The meeting opened with a show of force from the then ruler of the Majerteen, a man named Nur Uthman, where 'Nur' loosely translates as 'regent'. Nur Uthman chastised the chief of Alula – not for holding the crew of the *Memnon* captive but for not reporting the wreck immediately and for asserting rights of salvage without the 'consent of the Sultan's House'.[55] The Sultan reminded the assembled crowd of Majerteen notables that his brother, Uthman Semantar, was governor of Bandar Maryah in the Sultan's absence. In a further affirmation of the Sultan's sovereignty, Nur Uthman elevated six other brothers to the role of councillor in court.[56] The Majerteen regent also nominated the previous Sultan's mother's eldest and most able son – then a boy of about six – as heir apparent to the sultanate. He likewise imposed new taxes on Majerteen traders, including a 5 per cent tax on all imports, as well as creating a 'royal monopoly' over the trades in honey and amber.[57]

While the ruler of Alula, in not delivering the passengers of the *Memnon* directly to Bandar Maryah, had failed to properly

---

[54] Charles Rathbone Low, *History of the Indian Navy, 1613–1863, Vol. II* (London: Richard Bentley, 1877), pp. 161–165.

[55] IOR R/20/E/32, Letter, Cruttenden to Haines, Political Resident, Aden, 12/5/1848.

[56] Révoil, *Voyages*, pp. 126–127.

[57] Guillain, *Documents sur l'histoire*, pp. 444–445.

acknowledge the Sultan's authority in foreign affairs and in rights of salvage, Nur Uthman's actions left the assembled chiefs in no doubt that shipwrecks and relations with outsiders fell within Nur Uthman's conception of the royal prerogative. Uthman finished the meeting by inviting Cruttenden to enter into an agreement to the effect that the Majerteen should promise succour for stranded British ships along the Majerteen coast in exchange for a negotiable reward.[58] Cruttenden left the details of the treaty to a future delegation with the express backing of the British government.[59]

Cruttenden's informal agreements mirrored those of the Islamic world at large in affording a salvage fee in exchange for protection. Cruttenden and Uthman's negotiations integrated the Anglo-Adenis into a regional network of reciprocity – as the promise of gifts and money in exchange for protection suggests – but also into the *dar al-ahd*, the abode of treaties with non-Muslims, which permitted Muslims and non-Muslims to converse, transact and mingle for mutual gain. Indeed, the treaty set a precedent in the region as a favourable document worthy of emulation – contrary to later perceptions of European action in Africa coloured by events later in the century. As Cruttenden reflected, in the years that followed the East India Company's agreement with Nur Uthman, the clans bordering Majerteenia sent the EIC men in Aden a flurry of 'friendly letters' requesting instruction on how to get their 'name written in the books of the English ... as [their] Mijjerthaine brothers had done'.[60]

However, the period of British accommodation to Majerteen-Islamic norms did not last long. By the mid-1850s, the port of Aden had grown substantially, attracting ever-larger volumes of shipping to pass through the Gulf of Aden, spurred on by the introduction of steamships between Europe and Asia as well as by the advantages of customs-free trade with the region following the relaxation of duties in the port of Aden. With more traffic, so the number of shipping casualties rose. One such casualty was the British steamer *Telegraph*, becalmed one and a half miles off the shore and eight miles to the east of Bandar Maryah in late January 1858. On sighting the boat, the new sultan, Sultan Uthman Mahmud Yusuf (see Figure 1.1), dispatched

---

[58] IOR R/20/E/32, Letter, Cruttenden to Haines, Political Resident, Aden, 12/5/1848. See also, IOR R/20/E/64, Affairs at Berbera, re: wreck of Cruttenden.

[59] Cruttenden, 'Report on the Mijjertheyn', p. 115–116, 124.

[60] Cruttenden, 'Memoir of the Western or Edoor tribes', p. 67.

Figure 1.1 The Sultan of Majerteenia (centre) accompanied by his counsellors and Italian soldiers and officials, 1910.
(DEA/BIBLIOTECA AMBROSIANA/De Agostini Editorial/Getty Images.)

two large skiffs, each carrying some 40 to 50 armed men. On reaching the *Telegraph*, Uthman's men ordered the crew to abandon the ship, effectively requiring them to heed the informal agreement Cruttenden had made with his regent, Nur Uthman, a decade before. The crew of the *Telegraph* surrendered the ship. Uthman's men took a significant amount of the ship's moveable property, from its papers to the master's stash of currency. One of Uthman's retainers even took the master's coat, draped it over his own shoulders and paraded the deck of the Telegraph as the self-appointed Captain, to the mirth of his fellow soldiers. The crew of the *Telegraph*, however, took fright. Insisting on using their life rafts rather than one of Uthman's boats to find a tug in Aden, they drifted for five days before they were found by the Indian Navy patrol ship *Elphistone*, which plucked them from the sea and transported them to Aden.[61]

The events that followed signalled an important shift in Anglo-Majerteen relations. Until the 1850s, Britain and the EIC had tacitly accepted their place in the regional *dar al-'ahd*. But in the years since, the EIC had become increasingly imperious in its approach to domestic sovereignty. In response to the great uprisings against Company rule that had occurred across much of the Indian subcontinent in 1857, the British Parliament had elected to take India under direct rule. These high-level shifts in Britain's approach to the Indian Ocean empowered the British rulers of Aden to become increasingly aggressive. William Coghlan, the British ruler of Aden, ordered the *Elphistone* back to Maryah with the Master of the *Telegraph* aboard to identify and 'avenge the population' for an incident he framed as an illegitimate act of piracy, banking on his forces' superior firepower in a battle against the Majerteen.

On reaching the coast, the crew of the *Elphistone* waited below deck while the *Elphistone*'s Commander and the Master of the *Telegraph* surveyed the shore with his telescope. What the Commander saw was an off-season coastal market town with some five forts, one flying the Ottoman flag, while some fisherman worked on their nets. The quietness of the scene made the *Elphistone*'s Commander suspicious. Fraudulent claims for the compensation of self-inflicted or even non-existent shipwrecks, or for compensation for pirate attacks against stranded shipping, were not uncommon in cases where a crew member's negligence had caused an accident or even where the crew had sold their cargo for their own profit. However, after scouring the shore for an hour or more, they finally found the remains of a ship –

---

[61] IOR R/20/E/57, Letter, W. M. Coghlan, Political Resident, Aden, to H. L. Anderson, Secretary to the Governor, Bombay, 7/2/1858.

half dismantled, a number of men picking over the wooden ribs of the frame. The Commander led a party of men to investigate more closely.

The party found the *Telegraph* stripped to its beams and the town of Bandar Maryah almost devoid of people. The *Elphistone*'s crew spent an anxious night waiting, the ship's lookout anxiously waking the Captain on several occasions to report fires lighted on different parts of the shore. The fires, it soon transpired, signalled for the fighting men of the region to assemble. By daybreak Uthman's men had gathered along the beach, many having arrived from the hinterland that same night on horses and camels. According to the *Elphistone*'s Captain, this was proof of the Majerteen's belligerence – an indication that they intended to attack the British ships for loot. But it was the British who made the first move. At daybreak, the *Elphistone* launched a volley of cannon fire on the town. 'By eleven o'clock', the commander reported, 'almost all the forts and the houses had been struck several times, and the inner side of the forts were battered down.' The crowd on the beach huddled about two small boats for shelter and ran for cover behind the dunes; some replied to the assault with bursts of inconsequential rifle fire. 'Several of the natives suffered', the commander concluded imperviously, 'but how much, or how many, I cannot say'.[62]

The destruction was not, however, merely physical: it detrimentally affected the spirit of negotiation and diplomacy which normally patterned the region's international relations. The full impact of the *Elphistone*'s bombardment began to be felt a few months later, when another British merchant ship was stranded farther east along the Majerteen coast. In July of 1858 a British merchant brig named the *Henry Tanner* hit a sandy ridge in bad weather off Cape Guardafui, causing the vessel to break up and killing a number of the crew. When the seven survivors made landfall, about a hundred Majerteen men took them hostage at knifepoint. Now in captivity, the crew spent six weeks on the remote stretch of the Majerteen coast before a local chief rounded the crew members up and took them to Alula. A few days later, Uthman sent for the men, whom he transported to Bandar Maryah, where he kept them as hostages in various forts throughout the town. Here the men languished indoors, eventually learning enough Somali to converse with their captors. In October 1858,

---

[62] IOR R/20/E/57, Letter, J. Frushard, Senior Naval Officer, to Coghlan, Political Resident, Aden, 19/2/1858.

Figure 1.2 Portrait of Sir Robert Lambert Playfair, K.C.M.G., by John Adamson, 1865
(Reference number ALB-8-16, courtesy of the University of St Andrews Library)

meanwhile, the Resident at Aden sent a mission to inspect the Majerteen coast under his assistant Robert Playfair (see Figure 1.2). When their ship, the British Navy ship HMS *Chesapeake*, neared the area around Bandar Maryah, a small boat appeared alongside them carrying two European sailors aboard. The *Chesapeake* took the men aboard, where they introduced themselves as the Master and First Mate of the *Henry Tanner*. Playfair's first response was to threaten to bombard Bandar Maryah, thwarting any prospect of a renewal of the Anglo-Majerteen agreements. But the Master of the *Henry Tanner*, who had learned something of the politics of Majerteenia during his captivity, cautioned against such a heavy-handed response. Uthman regarded the British assault on Maryah as a 'serious calamity', the Master argued, and intended to play the hostages as bargaining chips with the British. The Master's poise brought the officials around; instead of bombarding the place again, they sent a delegation ashore to meet with Nur Uthman.[63]

In response, Uthman called a political meeting on the beach at Bandar Maryah. Playfair, officers from the *Chesapeake*, the crew of the *Henry Tanner*, Nur Uthman and a number of Uthman's counsellors were all present. The Sultan restated his commitment to cooperation, respect and an orderly process of treaty-making. He explained that in their dealing with the crew of the *Telegraph*, his men had intended to offer assistance, but the crew fled without warning. This had confused his men, he said, because he thought all British sailors would be aware of the terms of their relationship – the vast majority of sailors he encountered on his shores were. When the *Elphistone* visited Maryah and opened fire on the town two weeks later, Uthman believed at first that the British intended to salute him prior to opening negotiations over the division of the value of the wreck of the *Telegraph*. He was dismayed to see the cannon fire strike his forts. After some deliberation among the British officers and sailors, Playfair took Uthman's testimony at face value. On behalf of the British in Aden, he asked Uthman to relay to his followers, and they to their children, that the British would show restraint. The Sultan's kindness toward the British subjects aboard the *Henry Tanner*, Playfair said, had 'saved them from utter destruction'.[64] Playfair returned to Aden as a 'humane and politic' diplomat who not only secured the release of more British sailors, but also restored friendly relations with Bandar Maryah.[65]

---

[63] IOR R/20/E/57, Letter, Lt. Parkin to William Coghlan, 10/10/1858.
[64] IORR/20/E/57, Letter, Lt. Playfair, Assistant Resident Aden, to William Coghlan, 10/10/1858.
[65] IOR R/20/E/57, Letter, Coghlan to Anderson, Secretary to the Government of Bombay, 11/10/1858.

For Uthman, by contrast, treaty relations with the British entailed a markedly different conception of international relations. Alongside the destruction of numerous forts, Nur Uthman's insistence on negotiation made the Sultan look increasingly weak. For representatives of the British establishment such as Coghlan and Playfair, freedom of commerce and Britain's pre-eminent role in the commerce of the Indian Ocean region took priority. Other concerns paled in comparison with the importance of free trade and the projection of British power. Yet even Playfair himself acknowledged, at least half-consciously, that such a bullish approach to international relations might paradoxically diminish the relative security afforded to colonial commercial ships under existing principles of *aman*, and the *dar al-'ahd*. In his final assessment of the incident, Playfair opined that the absence of 'regular government' in Somalia could easily make the Red Sea shipping route impassable.[66] But Playfair did not make the link; colonial chaos appeared to Playfair as the cure, not the cause, of the troubles.

Meanwhile, Uthman continued to approach the British in Aden in terms of *aban*, *aman* and the *dar al-'ahd*. In September 1862, a becalmed British Navy Anti-Slavery steamboat named HMS *Penguin* ran out of coal close to the southern Somali port of Brava. As was common in the early days of steam the crew hoisted sails, but the southwest monsoon was in its last days, and the steel-hulled boat was heavy. The sailing was slow going and the crew had been without supplies for over a week when the winds failed them close to the port town of Baraada, adjacent to Alula. The chiefs of Alula sent a party to rescue the crew of the steamer. Although the men's intention was likely to have been to offer salvage or assistance, the British crew treated Alula's men as pirates. A fight broke out, resulting in the disappearance of all fifteen British sailors. When news of the fate of the crew of the *Penguin* reached Aden, Resident Coghlan sent Captain Playfair back to the Majerteen coast to investigate.

The scene on the beach at Baradaa in October 1862 was ominous but provided few clues as to the fate of the sailors. The village was situated in the middle of a great plain of beach, wrote Playfair,

[66] IOR R/20/E/64, Letter, Captain R. L. Playfair, to A. Kinloch Forbes, Acting Secretary to Government in Bombay, 26/10/1861.

surrounded by an amphitheatre of hills. Its few huts had recently been abandoned, and with every step he took through the deserted encampment 'a trace of the [crew of the *Penguin*] met our eyes; here a scrap of canvas, there a morsel of clothing, the ribbon from a seaman's hat and other articles, many of them stained with blood.' There were no bodies; the British sailors leapt to the conclusion they had been murdered and pushed out to sea or buried in unmarked graves.[67] Their actual fate, however, is uncertain. It is just as likely they abandoned ship as were murdered. Indeed, given the generally peaceful tenor of relations between the Majerteen and British until this point, a combination of death by shipwreck and desertion seems the more likely explanation. But Playfair failed to restrain his men. The British set fire to all the property they could find before embarking for Maryah for negotiations with Nur Uthman and the young Sultan.

In Maryah, under the shade of a tent erected on the beach specifically for the occasion, Sultan Uthman, Nur Uthman and his counsellors sought to repair their damaged relations with the British. The people of Alula, Uthman explained, opposed him, in part because Coghlan and Playfair had made the sultanate look weak. While Uthman insisted that he was not responsible for the attack, he promised to punish the culprits. The British demanded he turn over not less than twenty men and return all the plundered property and apologise 'to the British flag' on the deck of a British warship within ten days. Playfair proceeded to prowl up and down the Majerteen coastline in a British Navy gunship, towing the *Penguin* behind her. When he arrived at Baraada a month later, Uthman had managed to round up only eight alleged culprits and had seized only two rifles, a pistol and a sword belonging to the *Penguin*'s crew. Playfair later wrote of his crew's reaction that he was forced to pull rank to restrain them from 'proceeding to extremities' and running amok.[68]

---

[67] University of St. Andrews Library. Lt. Playfair's Private Papers, msdep14/6/4. Letter, Playfair, Assistant Political Resident, Aden, to Major General Honner, Acting Political Resident, Aden, 1/11/1862.

[68] IOR L/PS/6/526, Correspondence of the Government of India with the Bombay Government regarding the measures taken to obtain satisfaction from the Mijyrteyn tribe of Arabs in Somaliland for their massacre of fifteen sailors belonging to HMS *Penguin*.

The incident brought to a head the issue of Majerteen sovereignty, British power and the Majerteen Sultan's approach to diplomacy. Uthman informed Playfair that while he could identify the culprits, the matter of avenging their deaths fell to the offended party – to the British. If Uthman put the men to death himself, tensions with Alula were bound to escalate. If Playfair wanted to mete out punishment for the British deaths, he should undertake the act of execution himself. But Playfair would not listen to Uthman's reasoning; he insisted the Sultan take responsibility for their punishment. For Playfair, it was a matter of Uthman making clear his hostility to internal opponents of free trade and British power. Facing another humiliating bombardment, Uthman decided to personally undertake the grisly task of beheading the eight suspects from Alula on the beach at Baraada before an audience which consisted of Playfair's crew and the crews of eight other British frigates who sailed in for the occasion.[69] To make matters even worse for Uthman, a few months later the British proceeded to demand he stand on the deck of a British Navy ship, beneath a Union Jack flag, just off the coast of Maryah and before a crowd of British officials and acknowledge his 'sorrow' for the 'foul and cruel massacre' which his 'subjects dared to commit at Baraada' and whose conduct was 'so contrary to my wish and practice, and also contrary to the friendship which has so long existed betwixt my people and the British government'.[70]

In exchange for playing Britain's game of diplomacy, Uthman received the rather empty reward of recognition of royalty in the form of a seven-gun salute – a South Asian head of state conventionally received twenty-one.[71] Indeed, only two years later the British created

[69] University of St. Andrews Library. Playfair's Private Papers, msdep14/6/4. Letter, Playfair, Assistant Political Resident, Aden, to Major General Honner, Acting Political Resident, Aden, 1/11/1862.

[70] University of St. Andrews Library. Playfair's Private Papers, msdep14/6/4. Annex A., enclosed in Letter, Playfair, Assistant Political Resident, Aden, to Major General Honner, Acting Political Resident, Aden, 1/11/1862. See also IOR R/20/E/69, Letter, Brigadier Coghlan, Political Resident, Aden, to H. L. Anderson, Chief Secretary to the Government, Bombay, 27/1/1863. The treaty was concluded in the same year as the British signed treaties with the rulers of Mukalla: IOR R/20/E/69, Treaties with the Naqibs of the ports of Shihr and Mukalla, 1863.

[71] IOR R/20/E/102, Précis of the Aden Residency records. 1874. Also, Low, *History of the Indian Navy*, pp. 550–555.

the alqabnama register in India, which listed all of the 'native princes', their specific forms of address, and their associated privileges from the colonial state – including, after 1867, the use of gun salutes as a mark of honour according to the hierarchy established in the alqabnama. The register, which speaks volumes about Britain's hierarchical approach to international relations, included some rulers from the vicinity of Aden but not the Majerteen.[72] While the British thus nominally recognised Majerteen sovereignty, the act of incorporation was predicated on Britain's superiority and Majerteenia's submission to its interests in free trade and unfettered protection for its ships.

Playfair's cruel negotiating tactics succeeded in changing the tone of the conduct of diplomacy. After Baraada, Uthman signed an anti-slavery treaty, which saw him cede his rights as a local maritime power, and which left the question of his rights of salvage conspicuously absent. Moreover, even this radical break with the recent diplomatic past failed to satisfy Coghlan's superiors in India, who insisted that he return to ensure that the treaty made explicit that the Majerteen not only agreed to prohibit slavery but also that they conceded to the British Navy the right to search all Majerteen boats.[73] Uthman later agreed that all slaves may be confiscated but insisted his boats and crew could not be detained or taken from the high seas back to Aden.[74]

The Suez Canal

It was against this backdrop of growing hostility between Britain and Majerteenia that the Suez Canal was inaugurated in 1869, transforming the Red Sea into a global commercial transport artery. Within a few years of the Canal's opening, the Majerteen ports saw between two and four steamers passing their shores each day on their way to India, Southeast Asia, China and Australia. By the turn of the century, this figure had risen to some one hundred vessels a day circumnavigating

---

[72] John M. Willis, 'Making Yemen Indian: Rewriting the boundaries of imperial Arabia', *International Journal of Middle East Studies*, 41 (2009), p. 30.

[73] IOR R/20/E/64, Letter, Secretary of State for India, to Political Resident, Aden, 30/12/1859.

[74] A copy of the text of the treaty may be found in the Appendix. IOR R/20/E/69, Letter, Brigadier Coghlan, Political Resident, Aden, to HL Anderson, Chief Secretary to Government, Bombay, 27/1/1863 and Letter, the Governor General of India to Chief Secretary to the Government of Bombay, 20/3/1863.

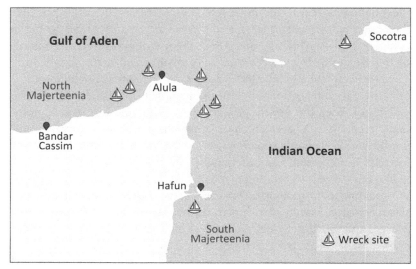

Map 1.3 The location of European steamships wrecked along the Majerteen coast between 1870–1874

(© 2021 Nicholas W. Stephenson Smith. All rights reserved)

the Canal and the southern Red Sea.[75] The rise in steam traffic also led to an increase in the number of ships stranded on Majerteen shores, with one British official recording seven British steamships wrecked along the Majerteen coast between 1870 and 1874 (see Map 1.3).[76] At the same moment, several other European powers arrived on the scene. Like Britain, they adopted a combative approach to diplomacy and the defence of free trade. By the late 1870s, matters reached boiling point.

In June 1877, a French Messageries Maritimes ship SS *Mei-Kong* was sailing from Saigon to Marseilles when it struck the rocky shoreline just east of Alula at night, stranding one hundred passengers and a valuable cargo that reputedly included ancient Cham statues from Vietnam.[77] (The French Messageries Maritimes, based in Marseilles,

---

[75] MAESS ASMAI – Volume 1 (1857–1939), Posizione 59/ Numero 2 – Somalia Settentrionale – 1887–1909, Fasciolo 15 – Vaire, 1897–1900. Report of Captain Pestalozza on the coast of Somalia north of Benadiir, 1/6/1900 and Anon, 'Suez Canal Traffic', *The Montreal Gazette* (July 2, 1903).

[76] Hunter, *An Account*, pp. 179–180.

[77] See Jean-François Hubert, *The Art of Champa* (New York: Parkstone Press, 2005), pp. 12–14.

was founded in the mid-nineteenth century and was analogous to the British Postal Office's older packet service, which ferried people and mail across the world's oceans). The impact of the collision drove a hole in the hull, forcing the passengers to abandon the sinking ship in life rafts. The Captain sent out a distress signal, which a passing British packet ship and a French passenger steamer answered, rescuing all the passengers on board.[78] But even as the passengers abandoned the *Mei-Kong*, the governor of Alula, Yusuf 'Ali, led a flotilla of boats from Alula towards the floundering wreck.[79] Uthman Mahmud Yusuf responded by laying siege to Alula, bringing Majerteenia to the brink of civil war. Uthman only managed to maintain a semblance of unity by relinquishing his claim to the *Mei-Kong*'s loot – since the boat had in any case sunk to inaccessible depths, the people of Alula had salvaged relatively little – and rallying Alula's forces to fight in a clan-wide conflict with another branch of the Darood over access to water wells.[80]

The *Mei-Kong* incident highlighted the tense, even chaotic state of international relations in the region. With France threatening to interfere in Majerteenia, Anglo-Majerteen relations at a low and given the continued risks to shipping in the region, Britain sought vainly for a solution to the sovereignty problem by reasserting Ottoman control. Under the influence of the British Ambassador Evelyn Baring, the Egyptian government reasserted its authority over the northeastern Somali coast as far as Ras Hafun in September 1877.

In other words, Britain used its influence over Egypt to expand its empire informally, without the need for expensive military

---

[78] d'Angremont, 'Le naufrage du «Mei Kong»' *Le Monde Illustré*, 28/7/1877, p. 54. Available at: https://gallica.bnf.fr/ark:/12148/bpt6k6384381v/f7.item. Accessed 12/11/2015; Paul Bois, *Le grand siècle des Messageries Maritimes* (Marseilles: Chambre de Commerce, 1992), p. 206.

[79] MAESS ASMAI Posizione 59/ Numero 1 – Somalia Settentrionale – 1886–1889, Fasciolo 7, 'Riforma, 24 June 1890'.

[80] IOR R/20/E/152, Letter, Brigadier General James Blair, British Resident, Aden, to the Chief Secretary to Government of Bombay, 22/1/1885; MAESS ASMAI Posizione 59/ Numero 2 – Somalia Settentrionale, 1887–1909, Fasciolo 25 – Ostilita tra I dui Sultani, Yusuf Ali di Obbia e Osman Mahmud dei Migiurtini. 1899–1901. Letter, Cap. Pestalozza, Italian Consul General in Zanzibar, to the Minister for Foreign Affairs, Aden [sic.], 1/12/1899; MAESS ASMAI, Posizione 59/ 4 – Somalia Settentrionale – Azione Italiana su Obbia e Migiurtinia, 1904–1908, Fasciolo 57 – I due Sultani protetti di contendono Durbo.

conquests.[81] But the effectiveness of Britain's 'indirect' strategy in the Somali context was mixed. First, Egypt had to ratify its claim to the northeastern Somali coast with Constantinople.[82] Second, both the Ottoman and the Egyptian claims to exercise sovereignty over the Somali coast were far from certain. British sources reported that the Ottoman flag was flown in Uthman's port of Bandar Maryah as well as at Alula. However, rulers in the region believed flag-flying signified nothing more than their affiliation to the Porte in religious matters, or even a simple diplomatic courtesy, since they raised and hauled down the flag at will depending on which foreign powers visited.[83] The British recognised that indigenous Ottoman notions of sovereignty in parts of Africa and the Middle East 'meant nothing beyond the ceremonial acknowledgement of friendly protectors or neighbouring parties' and more particularly signalled the flag-fliers membership of the Islamic ecumene.[84] Third, the Ottoman Empire was, if not enfeebled, then certainly waning. By the terms of the Treaty of Berlin in 1878, the Ottoman Empire had ceded almost a fifth of its territories to Russia in an effort to forestall a Russian military attack on the Ottoman capital of Constantinople itself. While a success on paper, in practical terms, Baring's effort to rehabilitate Ottoman influence over Somalia was a failure.

In this increasingly unsettled diplomatic climate, the wreck of the British steamer the *Vortigern* near Ras Hafun in 1878 caused the Majerteen political community to break apart. Where before Uthman managed to contain competition over the division of the spoils of shipwrecks with his various family members, the new governor of Alula Yusuf 'Ali began directly challenging Uthman's royal authority. The *Vortigern*, at 285 feet long, sailed from Britain with a cargo of 1,000 tons of coal, 500 tons of piece goods, 90 tons of iron, 10 tons of arms, 30 tons of powder and 200 tons of liquor. In February, in fine weather, the ship's mate misjudged the depth of the sea, running the *Vortigern* aground; the keel sunk some four feet into the sand. When a British Navy vessel arrived

---

[81] John Gallagher and Ronald Robinson, 'The imperialism of free trade', pp. 1–15.

[82] IOR R/20/A/1171, Letter, Lord Roseberry, British Foreign Secretary, to Count Hazfeldt, German Ambassador to London, 5/3/1886.

[83] IOR R/20/A/1171, Letter, Aden, dated 28/12/1885. See also IOR R/20/A/4554, Circulars, Socotra and Kishn, Somali, Subehi, Turks in Yemen, 1886–1887.

[84] F. W. Buckler, 'India and the Far East 1848–1858', in Adolphus W. Ward and George P. Gooch (ed.), *The Cambridge History of British Foreign Policy 1783–1919*, Vol. 2 (Cambridge: Cambridge University Press, 1923), p. 404.

to investigate a week or so after the *Vortigern*'s grounding, officials found the wreck awash with men from the port of Alula and elsewhere picking over the cargo. Yusuf 'Ali's men had taken 'all the copper pipes and every particle of moveable brass and copper' along with some 800 tons of goods; Omanis from the port of Sur had looted many of the ship's arms; 'some Greek wreckers from Suez', in the area looking for loot from the *Mei-Kong*, were also present at the scene. The Navy Commander took charge of the hull, emptying it of water before towing it back to Aden, concluding that the captain and crew had abandoned the ship 'in circumstances that appear most discreditable'.[85]

The British Navy saw the case of the *Vortigern* as a straightforward shipwreck and Yusuf 'Ali and the Sur merchants' actions as little more than an overzealous salvage operation. But Yusuf 'Ali and the Aden administration saw the matter as more complex. In Yusuf 'Ali's account of events, recorded in detail in the India Office, the self-styled Sultan of Alula rowed out to the *Vortigern* to liaise with the Captain, offering to protect the wreck as well as to transport for the crew to Aden. The Captain refused Yusuf's offer, proposing instead to wait for four days to see if the ship would dislodge from the sandbank. On the fourth day a steamer passed the wreck, collecting the thirty-three crew and transported them to Aden. By this time, the *Vortigern* lay abandoned within sight of Alula. According to Yusuf's testimony, it was at this moment that sailors from the eastern Arabian port of Sur arrived to plunder the wreck. Yusuf 'Ali and his men attempted to fight them off, he asserted, but were overwhelmed. The Suris were not the only ones who had heard about the abandoned wreck. After much of the cargo had been plundered, a Frenchman from Aden named M. Suet bought rights to the hull from Yusuf 'Ali. Yusuf 'Ali's claim to the wreck was, however, tenuous. According to his testimony, Yusuf 'Ali's claim to the wreck was based in his customary right to charge for services rendered to a foundering ship.[86] Indeed, the French traveller Révoil told the story similarly: Yusuf 'Ali surrounded the ship, looted its cargo of arms, and refused to relinquish control of the wreck until

[85] IOR R/20/A/512, Vol. 810 Africa, Details Respecting Steamer *Vortigern* in Compliance with the Request of the Political Resident, H.M.S. *Daphne* at Aden, February 1879.

[86] IOR R/20/A/512, Statement of Sultan Yusuf bin Ali of Alulah, made before Major Goodfellow, in Letter, Political Resident, Aden, to the Secretary to Government, Political Department, Bombay, 21/2/1879.

the insurance paid him salvage per the terms of the Anglo-Majerteen agreements. To secure the *Vortigiern* and its crew's release, the salvage company paid Yusuf's demand.[87]

Unlike in their recent dealings with Uthman, British officials in Aden took a sympathetic view of Yusuf's claim. British officials observed that the wreck fell 'virtually' within Yusuf 'Ali's 'jurisdiction'. As a result, EIC officials reasoned, Yusuf was the 'sovereign' of the coast and of the ships stranded upon it.[88] Capitalising on the political support he enjoyed at Uthman's expense, Yusuf 'Ali petitioned officials in Aden for concrete recognition of his 'sovereignty' and his rights to a salvage payment. Travelling to Aden, Yusuf 'Ali made various claims against the authorities and the ship's owners. He suggested he had personally sold the wreck to a representative of a French company for £5,500 (about £689,000 today). When this total proved too ambitious even given the supportive mood in Aden, Yusuf 'Ali lobbied officials to pay him a reward of some £380 (about £48,000 today), equivalent to sums previously paid to Sultan Uthman for the protection of wrecks on Majerteen shores. Aden officials felt Yusuf 'Ali's claims warranted consideration 'politically' and recommended he lodge a case for his claim to salvage against the insurers in the Admiralty courts, or in Aden's court directly, since the wreck itself was by now in Aden, in the hands of The Liverpool Salvage Company, acting on behalf of the ship's insurers at Lloyds in London.

Quite apart from the fact that all previous salvage claims had passed through Sultan Uthman, and not through any chiefs in Alula, officials overlooked the fact that all previous arrangements were made on a political basis, without any recourse to the courts. Indeed, had the legal admissibility of the Anglo-Majerteen salvage agreements been tested in an Anglo-Indian or Admiralty court, it is highly unlikely that the outcome would have been in Yusuf's favour. Even if he could prove himself to be an independent ruler of the stretch of coast around Alula and argue that he had simply gone to the *Vortigern*'s aid, he would have been swimming against the current of common law precedent in regard to salvage. Moreover, while salvage law allowed the Captain considerable latitude to strike a bargain with his salvors, this applied

---

[87] Révoil, *Voyages*, pp. 9, 20, 24, 137.

[88] IOR R/20/A/512, Memorandum, Major Goodfellow, Assistant Resident, 16/2/1879.

only to the ship's cargo, given away in proportion to the immediacy and degree of peril the ship faced. The Captain's promise of the hull itself to Yusuf 'Ali was unprecedented. In fact, the Captain's desertion of the *Vortigern* might have landed him in prison if the case had gone to court. Thus, in reply to the Aden government's suggestions to start legal proceedings, British officials in India wrote witheringly that if the Aden government believed there was a case to be made on Yusuf's behalf, they should 'please submit [a] full statement of case showing grounds on which you consider chief's claim good at common law'.[89]

In practice, Aden's championing of Yusuf 'Ali's case had little to do with the law. On the contrary, their position stemmed from their ambitions to renege on their alliances with Sultan Uthman, to recognise Yusuf 'Ali as a coastal sovereign in his own right, and to aggravate an increasingly anarchic situation along the Majerteen coast. The Aden government's reasons for supporting Yusuf 'Ali's baseless claims to salvage served instead to stoke disorder in the maritime sphere and to undermine the Sultan, his networks, and his consensus-oriented style of diplomacy and international relations. British Aden officials' response also reflected the competitive colonial politics of the port city in the wake of the wreck. The Frenchman to whom Yusuf 'Ali sold 'his rights' to the hull of the *Vortigern*, it transpired, also gave him the right to build a lighthouse on Cape Guardafui.[90] The bond promised to pay Yusuf 'Ali a yearly stipend of $500 MT on condition that after ninety years the lighthouse should revert to local control. When they investigated the note, officials discovered that the Frenchman who had obtained it was the manager of a local hotel. He intended to form a company to raise the funds to pay Yusuf and build the lighthouse himself, failing which he planned to sell the bond to the Italian consul. This, the man reasoned, would give the Italians 'a footing on that part of the African littoral ... under the ostensible motive of becoming general benefactors to the whole of the shipping and trading portion of the world'.[91]

---

[89] IOR R/20/A/512, Letter, Resident at Aden to Secretary to Government, Bombay, 8/3/1879.

[90] IOR R/20/E/122, Letter, Francis Loch, Political Resident, Aden to Secretary of State for India, India Office, London, 28/1/1879.

[91] IOR R/20/A/512, Lighthouse, Letter Political Resident Loch, Aden, to Secretary of State, India, 5/4/1879.

The threat of French or Italian interference in Majerteenia gave Yusuf 'Ali's petitions a credibility and urgency which they otherwise might have lacked. The Resident bought the bond for $500 MT of the port's governmental budget. While the sum 'may seem large', wrote the Resident to his superiors in India, 'it must be admitted that we have no effective arguments to use with these chiefs against such a sale, nor can we, so far as I see, forcibly put a stop to such taking place at any time'.[92] Buying the bond and giving support to Yusuf 'Ali's claim to control the Majerteen coast, in other words, was a necessity if Britain intended to maintain its pre-eminence in the region.

But officials' acceptance – even encouragement of – politically ambitious actors such as Yusuf 'Ali was deeply disruptive to the culture of diplomacy in the region and to the stability of the Majerteen Sultanate. That Anglo-Adeni officials would even contemplate the validity in international law of a bond of such dubious provenance made between a private citizen and an upstart chief is a measure not only of the shortness of the Anglo-Adeni's institutional memory, but also the extent of their hostility to indigenous systems and networks of diplomacy in the region. In his notes, the Political Resident in Aden wrote that 'The action taken by the Alula Chief is that of an uncivilized ruler, and cannot be gauged by any civilized law, and hence, any parallel in justice cannot be drawn.' As a result, the Aden Resident concluded, 'superior force alone can be admitted as constituting right'. The Resident contemplated replying to Yusuf 'Ali on those terms, effectively encouraging him to wreck and loot ships and resist Uthman's claims to rule the coast. But in the event, he stopped short of sending such a clear incitement to violence in a region already slipping into civil unrest.[93]

Aden officials had shown themselves eager to jettison the historic mode and representatives of diplomacy in the region, but officials in Bombay – perhaps with the benefit of hindsight – sought to restore a semblance of the former diplomacy. The British Indian government responded to the Political Resident's ruminations that the only solution not 'contrary to international etiquette' was to draft an agreement with the Majerteen chiefs granting Britain rights of some kind or another

---

[92] IOR R/20/A/512, Lighthouse, Letter Political Resident Loch, Aden, to Secretary of State, India, 29/8/1879.
[93] IOR R/20/A/512, Letter, Political Resident, Aden, to the Secretary to Government, Political Department, Bombay, No. 64/313, 21/2/1879.

to the shore in exchange for money. Writing to his superiors in Bombay, the Resident in Aden reported, 'They may have a loose reputation on the score of being wreckers, but they have also a reputation of having, on many occasions, shown kindness and hospitality as in the present case, to those (our own country-men especially) thrown on their shores'. The British Resident continued that as a result, in 'judging' the Majerteen as a people, 'it should not be lost sight of that they are but little removed from savages but possessed of good points which merit our consideration.'[94] Aden officials shortly dispatched a treaty mission to the Majerteen coast and wrote to Constantinople to clarify the question of Ottoman authority in the region. The Ottomans duly affirmed the Ottoman Sultan's overarching sovereignty in the region and stated forcefully that no other 'chief ... had any right to enter into an engagement' with any government without the consent of the Porte.[95]

At the same time, Aden's Assistant Resident, Major Charles Goodfellow, travelled to Alula with Yusuf 'Ali with the aim of signing a new agreement giving Aden a more colonial relationship with the Majerteen coast. But Goodfellow also found that Yusuf 'Ali's assumption of control of the wrecks of the *Mei-Kong*, the *Vortigern* and another wreck referred to as the *Cashmere* had created a 'state of enmity' between the Sultan and the Governor. As Uthman pointed out to Goodfellow, the real source of disagreement between himself and Yusuf 'Ali lay in the fact that the Aden Residency addressed Yusuf 'Ali as 'Sultan', usurping Uthman's role as the chief-of-chiefs and as the primary point-of-call for foreign relations. Goodfellow dismissed Uthman's protest as owing to the irrational 'jealousness' of his advisors, in whose hands Uthman was a 'total puppet'. On the contrary, Uthman's concerns were significant and well-founded. His dispute with Yusuf 'Ali, and particularly his concern over the Anglo-Adeni's use of titles, was rooted in a practice of diplomacy and inter-state relations which held him, as Sultan, as the central personality along the whole northeast coast of Africa. Any effort to undermine Uthman's role threw into disarray the whole treaty system on which

---

[94] IOR R/20/A/512, Letter, Resident at Aden to Secretary to Government, Bombay, 24/2/1879.

[95] IOR R/20/A/512, Lighthouse, Letter, Sir Henry Layard, British Ambassador, Constantinople to Marquis Salisbury, Secretary of State for Foreign Affairs, 2/7/1879.

political and economic life in the southern Red Sea rested. Without Uthman as Sultan – or more properly, without a single, stable, acknowledged Majerteen figurehead – international action would be apt to descend into chaos.

Recognising the need for a return to the kind of diplomacy that affirmed the Majerteen Sultan's sovereignty, Goodfellow set about drafting a treaty that would grant reciprocal rights over international shipping stranded along Majerteenia's shores. Moreover, Goodfellow admitted that recognising Yusuf 'Ali's right to enter salvage treaties along the coast would lead the people of Alula to 'expect to derive a rich harvest on the occasion of [e]very vessel being cast on their shore'.[96] Yet Goodfellow could not resist seeing in Yusuf 'Ali an expedient solution to his diplomatic challenge – a man eager to sign an agreement of any description and willing to give Aden assurance he would protect their ships and crew in exchange for a fee. In support of his contradictory vision of Majerteen politics, Goodfellow mused that the 'system seems much the same as is the case in India where relatives of the chiefs receive towns as their portion [of the region's wealth], and in this way most of the seaports are in the hands of the elders'. Goodfellow continued that since the Sultan owned 'only few' ports, his 'loyalty' was of limited utility to the Aden administration. He therefore advocated that the Sultan 'delegate' his authority to Yusuf 'Ali, who was more often present on the coast, which Uthman and his advisors dismissed out of hand. Finally, Goodfellow contemplated abandoning Uthman altogether in favour of an agreement with the more 'useful' Yusuf 'Ali. But Goodfellow recognised in the end that jettisoning the Anglo-Adeni's historic relations with Uthman would do little but aggravate a conflict, which would render the agreement cheaper than the parchment on which it was written.

Conclusion

In a good example of Aden officials' capacity for blaming troubles of their own making on the purported dysfunctions of local politics, Goodfellow – who had done so much to sow division and anarchy in the diplomatic arena – concluded simply and without irony that he was

---

[96] IOR R/20/A/512, Letter, Resident at Aden to Secretary to Government, Bombay, 18/4/1879.

unable to 'eradicate the jealousy and ill feeling existing between these two chiefs'.[97] Nevertheless, it seems that the Sultan's entourage finally consented to sign a new treaty agreement which highlighted his duties towards stranded foreign sailors and ships on his shores. Goodfellow also recorded that the treaty included a clause which would finally allow the British to lease land to build a lighthouse on the Majerteen coast. Uthman allowed Yusuf 'Ali to be listed as one amongst a number of chiefly signatories.[98] But Uthman refused to partake in any symbolic activities which might further undermine his authority and resisted in particular the invitation to set foot on the treaty delegation's boat. Instead, Uthman sent his *qadi* – or Islamic judge – on the pretext that he was the only member of the retinue who could read English.[99]

After Goodfellow's departure, Uthman wrote in protest to the British in Aden that he objected to the use of the title 'sultan' for Yusuf 'Ali. Uthman sought to reassert the primacy of his own authority in the international and domestic spheres, insisting that the conflict between himself and Yusuf was an internal one, which should be settled within the Majerteen community.[100] Uthman need not have worried. Bombay and the Foreign Office, mindful of the larger geopolitical picture, refused to assent to the new agreement and the building of a lighthouse on the grounds that the Egyptians or Ottomans might object to Britain's encroachment on their empire. Instead, they proposed that Aden make an informal verbal agreement with the chiefs of Majerteenia to the effect that they would be rewarded financially for providing succour for wrecked ships; in other words, Bombay favoured an agreement that simulated the significance of a treaty but avoided questions of sovereignty and law. The Aden government objected as strongly as possible, notwithstanding their subordinate position within the hierarchy of British India. The British Resident replied that the Majerteen 'are not wanting in appreciating a position [and] would readily perceive that they are masters of the situation'. To ensure they kept the upper hand, and not allow the Majerteen to do

---

[97] Ibid.   [98] A copy of the treaty may be found in the Appendix.

[99] IOR R/20/A/512, Major Goodfellow's Report of proceeding at Muraya and Alula, undated, April, 1879.

[100] IOR R/20/A/512, Letter, Sultan Othman Mahomed, The Sultan of the Mijjertain, to General Loch C. B., Resident, Aden, 6 Rubea al Akhir, 1296 (30 March 1879).

'as they pleased' in regard to international shipping, the British must be 'prepared to use force'. As Goodfellow put it grandiosely, compared with other powers such as the Ottomans and rival Europeans, 'our interests are really universal'. As a result, it was incumbent on Britain not to be 'blind to our own interests in this matter'.[101]

Goodfellow's vision of the universal value of free trade and of Britain's strategic, even divine role in ensuring it, while zealous, was a far cry from the precolonial 'galactic' approach to diplomacy. Beneath Goodfellow's pompous claims about Britain's global mission to ensure free trade and commercial security was a clear intention to establish Aden's pre-eminent place in the regional order. The rise of wrecks and ships stranded along the northeastern coast of Somalia, and the ensuing British interference in their affairs, posed a challenge to Majerteenia's figureheads Nur Uthman and Sultan Uthman. By and large, the Majerteen sultans managed to maintain their primacy in international relations by creating agreements that saw them win financial reward and political recognition from the British in Aden in exchange for the protection of shipwrecks until the 1870s. But there was a significant shift in the tone of diplomacy, as well as the expectations of the British as diplomatic partners, which played out in dramatic fashion in the Playfair negotiations of the early 1860s. From the 1860s onwards, the British became increasingly pugnacious in their approach to international relations in the region. In Chapter 2, we see that by the 1880s a race towards an anarchic system of international relations in the region had begun, in which the weak and the powerful, the royal and the commoner alike battled for resources, power and recognition.

---

[101] IOR R/20/A/512, Letter, Brigadier-General Loch, Resident, Aden, to Secretary to Government, Bombay, undated, September 1879. See also IOR R/20/E/121, Ratification of Major Goodfellow's Convention with the Majertain Somalis and IOR R/20/E/123, 1884: Mijertteyn Chiefs: Agreement. Aden Residency, Memorandum, 2/4/84.

2 | *The Beginning of the End of Diplomacy*

In Chapter 1, we explored the precolonial history of the northeast African Somali peninsula, and its deep engagement in regional commerce and international relations. We saw that a tradition of royal government in the region dated back to at least the time of the Egyptian Middle Kingdom. We saw the continuation of this tradition of royal government and regional diplomatic engagement with the advent of the Majerteen Sultanate in the eighteenth and nineteenth centuries. In the 1800s, the Majerteen Sultanate blended local and Islamic ideas, notably *aban*, the integration of visitors into the Sultan's lineage, as well as *dhimmi*, *himaya*, and *aman* into its approach to the management of foreign relations at the local, everyday level. At the 'high', inter-state level, Majerteenia formed part of the Islamic *dar al-'ahd*, the realm of treaties, wherein written agreements with other coastal royal families in the region affirmed and reinforced the Sultanate's sovereignty. But with the arrival of the British in Aden in 1839, and particularly following the opening of the Suez Canal in 1869 and the increase in the number of European steamships wrecked along the northeastern Somali coast, Majerteenia was exposed to a sharply contrasting approach to diplomacy. While the Cruttenden agreements assimilated the British into a regional model and style of treaty-making and diplomacy, the atmosphere of international relations changed climactically in the early 1860s. Whereas Cruttenden had partaken in the meeting of chiefs as a guest, under the protection of an *aban*, Playfair forced Uthman to behead his people at gunpoint. Goodfellow, in turn, connived to exploit the rivalry between Uthman and Yusuf 'Ali, and then blamed the mounting tensions between the two men on the inherent discordance of Somali politics.

The stage was set for a radical shift in the international politics of the region. Not only was the culture of diplomacy about to be transformed, the map of regional sovereigns was about to be redrawn. In the late nineteenth century, the British upended the regional web of long-term alliances and mutual gift giving and recognition. The new regime of treaty making and international law was transactional; international negotiations were transformed into competitions, the discussions over the terms of treaties metamorphosed into contests for strategic advantages in the geopolitical realm. At the same time, violence – once the exception in inter-state relations in the region – evolved into a diplomatic strategy which could be instrumentalised for political and financial gain. The maritime arena became one of incessant war, the colonial powers' culture of diplomacy created chaos. As the nineteenth century progressed, the British reneged on their promises, relied on duress in negotiations, and engaged in double-dealing with Uthman's political rivals – especially Yusuf 'Ali. By the end of the century, as a result of Euro-African machinations, the Majerteen Sultanate would be split in two, carved into mutually antagonistic northern and southern spheres which continue to this day to be rivals, as can be witnessed in the contemporary tensions and rivalries between the Puntland and Galmudug federal administrations.

Imperial historians from Gallagher and Robinson to John Darwin have emphasised that the European colonial enterprise was persistently informal, even makeshift. Yet in the Somali case, its informality was more extreme. European colonies did not seek to create, they destroyed. Rather than building democracies, transforming economies and establishing legal systems, the thrust of European colonial action in the southern Red Sea was to create chaos. In Benton's words, Europeans used their limited power and resources to 'purposely undermine indigenous political structures and norms'.[1] In the place of stable, long-established international relationships between the Majerteen Sultans, and the rulers of Mukalla, Oman and elsewhere, Europeans left competition and violence. In the place of mutual recognition, they incited retaliation, one-upmanship and competition. The principles of *aman*, *aban* and the *dar al-'ahd* did not disappear, but they were hollowed out, transformed and repurposed to new, more adversarial methods of diplomacy and international relations.

---

[1] Benton, 'Legal spaces of empire', p. 700. See also John Darwin, 'Imperialism and the Victorians: The dynamics of territorial expansion', *The English Historical Review* 112(447) (1997), p. 619.

Lighthouses

At the end of Chapter 1, we saw the trail of failed Anglo-Majerteen treaties grow longer when the Goodfellow agreement stalled in 1879. Britain's response to this latest diplomatic calamity was to invoke Egyptian-Ottoman sovereignty in the Cape Guardafui region. British officials hoped, somewhat vainly, that where Uthman's authority appeared to be failing, the Porte might successfully interject.[2] Yet Ottoman sovereignty along the Majerteen coast did not conform with European notions of direct domination and exclusive territorial jurisdictions. Instead, Majerteenia's membership in the Ottoman Empire was rooted in a more fluid understanding of affiliation with the wider Islamic ecumene, which the Ottoman Empire represented. However, the Islamic world was not reducible to the Ottoman Empire; nor was Majerteenia simply a province of the Empire, or of the Islamic world. For the Majerteen, flying the Ottoman flag meant signalling their connection to the fluid international system of which the Ottomans were a part, not subordination to the Porte.

Any European effort to enforce Ottoman domination, or to trade Ottoman overrule for European overrule in Majerteenia, was doomed to failure. British officials were not unaware of this disjuncture between European and Majerteen ideas about sovereignty and the nature of international relations. Sensing Britain's desperation, France sent a survey mission to the coast; this was swiftly followed by a British-sponsored Egyptian-American expedition. Both missions set out to survey the region, make informal diplomatic overtures to Majerteenia's coastal power-brokers and (ideally) to settle the question of the coast's vexed sovereignty. At the same time, both the British and French expeditions should stay on the lookout for an opportune building spot for a lighthouse.

Far from allaying international concerns about the growing menace posed to international shipping by civil disorder in the region, the

---

[2] IOR R/20/E/107, Letter, Louis Mallet, Chief Negotiator with the Khedive at the India Office, to Under Secretary of State, Foreign Office, London, 27/1/1877, and Letter, Secretary of State for India, London, to the Government of India, Bombay, 15/3/1877. See also Col. E. A. Stanton, 'Secret letters from the Khedive Ismail in connection with an occupation of the east coast of Africa', *Journal of the Royal African Society* 34(136) (1935), p. 282, and Lt.-Col. Charles Graves, 'Le Cap Guardafui. Rapport à S. E. Général Stone-Pacha', *Société Khédiviale de Géographie* (9) (1880), p. 39.

missions confirmed European concerns that Uthman Mahmud Yusuf's control of the coast was in disarray. The leader of the French mission wrote particularly starkly on this point. In the wake of Yusuf 'Ali's attack on the *Vortigern*, the French mission discovered that Sultan Uthman had led some two thousand warriors in companies of archers, shieldsmen, cavalry armed with lances, swordsmen and a small number of Arab riflemen from Bandar Maryah to surround the port of Alula. In turn, Yusuf 'Ali sold loot to pay for foreign fighters, munitions and boats from the port of Mukalla, which he dispatched to Maryah harbour to destroy Uthman's ships.[3] The French surveyor wrote that Maryah was 'like a vast cemetery in which the dead had escaped from their tombs … in every corner reigns a disastrous drought'.[4]

There is some exaggeration for effect, and both reports entirely overlook the root of the civil disorder – Britain's systematic frustration of Uthman's sovereignty and the historic diplomatic order of the region over the previous two decades. But the expedition leader's assessment of growing disquiet in the region gives an important insight into the far-reaching effects of rising international disorder. Moreover, the influx of firearms to Yusuf 'Ali's retainers is corroborated by Goodfellow's confession that he had only secured the return of thirty-five rifles of the 1,000 lost from the *Vortigern*, suggesting Yusuf had recently come to control 950 or more firearms along with their ammunition and was claiming, contrary to Majerteen practice outlined in Chapter 1, that it was his followers' custom to lay claim to the entire cargo of a stranded vessel.[5] The Anglo-American and Egyptian mission to the coast reported similar findings about the disarray in which the Majerteen political system found itself. Seeing no political solution to the impasse, the report recommended the British focus on negotiations over the construction of a lighthouse to mitigate the risk of wrecks on the coast rather than becoming embroiled in bloody civil conflicts. However, the report concluded that if, as they recommended, Britain concentrated its diplomatic efforts on persuading the Majerteen to lease Britain a small section of land and allow British engineers to construct a lighthouse on Cape Guardafui,

[3] Révoil, *Voyages*, pp. 13, 21, 29, 164–170, 182.
[4] Révoil, *La Vallée*, pp. 20, 23, 27.
[5] IOR R/20/A/512, Letter, Resident at Aden to Secretary to Government, Bombay, 14/2/1879 and 18/4/1879.

Figure 2.1 A view of the town of Alula, circa 1890. Engraving by Ernesto Mancastropa from a photograph by Luigi Robecchi Bricchetti. (DEA/ICAs94/De Agostini Editorial/Getty Images.)

this would likely prove all but impossible in the current conditions of civil war.[6]

It was against this backdrop of stalled international negotiations and growing civil unrest that another British steamship, the *Consolation*, was wrecked on the coast close to Alula in 1882. In response, Yusuf 'Ali returned the crew to Aden unscathed and invited officials from Aden to visit Alula (see Figure 2.1) in the summer of 1882 to reopen negotiations for a treaty. The mission promised Yusuf 'Ali a $360 MT annual stipend, the same as was promised to Uthman in 1879. The new agreement also proposed to list Yusuf 'Ali as a 'Sultan of Alula'; in exchange, Yusuf agreed to concede land to the British for a lighthouse. When another British ship, the *Fleurs Castle*, was wrecked off Cape Guardafui later in 1882, the new British Resident in Aden dispatched

[6] Graves, 'Le Cap Guardafui', pp. 29–45.

another mission with the goal of obtaining Uthman's assent to the
agreement with Yusuf 'Ali and to the building of a lighthouse. If he
failed to make a concrete offer to lease land on the Somali peninsula,
British officials repeatedly threatened to demote Uthman to the status
of chief and recognise Yusuf 'Ali as Sultan.[7] If he complied and signed
a fresh treaty, by contrast, British officials promised Uthman $500 MT
in recognition of the Majerteen's assistance to the *Fleurs Castle*. But the
terms of the treaty proved too disagreeable.

As Britain's chief representative Captain Sealy described it after the
event, the British government translator rendered the proposed treaty
into Somali in front of the assembled elders. The treaty contained
provisions for the cession of a lighthouse and the recognition of
Yusuf 'Ali as 'Sultan of Alula'. After the treaty had been read aloud,
a long, uncomfortable pause followed. Uthman eventually replied, at
length, in his conciliatory way, that on reflection he wanted to withdraw from the treaty negotiations altogether. Uthman thanked the
delegation from Aden for their offer. He did not close the door to
diplomacy. 'God willing we will send some men to you', Uthman wrote
to Aden after the mission left his shores, 'and on meeting together we
will converse.'[8] But he left the British delegation with little choice but
to leave, lamenting Uthman's obstinacy, his jealousness of his status,
and his venal self interest in shipwrecks.

It is true there was a long-standing resistance on the part of the
Majerteen Sultans to taking measures to improve the safety of shipping
passing their shores. As early as the 1840s, the French explorer Charles
Guillain noted that the Sultan of Muscat had sent 'considerable presents to this Majerteen tribe and asked them permission to create a
small light-house on the promontory of Gardafui' – perhaps under
pressure from the Omanis' British advisors – but that the presents were
returned and the offer declined.[9] The French mission to the Majerteen
coast in 1878 wrote that the Majerteen Sultans had long believed that

---

[7] IOR R/20/E/137, Letter, James Blair, Resident, Aden, to Secretary to the
Government of Bombay, 13/2/1883, and Letter, James Blair, Resident, Aden, to
Secretary to the Government of Bombay, 24/2/1882.

[8] IOR R/20/E/137, Letter, Captain Sealy, Bunder Maryah, to James Blair, Aden,
23/2/1883, and Letter, Sultan Othman Mahmood, to James Blair, Resident,
Aden, 19/2/1883. See also IOR R/20/E/123, Aden Residency Memorandum, 19/
4/1884.

[9] AOM FM SG Océan Indien OIND/ 22, dossier 117. Charles Guillain, 'Note sur
Abd-al-Gouri et la presqu'ile de Raz-Khafoun', 22/3/1848.

shipwrecks were much too great a source of wealth and prestige to abandon.[10] An Italian observer likewise noted in the early 1900s that 'the head and front of the opposition' to the lighthouse was the Sultan, who sponsored the tradition of 'a [saint] praying day and night for the shipwreck of the infidel on that iron-bound coast'.[11]

But the reasons for Uthman's objections to a lighthouse, and his refusal to sign the treaty with the British, were more substantial. Uthman did not seek to encourage shipwrecks. Rather, he saw ship-wrecks as an important precursor to his membership in a reciprocal system of treaty obligations with other local rulers, which were based in part on agreements around salvage and other questions of maritime law. Shipwrecks were an opportunity to engage in international diplo-macy and mutual assistance. British officials, by contrast, had shown themselves committed to hard bargaining, gunboat realpolitik and competitive one-upmanship, which undermined Uthman's authority. Indeed, the British had gone so far in the opposite direction of permis-sive and deferential indigenous forms of diplomacy as to demote Uthman and give Yusuf 'Ali the title Sultan. In other words, the problem lay not in the environment or in the ambition of individual leaders, but in the competitive and adversarial system of international competition that the British and other European powers had created. It lay in colonial chaos.

Yet British officials continued to conflate cause and cure in the emerging colonial chaos. They became only more persuaded that a policy of division and adversarial diplomacy was the solution. 'Should any European power wish to establish a footing on the North-East coast of Africa', Sealy smarted after returning defeated to Aden, 'it would not be a difficult task as it would be easy to avail oneself of the jealousies existing among the various chiefs who hang together by rather a slender connection'.[12] In October 1883, the British dispatched a Somali envoy to Sultan Uthman at Bandar Maryah to obtain

---

[10] Révoil, *Voyages*, p. 172.
[11] See Reclus, *Earth and Its Inhabitants*, p. 396; Cruttenden, 'Report on the Mijjertheyn', p. 120; Rigby, 'On the Origin', p. 93; Baldacci, 'The Promontory', p. 71. See also R. B. Serjeant, 'Hadramawt to Zanzibar: The Pilot Poem of the Nakhudha Sa'id Ba Tayi' of al-Hami', in R. B. Serjeant and G. Rex Smith (eds.), *Farmers and Fishermen in Arabia* (Aldershot: Variorum, 1995), p. 121.
[12] IOR R/20/E/137, Letter, Captain Sealy, Bunder Maryah, to James Blair, Political Resident, Aden, 23/2/1883.

Uthman's signature to Sealy's treaty – still allowing for the building of a lighthouse and recognising Yusuf 'Ali as a 'Sultan' – but this time sharpened by the threat that the British would proceed to sign a contract and offer Yusuf 'Ali $500 MT if Uthman refused to consent. This time Uthman Mahmud Yusuf's response was less restrained. His retainers ran the dragoman out of the port, looted the ship, and stripped him of his property, clothes and letters.[13]

To salvage their relationship with Uthman, British officials had little choice but to revert to the original terms of the agreement, based on the informal agreement between Cruttenden and the Majerteen elders at Bandar Maryah in 1844, and reiterated a number of times thereafter, including by Playfair.[14] Major J. S. King, the Assistant Resident in Aden, travelled to Majerteenia in 1884, paid Uthman his stipend – backdated four years as promised by the 1879 agreement – and obtained his signature to a treaty which promised the Majerteen Sultans present and future would offer assistance to stranded shipping in exchange for a stipend paid by Aden. Major King then proceeded to Alula to obtain Yusuf 'Ali's signature as a chief rather than a Sultan. When Yusuf requested that he be entertained in Bombay as an official visitor of the British government, the Bombay government ventured that 'some subordinate official' might accompany him on his visit to the city.[15]

For a moment in the mid-1880s, the old system of sovereignty and diplomacy seemed to have been restored. But the return of a calm and cooperative model of diplomacy proved short-lived. In 1883, British forces occupied Sudan in response to the uprisings led by Muhammad Ahmad bin Abd Allah – more popularly known as the Mahdi. As Egypt's major creditor and de facto rulers, Britain compelled Egypt and the Ottomans to formally withdraw their imperial claim to rule northeast Africa, conclusively ending the Egyptian-Ottoman imperial

---

[13] IOR R/20/E/137, Letter, James Blair, Aden, to Chief Secretary to the Government of Bombay, 21/11/1883.

[14] Copies of the Anglo-Majerteen treaties (which made it to signature) arranged in chronological order may be found in the Appendix.

[15] IOR R/20/E/123, Letter, Resident, Aden, to Secretary to Government, Bombay, 23/1/1884, and Extract from a Report dated 23/1/1884, and Letter, Secretary to the Government of India, to the Chief Secretary to the Government of Bombay, 30/7/1884.

claim to govern the Somali-speaking lands.[16] In 1884, the British Foreign Office demanded the Egyptian government formally withdraw its claims to govern the coast from Cape Guardafui to Zeila and cede sovereignty to the British government of India.[17] In turn, Britain took over the Egyptian garrisons in Zeila and Berbera further west, as well as signing a treaty of protection with the extant Warsengali rulers of the port of Las Khorai. This political reorganisation, which essentially confronted the reality of the Ottoman and Egyptians' ineffectiveness in influencing the wider north-east African zone, led directly to the establishment of the coastal limits of what became British Somaliland.[18] Britain also signed agreements with various clan leaders from the north-western coast of the Somali-speaking zone, including the leaders of the Gadabursi, Habr Awal and Issa clans, constraining them never to 'cede, sell or mortgage' their country to another power.[19]

New Men

The short-lived restoration of the old order, of the concept of *aman*, in the tradition of the *dar al-'ahd*, turned out to simply prove the extent to which the new rules of diplomacy were really driven by competition, retaliation, power and violence. In 1884, a French merchant marine ship travelling from Singapore to Marseille ran aground near Alula, stranding some 400 French soldiers. The ship, the *Aveyron*, sent out a distress signal, to which a nearby German steamer responded, plucking some 300 soldiers from the half-sunk steamer during the night. Next morning, the British sent a naval patrol boat to the spot, carrying

[16] Sir Rawson W. Rawson, 'European territorial claims on the coasts of the Red Sea, and its southern approaches, in 1885', *Proceedings of the Royal Geographical Society*, 7(2) (1885), pp. 102–103.

[17] NA FO 403/ 83, Letter, Arthur Godley, Under Secretary of State for India, to Sir Julian Pauncefote, Under Secretary of State for Foreign Affairs in the India Office, 28/1/1885, and Letter, Arthur Godley to Julian Pauncefote, 10/2/1885.

[18] Healy, 'British Perceptions', pp. 176–180.

[19] Sir Charles Aitchison, *A Collection of Treaties, Engagements and Sandads Relating to India and Neighbouring Countries, Vol. XIII, the Treaties &c Relating to Turkish Arabia, Aden and South Coast of Arabia, Somaliland, R. Shoa, and Zanzibar* (Calcutta: Superintendent Government Printing, 1909), pp. 204–218.

copies of the 1884 King agreements.[20] But the ship was by now under water; Yusuf 'Ali's men had arrived at the spot where the Captain of the ship landed in life boats on the Somali shores. Yusuf 'Ali demanded $2,000 MT in recognition of the assistance he had provided to the French.[21]

Seeking to capitalise on the importance of the military crew of the *Aveyron*, Yusuf immediately sailed to Aden accompanied by the *Aveyron's* Captain and crew, where he vigorously petitioned British and French officials for recognition. On the face of things, Yusuf 'Ali sought recompense for the services he provided for the crew of the *Aveyron*. But in truth Yusuf 'Ali's assistance to the *Aveyron* was limited. Underneath Yusuf's demands for restitution lay an overarching desire to reanimate his relations with the French and the British. In the course of his meetings with officials, a conspiratorial plan emerged. Yusuf proposed that he would seek the support of Sultan Barghash, the ruler of the Sultanate of Zanzibar, who – in addition to being heavily indebted to the British – made historical claims to sovereignty over the far southern Somali coast as far as the Wadi Nogal valley, which met the Indian Ocean close to Hobyo. With Britain's backing, Yusuf obtained Barghash's approval to create a new port near the mouth of the Wadi Nogal. Under pressure from Britain, Barghash agreed to acquiesce in Yusuf's proposals to establish a rival Majerteen state to the south of Cape Guardafui. Barghash, for his part, asserted that he would retain all the income and duties derived from his expanded coastline, stating that Yusuf was 'leasing' the coast to 'watch over' Zanzibari interests.

In the course of a few feverish weeks of international scheming between Yusuf 'Ali, Sultan Barghash, the British and the French, the historical Majerteen-Omani-Zanzibari treaty alliance was rekindled. While ostensibly a mirror of the relations that existed between Sultan Uthman and the Sultan of Oman in the early nineteenth century, the new coalition was not built on mutual commercial interests and the reinforcement of royal networks. It was predicated instead on power politics, aggression and British imperial control. In early 1885, Yusuf

[20] ADP – 1815–1896, Sous-serie: Afrique, Erythree, Somalie Italienne, 1872–1895, Côte: ADP1/ 24. L'Aveyron: Naufrage au Cap Guardafui. Letter, Ambassador of France in England, to Jules Ferry, Foreign Minister, 24/9/1884.

[21] J. M., 'L'Affaire de l'«Aveyron»', *Bulletin - Société de Géographie Commerciale de Bordeaux*, Série II, Annèe VII (1884), pp. 654–658.

'Ali set sail a flotilla to the mouth of the Wadi Nogal, some 200 miles south of Alula, to extend his territory far into the south of Somalia and founded the port of Hobyo.[22] By placing himself in a new port under the umbrella of Zanzibari sovereignty and outside Sultan Uthman's historical sphere of influence, Yusuf hoped to finally put an end to Uthman's stranglehold on the diplomatic process in the region.

But exigence and opportunity prevailed over history and tradition in the new diplomatic order, at the cost of stability. When he travelled to Zanzibar to meet with Barghash, Yusuf 'Ali found himself shunned by the Sultan and driven into the orbit of the German Consul in Zanzibar. In spite of the fact that the Berlin Conference – which took place almost concurrently with Yusuf's visit to Zanzibar – excluded the Germans from Somalia, and that he had agreed with the British to govern north-eastern Somalia from Hobyo as their ally, Yusuf consorted with the Germans. Thus, during the monsoon trading season of 1885, two German representatives of the German East Africa Company (GEAC) travelled to Hobyo, where they agreed with the Yusuf that he, as Sultan of Hobyo, would protect them and allow them to trade in the area in exchange for $2000 MT annually. In October, the Germans continued to Alula, which Uthman had now occupied, where they signed a much more limited agreement that allowed the Germans to trade with Uthman's coast and in which Uthman 'renounced his rights to the foreshores' – his right to salvage – in exchange for $1,900 MT annually. Yet as a later British mission to Uthman's coast confirmed, this treaty in no way conferred any colonial rights upon the GEAC and indeed, Uthman was still flying the Turkish flag at Alula, although this was taken down when the news of Egypt's withdrawal from the Somali coast had been delivered.[23]

In spite of the treaties' manifestly limited description of Germany's rights in Majerteenia, the German government interpreted them widely. In 1886, the German Ambassador to London, Count Paul Von Hatzfeldt, presented treaties to the Foreign Office apparently signed by Yusuf 'Ali and the GEAC, as well as a separate agreement between Uthman and the GEAC, ceding 'the whole Majerteen coast,

---

[22] IOR R/20/E/152, Letter, Sir John Kirk, HM's Agent Consul General, Zanzibar, to Brig-Gen James Blair, VC, Political Resident, Aden, 13/4/1885, and Letter, Sultan Barghash bin Said to Earl Granville, Secretary of State for Foreign Affairs, 10/4/1885.

[23] The text of both treaties is included in the Appendix.

from Berbera to Ras Asir ... to the Germans'.[24] The GEAC sought the Reichstag's backing for the creation of a protectorate on the coast, with the exception of the towns of Berbera and Ras Hafun, which they misunderstood as being under Ottoman sovereignty. The British Foreign Secretary, the Earl of Rosebery, smartly rebuffed the Ambassador's claims, claiming – misleadingly – that Britain had engaged in protectorate agreements with all the Somali peoples of that coast in 1884 and that the British government would announce internationally once they had agreed the borders of their Somali possessions with the French. In fact, Sultan Uthman had expressly refused the offer of a protectorate during his treaty negotiations with Captain King.[25] It was true, however, that British officials had spoken with the Majerteen chiefs, who stated that no protectorate arrangement existed between them and the GEAC. Majerteenia east of the forty-ninth degree of longitude was independent of any external power, while Hobyo, Rosebery emphasised, was under the Sultan of Zanzibar in April 1885. Rosebery continued that the British would 'welcome' a German protectorate over Majerteen, which would tend to introduce 'trade and civilization ... and put a stop to the pillage of vessels wrecked on that dangerous coast'. But the Germans, Rosebery insisted, would need to refer to the Sultan of Zanzibar on the matter of Obbia and to check the trade in arms to Majerteenia.[26]

Rosebery's approach was a perfect example of Foreign Office obfuscation. The Germans would be welcome to Majerteenia, he stated, but they should ask the Zanzibaris, not the British, in spite of the fact that Rosebery would have fully understood that asking the Zanzibaris would lead back to the British. Rosebery's delay tactics proved strategic. Not long after 1885, Britain began negotiating with the German government and the GEAC to abandon some of their claims to coastal

---

[24] IOR R/20/E/159, English Translation of a German Translation of the Arabic Text of a Treaty concluded on the 26th November 1885; Letter, Archibald Primrose, Earl of Rosebery, Secretary of State for Foreign Affairs, to Sir Edward Malet, British Consul General, Egypt, 24/3/1886, and Draft Memorandum, Count Hatzfeldt, signed Archibald Primrose, Earl of Rosebery, Secretary of State for Foreign Affairs, 5/2/1886. See also IOR R/20/E/159, Translation of the German Translation of the Arabic Text of a Treaty concluded with the Sultan of the Medchertin Tribe, included in letter from Baron Plessen to Archibald Primrose, 17/5/1886.

[25] IOR 20/A/1171, Printed Papers, The Mijjerteyn Somali refuse a British Protectorate.

[26] IOR 20/A/1171, Printed Papers, Letter, Lord Rosebery to Count Hatzfeldt, 5/3/1886.

East Africa in exchange for Britain's withdrawal from the Heligo islands in the North Sea. In the 1890 Heligoland Treaty, Germany agreed to confine its interests in East Africa to the area around Dar es Salaam. As the threat of German interference in coastal East Africa receded, so British support for Yusuf 'Ali ebbed. Britain thus snubbed Yusuf's offer of a new and more formal treaty between Yusuf as the 'Sultan of Hobyo' and Britain as 'hardly worth the outlay'.[27]

However, this increasingly unsettled diplomatic environment proved fertile ground for other prospectors and opportunists. As soon as German interest in the region receded, an Italian naval captain and shipping line owner named Vincenzo Filonardi stepped into the vacuum. Having suffered setbacks in their efforts to expand their African Empire from their base on the Eritrean coast of Massawa further north, the Italians under Prime Minister Crispi promoted a proactive imperial policy in the Somali region.[28] Filonardi used Zanzibar as a base to expand his shipping line, running commercial routes between East Africa and Italy. In 1888, Filonardi visited Yusuf 'Ali in Hobyo, offering him a stipend in exchange for a treaty. But Filonardi did not seem to have been expecting Yusuf to agree so readily. He had neither worked out the terms of the treaty he would offer, nor did he have anything other than some scraps of consular paper on which to draft the treaty.[29]

When the Italian government-backed Benadiir Company was formed to govern southern Somalia, however, they took over Filonardi's treaties in 1894 and consolidated their links with Yusuf 'Ali, which became the basis for Italy's protectorate in Somali north of Mogadishu.[30] Where once diplomatic negotiations took months, involving all the paraphernalia of royal ceremony, actors like Yusuf 'Ali allowed agreements affecting the governmental future of whole

---

[27] IOR R/20/E/159, Statement of Yusuf Ali of Alula, 26/3/1886, and Letter, Consul Frederick Hunter, to Brigadier General Adam Hogg, Resident, Aden, 27/3/1886, and Telegram, Resident Hogg to Richard Cross, Viscount Cross, Under Secretary of State for India, 13/9/1886.

[28] See Aldo Cairoli, *Le origini dei protettorati italiani sulla Somalia settentrionale, 1884–1891* (Trieste: University of Trieste, 1987).

[29] See MAESS ASMAI Posizione 59/ Numero 1 – Somalia Settentrionale, 1886–1889, Fasciolo 5, Trattato col Sultano di Obbia.

[30] NA ADM 116/929. Telegram, Sir Francis Bertie, British Ambassador in Rome, to Minister for Foreign Affairs, London, 1/09/1903, and Telegram, SNO, Aden, to Major Egerton, Military Official of the Somaliland Field Force, 29/12/1903, and Letter, Major Egerton, to SNO Aden, 14/12/1903.

swaths of territory to be concluded on scraps of paper. As the Italian historian Francesco Battera observed, the only political logic which Yusuf 'Ali obeyed was that of accumulation.[31] The new international regime which emerged as a result of Britain's machinations in the region, combined with the uptick in shipwrecks and a growing availability of military patronage, had allowed a peripheral member of the Majerteen ruling class to insert himself into the international regime.

With Britain losing interest in Majerteenia, and in the absence of any new shipwrecks as a pretext for initiating another round of treaty negotiation, Uthman was left with little choice but to accommodate Italian advances, in spite of their closeness to Yusuf. In 1888, Uthman signed a protectorate agreement with Filonardi.[32] This was a significant concession from Uthman, who had steadfastly defended an old order of mutual respect, courtesy, diplomacy, gentility and consensus-seeking. Conventionally, historians have explained the willingness of African sovereigns such as Uthman to sign colonial treaties in terms of misunderstanding of the treaties' actual implications, or even fraud. For example, the historian Robert Hess argued that Italy deliberately mistranslated the terms of their alliance with Abyssinia's rulers at the 1889 Treaty of Wuchale, describing themselves as the colonial 'protectors' of Abyssinia only in the Italian copy, which Emperor Menelik did not understand nor assent to. Hess likewise suggested that Filonardi's translator obfuscated the thorny question of Uthman's sovereignty in its treaty with Uthman in 1889.[33] But taking a similar view in this case would overlook the careful attention Uthman paid treaties and the process of treaty making in the past. He was attuned to the dangers of mistranslation in treaty negotiations and generally insisted on using his own brokers' renderings in his past dealings with Britain so as to avoid ambiguity.

We cannot know for sure what motivated Uthman's uncharacteristically meek response to the aggressive terms of the Italian protectorate treaty. However, reading between the lines of the colonial sources, we can easily imagine that Uthman felt trapped: he was increasingly unable to defend the old order of salvage and mutual respect for sovereignty, but nevertheless remained committed to a historic

---

[31] Battera, *Della tribù*, p. 98.
[32] Copies of both treaties can be found in the Appendix.
[33] Robert Hess, *Italian Colonialism in Somalia* (University of Chicago Press, 1966), pp. 51, 54.

programme of diplomacy and permissive, inclusive international relations. Uthman did not yet have good enough reason to give up on the
old order. Previous agreements – recently the King treaty – had
recognised and secured rather than eroded Uthman's claim to rule
the coast. They had guaranteed him salvage payments. They made
Uthman – rather than Yusuf 'Ali – the central figure in Majerteenia's
foreign relations. Uthman cannot have seen what would emerge from
his new relationship with the Italians. Uthman was instinctively
inclined to cooperate; with Yusuf 'Ali poised to take advantage of
Uthman's concessions, he had little option but to involve himself in
the new international politics, or face the total eclipse of his
sovereignty.

Firearms for Loyalty

By 1890, Majerteenia's domestic and international politics had been
dramatically transformed. Nowhere was this transformation more
evident than in the addition of firearms as an important element in
the negotiations between Uthman, Yusuf and the Italians. Within a
month of signing a treaty, the Italians supplied Yusuf 'Ali with arms 'as
tokens of support' against 'anti-Italian elements' among his population. Uthman soon demanded he too receive arms in recognition of his
standing as a coastal ruler.[34] Officially under international law, the
provision of arms to northeast African rulers was banned under the
terms of the Brussels Conference in 1890. Moreover, the Italians had
ratified the ensuing agreement alongside the British and the French.[35]
Indeed, the anti–arms trading clauses in the Brussels Acts, namely
Articles VIII–XIII, built on earlier British-led efforts to oppose the
trade, including British-organised agreements between Britain, France
and Italy in 1884 and 1887.[36] The Abyssinian ruler Menelik, by
contrast, was exempt from the continental embargo, as were members

---

[34] MAESS ASMAI Posizione 59/ Numero 1 – Somalia Settentrionale, 1886–1889,
Fasciolo 4, Letter, Signor Crispi, Minister for Foreign Affairs in Rome, to Signor
Cecchi, Consul-General in Aden, 23/3/1889; IOR R/20/E/173, Letter, Secretary
of State for Foreign Affairs, London, to Viceroy, Calcutta, 3/1/1889, and Letter,
Adam Hogg to Secretary to the Government of Bombay, 18/2/1889.

[35] See especially Articles XX–LXI, chapter 3, *Actes de la Conférence de Bruxelles
(1889–1890)* (Bruxelles: F. Hayez, 1890), pp. 641–644, 652–663.

[36] IOR R/20/E/170, Letter from the Assistant Secretary, Political and Secret
Department, India Office, London, 7/10/1887.

of his court including Ras Makonnen, ruler of Harar and father of
Abyssinia's future leader Haile Selassie. At Italy's instigation, Uthman
made repeated requests to the Italians in the early 1890s for 'ammuni-
tions and rifles' with which to support his ally, the new ruler of Harar,
Ras Makonnen.[37] But when Italy faced defeat at the hands of a well-
armed Abyssinian military at the battle of Adwa in 1896, their policy
of arming renegade Abyssinian rulers via clandestine channels in
Majerteenia proved self-defeating. Italy considerably reduced the
scale of arms exports to Africa, channelling arms in a clandestine
way to Uthman.[38]

But by now Uthman was entrenched in the regional arms trade. The
late nineteenth century saw the advent of an anti-European Sufi
brotherhood known as the *Salihiyyah* in the Majerteen hinterland
and Ogaden, led by the cleric Sayyid Muhammad Abdille Hassan.
Strongly anti-European and broadly linked to the Idrisi of Libya and
'Asir, the *Salihiyyah* incited its followers to take up arms against the
colonial incursions. Firearms, however, could not be obtained except
from Europe, and Uthman intermediated between European sources of
mechanised weaponry and the Sayyid's followers.[39] Indeed, Uthman
invoked the spectre of an alliance with the Sayyid to goad the French
and Italians into reopening the supply of arms, purported to hold off
the emerging *jihad*.[40] If he could not defend his territory with an
arsenal of his own, Uthman claimed, he would have no choice but to
fraternize with arms dealers in French Somaliland such as the Zeila
merchant Abu Bakr, a descendant of the Turco-Egyptian Pasha of
Zeila, whom the French poet-turned-trader Arthur Rimbaud described

[37] MAESS ASMAI Posizione 59/ Numero 1 – Somalia Settentrionale – 1886–1889,
Fasciolo 11, Letter, Sultan Osman Mahmud Yusuf to Signor Cecchi, Consul for
Italy in Aden, 10/6/1894.
[38] Jonathan A. Grant, *Rulers, Guns and Money: The Global Arms Trade in the
Age of Imperialism* (Cambridge, MA: Harvard University Press, 2007),
pp. 50–56.
[39] IOR R/20/E/236, Letter, P. J. Maitland, Resident, Aden, to Captain Cartwright,
Senior Naval Officer, Red Sea Patrol, 4/3/1902.
[40] See MAESS ASMAI Posizione 60/ Numero 1 – Somalia Settarionale – Traffico
d'armi e repression (1897–1903), Fasciolo 1, Letter, Italian Consul, Zanzibar, to
Foreign Minister, Rome, 19/4/1899; AOM FM 1/AFFPOL/3144, Letter, Adrien
Bonhoure, Governor of Côte Française des Somalis, to Albert Decrais, Minister
for Colonies, Paris, 1/10/1901.

as 'the plague'.[41] If Uthman refused to deal with the Sayyid directly, Abu Bakr would demand he supply the Sayyid as the cost of doing business.[42] In reality, Uthman simply sought to maintain a connection with Europeans, to save the vestiges of an increasingly moribund form of inclusive diplomacy.

That Uthman had adopted such a Machiavellian approach to diplomacy must be understood through the optic of disarray and disorder in the diplomatic sphere. By the late 1890s, the British had all but withdrawn from the Majerteen coast. There had not been a British diplomatic mission to Bandar Maryah or any of the Majerteen ports since 1884. Rather than acting as universal arbiters of the shipping industry on behalf of shipowners of all nations, the British increasingly referred the victims of shipwreck either to the Italians, to the Sultan of Zanzibar, or to the nearest ambassador of the country whose flag the distressed vessel carried. The situation was, in other words, one in which every nation, every ruler, every shipowner and every sailor fended for themselves. In allying with Muhammad Abdille Hassan, Uthman was simply fighting his corner in the free-for-all battle for survival – using the relationship to extract arms and favours from regional powers. The fractious, ephemeral, transactional and increasingly competitive tenor of international relations, which the British introduced and the Germans and Italians had perpetuated, now included the French, who via their colony in French Somaliland (explored in more detail in Chapter 4) became the region's premier arms market. Indeed, French Somaliland sent some 3,000–4,000 rifles to Majerteenia each year.[43] Moreover, the trade was profitable, and the retail value of a single rifle on Majerteen shores was around $40 MT, indicating an overall value of the arms market in the range of

---

[41] See Marc Fontrier, *Abou-Bakr Ibrahim: Pacha de Zeila, Marchand d'esclaves; Commerce et diplomatie dans le Golfe de Tadjoura, 1840–1885* (Paris: Harmattan, 2003), pp. 242–243.

[42] MAESS ASMAI Posizione 60/ Numero 1 – Somalia Settarionale – Traffico d'armi e repression (1897–1903). Fasciolo 2, Letter, Cav. Pestalozza, Italian Consul in Zanzibar, to Prinetti, the Foreign Minister, Rome, 28/11/1899.

[43] See IOR R/20/E/236, Letter, Consul Harry Cordeaux, Consul-General, Berbera, to the Secretary of State for Foreign Affairs, London, 19/11/1901, and Letter, Consul Harry Cordeaux, Consul-General, Berbera, to the Secretary of State for Foreign Affairs, London, 19/11/1901. See also NA FO 2/970, Letter, British Vice Consul, Zeila, to Eric Swayne, Consul General, Berbera, 2/10/1902.

$120,000 MT – or around one-third to one-half of Majerteenia's annual foreign currency earnings.[44]

Uthman likewise approached salvage in an increasingly self-serving fashion in the 1890s. In November 1898, Uthman sent ships to loot the remnants of a P&O steamer, the SS *Aden*, which had run aground in bad weather off the coast of Socotra, some 150 miles off the coast of Cape Guardafui, in 1897.[45] Never before had Majerteenia sent sailors out of their way to attack ships. Yet the following year Uthman launched an attack against Omani pearl fishermen close to Socotra, killing three and wounding more before taking a handful of hostages to Somalia.[46] In August 1900, an American cargo ship, the *Indra*, carrying a cargo of around 5,000 tons of sugar worth some $500,000 US (around $13 million US today) between Java and New York, ran aground close to the peninsula of Ras Hafun, just south of Cape Guardafui. Uthman and his followers initially protected the wreck, reassuring the crew that they would guard their cargo until help could be obtained in Aden. When the crew left in search of rescue, however, Uthman lifted in excess of 1,000 tons of sugar to the shore – an amount worth some $100,000–200,000 US, or in contemporary terms, some $2.5–5 million US. According to the Aden Gazette, 'a small village' sprang up close to the wreck reminiscent of a 'sudden swoop of a mining camp of prospectors, where gold has been struck'. While salvage had long played a role in the Majerteen approach to managing shipwrecks, looting on this scale was unprecedented.[47] Then in June

---

[44] Based on valuations of rifles sold in Majerteenia at $40 MT each. IOR R/20/E/236, Letter, Commander Cartwright, HMS Cossack, Red Sea Patrol, to Rear Admiral Bosanquet, Commander of Mediterranean Fleet, 3/2/1902; IOR R/20/A/1221, Somaliland Intelligence Report, 5/12/1905.

[45] MAESS ASMAI Posizione 62/ Numero 1 – Somalia Settentrionale – Naufragi sulle coste di Obbia e dei Migiurtini (1898–1909), Fasciolo 1, Letter, British Ambassador, Rome to Count Canevaro, Foreign Minister, Rome, 21/11/1898. See also SS *Aden* (II) (+1897), www.wrecksite.eu/wreck.aspx?134430, accessed 12/1/2020.

[46] MAESS ASMAI Posizione 59/ Numero 2 – Somalia Settentrionale – 1887–1909, Fasciolo 26, Letter, Arthur Hardinge, British Consul, Zanzibar, to Signor Dulio, M. le Gouverneur de la Somalie Italienne, Magadoxo, 8/09/1900; MAESS ASMAI Posizione 60/Numero 1 – Somalia Settarionale – Traffico d'armi e repression (1897–1903), Fasciolo 1, Letter, Italian Consul, Zanzibar, to Foreign Minister, Rome, 19/4/1899.

[47] MAESS ASMAI Posizione 62/ Numero 1 – Somalia Settentrionale – Naufragi sulle coste di Obbia e dei Migiurtini (1898–1909), Fasciolo 3, Aden Weekly

1901, Uthman's men looted a German steamship named the *Asturia*, carrying a large cargo of tin, copper, silk and hides from China to New York which had run aground east of Maryah. Only when a British warship called at Maryah did Uthman agree to return some of the goods.[48]

Following the wrecking and looting of the *Indra* and the *Asturia*, the Italian Consul in Zanzibar, Cavaliere Giulio Pestalozza, sought to reopen negotiations with Uthman for a new treaty in 1901. Uthman replied to Pestalozza that the coast was under both British protection and the protection of the Germans in Dar es Salaam.[49] Pestalozza returned to Zanzibar, where he persuaded the Italian Navy to dispatch an occupying force using troops raised from among Yusuf 'Ali's guard in Hobyo. Even as gunboats loomed off the coast of Majerteenia, Uthman continued to resist a meeting, instead smuggling an envoy to Aden to request British support against the impending Italian invasion.[50] After withstanding months of siege conditions, Uthman submitted to a meeting with the Italians. In the course of the negotiations, Uthman repeatedly threatened the Italians with the fact that Muhammad Abdille Hassan wrote to him 'daily' enjoining him to wage war 'against the white men'. 'Such a war', Uthman continued, 'would very much please the Bedouin people of the Sultanate'. By threatening the spread of violence to his ports, Uthman rejected Italian demands for an Italian agent in his ports and successfully challenged the Italians' demand to surrender his arms, which might leave him unable to resist the Muhammad Abdille Hassan's advances. Uthman also retained his rights of salvage and traditional payments for

Gazette, Aden, 30th October, 1900, pp. 8–9, and Letter, United States Ambassador, Rome, to M. Prinetti, Foreign Minister, Rome, 3/4/1901.

[48] MAESS ASMAI Posizione 62/ Numero 1 – Somalia Settentrionale – Naufragi sulle coste di Obbia e dei Migiurtini (1898–1909), Fasciolo 6, 'La Sottomissione del Sultana dei Migiurtini, in seguito al saccheggio dell'Asturia', *La Sera di Milano* (26–27 Agosto 1901), and Fasciolo 7, Letter, Resident, Aden, to Sultan Othman Mahmud, Mijertain, through the Consul General for Italy, 18/03/1902.

[49] MAESS ASMAI Posizione 59/ Numero 2 – Somalia Settentrionale, 1887–1909, Fasciolo 33, Letter, Giulio Prinetti, Minister for Foreign Affairs, Rome, to M. Pausa, London, 8/2/1902.

[50] MAESS ASMAI Posizione 59/ Numero 2 – Somalia Settentrionale – 1887–1909, Fasciolo 30, 31, 32, Letter, Giulio Prinetti, Minister for Foreign Affairs, Rome, to Cav. Pestalozza, Consul General, Zanzibar, 20/07/1901.

services to stranded ships, though he permitted the insertion of a clause that the Italians be allowed to erect a lighthouse at Alula.[51]

The resulting treaty was so unfavourable to the Italians' interests that the Governor of Eritrea argued the Foreign Ministry should refuse to sign it and suspend all colonial relations with Uthman. The Governor of Eritrea wrote disparagingly that the agreement posed 'no advantage whatsoever' for Italy and would be a 'grave error'. Majerteenia's ports, he wrote, have an annual trade with Aden valued at only 1.2 million rupees, or 2 million lire. While double what it had been some twenty-five years earlier, the amount was still not enough to persuade the Italian Governor of the value of a colony. In exchange for a modest customs revenue, the Governor observed, Italy would find itself responsible for both shipwrecks and for the impossible task of policing the arms trade.[52] Pestalozza returned to Majerteenia and renegotiated the treaty for one which allowed an Italian agent to reside permanently in Bandar Cassim to monitor and check the expansion of the arms trade.[53]

In effect, Uthman had played the colonists at their own game of geostrategy and won. Indeed Uthman responded to the increasing diplomatic pressure from Italy and the threat to his sovereignty by redoubling his involvement in the arms trade with the interior. By the end of 1901, the British reported '"droves of upwards of 1,000 camels at a time" arriving in the Majerteen ports for purchasing rifles and ammunition'.[54] A British patrol ship captured a Majerteen dhow smuggling 7,000 cartridges and 80 arms of various kinds to the Somali coast directly from Djibouti.[55] When the British confronted the Italians with Uthman's role in the war in early 1902, the Italians protested that arms were sold only in small numbers in Majerteenia, largely by private traders, and only in response to the very high prices

---

[51] MAESS ASMAI Posizione 59/ Numero 3 – Somalia Settentrionale – Azione Italiana su Obbia e Migiurinia, 1902–1904, Fasciolo 33, Extract from Pestalozza's diary.

[52] MAESS ASMAI Posizione 59/ Numero 2 – Somalia Settentrionale – 1887–1909, Fasciolo 28 e 29, Letter, M. Martini, Governor of Eritrea, Asmara, to Minister for Foreign Affairs, 13/06/1901.

[53] The full text of the treaty can be found in the Appendix.

[54] Ray W. Beachey, 'The arms trade in East Africa in the late nineteenth century', *Journal of African History*, 3(3) (1962), pp. 464–466.

[55] MAESS ASMAI Posizione 60/Numero 1 – Somalia Settarionale – Traffico d'armi e repression (1897–1903), Fasciolo 7.

they obtained in the interior.[56] But the trade was not small; internal Italian reports indicated that some 20,000 French Gras rifles had arrived in Majerteenia from the port of Djbouti during the trading season of 1901. Britain was convinced many of these arms had fallen into the hands of the Sayyid's supporters.[57] Bandar Casim, one British official observed, was 'notoriously the centre of the traffic'.[58]

But Uthman's adoption of the colonial style of diplomacy, while successful in holding the Italians at bay, was not without deleterious side effects. The increasingly fractious state of international politics in the region affected Uthman's ability to govern in the domestic realm. The large numbers of rifles imported via Bandar Cassim had increased Muhammad Abdille Hassan's prestige, making his jihadi movement a growing military and ideological threat to the Sultanate.[59] Likewise, as one of Uthman's lieutenants put it, the proliferation of arms turned Uthman's domestic opponents into belligerents who 'threatened Uthman's sovereignty and independence'. The Sultan now lacked the 'moral and material means', as Ahmad summarised the situation, to survey his coastline and to ensure that his followers maintained their allegiance to him.[60] More seriously for Uthman, his involvement with Muhammad Abdille Hassan concentrated international attention on policing Majerteen shores like never before. The British, Italian and Ottoman rulers had all increased their naval patrols of the Red Sea in response to the jihad, with a combined patrol of some eight gunboats of the Majerteen coastal area in the early 1900s, mandated to prevent

---

[56] IOR R/20/E/236, Letter, Minister for Foreign Affairs, to Secretary of the Political and Secret Department, London, 23/1/1902, and Letter, P. J. Maitland, British Resident, Aden, to Captain Cartwright, SNO, 4/3/1902.

[57] MAESS ASMAI Posizione 60/Numero 1 – Somalia Settarionale – Traffico d'armi e repression (1897–1903), Fasciolo 3, Letter, Italian Consul, Aden, to Minister for Foreign Affairs, 28/9/1901.

[58] IOR R/20/E/236, Letter, Harry Cordeaux, Consul General, Berbera, to Minister for Foreign Affairs, London, 19/11/1901, and Letter, P. J. Maitland, British Resident, Aden, to Captain Cartwright, SNO, 4/3/1902.

[59] MAESS ASMAI Posizione 60/ Numero 2 – Somalia Settrionale – Traffico d'armi e repressione, 1902–1910, Fasciolo 9, Copy of Report Compiled by the Foreign Office, London, 13/08/1902. See also NA ADM 116/930, Final Report on the Operations Conducted by Lieutenant Colonel Eric Swayne, Somaliland Field Force, 18th January to 1st November 1902.

[60] IOR R/20/E/236, Letter, M. Prinetti, Ministry of Foreign Affairs, Rome, to Lord Currie, Rome, 1/3/1902, and Report of Cav. Sola, Commander of the Governolo, Italian Navy, to the Minister of the Marine, 4/2/1902.

arms dealing or any other threats to international shipping emanating from Uthman's coastline.[61]

In late 1904 rumours reached the British in Berbera that Muhammad Abdille Hassan was preparing a new offensive against the British and Italian colonial occupations. In response to the news, the British prepared an attack on Muhammad Abdille Hassan's strongholds in the Ogaden hinterland. Meanwhile, Italian and British naval officers apprehended one of the Muhammad Hassan's chief allies, a Majerteen broker named Abdullah Shehri, during a visit to Bandar Cassim. Questioned by the Italians, Abdullah Shehri revealed a host of information about the arms trade between the Sultan Uthman and Muhammad Abdille Hassan, implicating the German agents and the French firms in the supply of arms to Britain's enemy. Abdullah Shehri admitted that he personally had imported thousands of French Gras and British Martini–Henry rifles to Muhammad Abdille Hassan in the last five years. Wishing to forestall any cooling of relations with the British, Italian officers counselled Abdullah Shehri to declare before British officials that he was 'a thief', with no other motive to engage in the arms trade than to make money.[62] British officials questioned Addullah Shehri's defence, but did not press the issue of Italian complicity, instead pressuring the Italians to increase their patrol of Uthman's coastline, recommending that at least six armed dhows concentrate on Uthman's ports of Bandar Casim and Bandar Maryah.[63]

Yusuf 'Ali capitalised on Uthman's misfortune. Yusuf proposed in early 1904 that British and Italian forces use the port of Hobyo as a launching point for their offensive against Muhammad Abdille Hassan – on condition that the colonists blocked all arms imports to Uthman's ports.[64] Yusuf's overtures to the British and Italians met with a mixed response among British officials, who cautioned that Yusuf 'Ali was unreliable and that the harbour was unfit for a major

[61] IOR R/20/A/1300, Letter, Commissioner's Office, Somaliland, to Secretary of State for the Colonies, 10/04/1906; Letter, SNO, Aden Division, to the Commander-in-Chief, East Indies, 01/09/1905.
[62] IOR R/20/A/1214, Memorandum compiled by Lt-Col Forestier-Walker, Somaliland Field Force; NA ADM 116/931, Information regarding the Mullah.
[63] NA FO 2/970, Telegram from Eric Swayne, Commissioner, Berbera, to Minister for Foreign Affairs, London, 17/10/1903.
[64] NA ADM 116/931, Correspondence re. Return of Yusuf Ali's son to Obbia. 16/05/1903.

disembarkation of troops from naval steamships.[65] Eventually Yusuf
'Ali's proposal was accepted, but the disembarkation of British and
Italian colonial forces in Hobyo – including some 4,500 troops and
3,000 animals – took over a month and resulted in the total loss of
three naval steamboats, which broke up against rocks in the harbour in
poor weather.[66] To make matters worse, Yusuf regularly fined the
landing forces for petty misdemeanours while refusing to constrain
his followers, who harassed the sentries during the night.[67] Under
mounting British pressure to establish order, the Italian representative
arrested Yusuf 'Ali and his son, sending them first to a military prison
in Aden, and thence to Massawa.[68] In Yusuf's absence, the Italians
established a political residence in Hobyo to oversee Yusuf's affairs.[69]

In response, Uthman made his own belated effort to weigh in on the
side of the Europeans and, in the spring of 1905, sent two columns
consisting of a few hundred of his own men in support of Britain's war
with the Muhanmad Abdille Hassan in exchange for arms and a
payment of £1,000.[70] In the early summer of 1905, Muhammad
Abdille Hassan agreed to peace with the British and the Italians at
Illig.[71] But Uthman's efforts to reposition himself alongside the British
in the war against the Sayyid proved too little, too late. As one British

---

[65] NA ADM 116/930, Final Report on the Operations Conducted by Lieutenant
Colonel Eric Swayne, Somaliland Field Force, 18th January to 1st
November 1902.

[66] NA MT 23/160/2, Letter, Captain Bethell, SNO, Obbia, to Admiral Drury,
Commander in Chief, East Indies, 17/2/1903.

[67] NA ADM 116/930, Final Report on the Operations Conducted by Lieutenant
Colonel Eric Swayne, Somaliland Field Force, 18th January to 1st
November 1902.

[68] NA ADM 116/929, Letter, Marquess of Lansdowne, Secretary of State for
Foreign Affairs, to Sir Francis Bertie, British Ambassador to Italy, Rome, 13/2/
1903, and Telegram, Sir James Rennell Rodd, First Secretary, British Embassy,
Rome, 17/2/1903, and Cypher, Sir James Rennell Rodd, First Secretary, Rome,
27/2/1903, and Letter, Marquess Lansdowne, Secretary of State for Foreign
Affairs, London, to Sir James Rennell Rodd, British Embassy, Rome, 6/3/1903.
See also Anon, 'Sultan of Obbia a Prisoner', *New York Times* (1903).

[69] NA ADM 116/931, Correspondence regarding arms found in Yusuf Ali's
House. 15/02/1903.

[70] IOR R/20/E/245, Letter, Brig-Gen. Maitland, Political Resident, Aden, to
Secretary to Government of Bombay, 1/4/1903; NA ADM 116/929, Telegram,
Sir Francis Bertie, British Ambassador, Rome, to [unknown], 9/4/1904; IOR R/
20/A/1221, Letter, Sultan Uthman Mahmud, chief of the Majerteen Somali, to
Political Resident, Aden, undated, 1905.

[71] Martin, *Muslim Brotherhoods*, pp. 186–188.

officer put it, Uthman 'only pretends that he means to help us, in the hope of receiving money, supplies and rifles from us'.[72] In a brazen show of force even after hostilities had officially ended, the Italians blockaded Uthman's coast between Bandar Casim and Ras Hafun, bombarded his forts and seized his dhows.[73] The British and Italians also agreed to support one another in blockading any ports in their respective spheres that refused to pay customs dues.[74]

International relations had transformed quite literally into a battleground. The Italians were quick to capitalise on Uthman's manifest weakness as the losing party. The reparations the Italians sought were more direct control of Majerteenia's foreign affairs. Shortly after the end of the war with the Sayyid, the Italians formally colonised both north and south Majerteenia. They set up residences in Uthman's territory as well as in Yusuf 'Ali's. They built forts, erected lighthouses, dredged harbours, registered Majerteen ships with Italian customs houses and distributed Italian flags.[75] Nevertheless, the actual physical impact of formal colonial rule in Majerteenia was belated and limited in scope to a handful of personnel in a few coastal outposts, largely concentrated on the management of the Majerteen maritime sphere. Thus when a large French passenger steamer named the *Chodoc*, travelling between Indochina and France, ran aground to the west of Bandar Casim in June 1905, Uthman assisted all 500 passengers to safety. In a small-minded and needless confirmation that Uthman had lost his independence, the Italians blocked French efforts to provide Uthman with a naval medal for his efforts. In the circumstances, the

---

[72] NA ADM 116/929, Letter, Naval Commander of *Hyacinth*, to Admiral Atkinson-Willes, the Secretary to the Admiralty, 13/4/1904.

[73] MAESS ASMAI Posizione 59/ Numero 3 – Somalia Settentrionale – Azione Italiana su Obbia e Migiurinia, 1902–1904, Fasciolo 48, Letter, Commander of the Italian Naval Ship the *Volturno* to Sultan Uthman Mahmud, Sultan of the Majerteen, 21/06/1904; Letter, Sultan Uthman Mahmud, Sultan of the Majerteen to Commander of the Italian Naval Ship the *Volturno*, 21/06/1904. See also NA ADM 116/929, Telegram, Captain of HMS *Pomone*, to Senior Naval Lord, 30/1/1904, and Telegram, Marquess Lansdowne, Secretary of State for Foreign Affairs, to Francis Bertie, British Ambassador, Rome, 1/2/1904.

[74] IOR R/20/A/1280, Office Notes, 1906.

[75] MAESS ASMAI Posizione 59/ Numero 4 – Somalia Settentrionale – Azione Italiana su Obbia e Migiurtinia, 1904–1908, Fasciolo 59, Letter, Captain Pestalozza, Aden, to Minister for Foreign Affairs, 12/12/1905, and Fasciolo 64, Letter, Minister for the Marine, Rome, to Foreign Minister, Rome, 6/5/1905, and Fasciolo 81, Letter, Piantini, Consul General for Italy in France, to Minister for Foreign Affairs, Paris, 6/2/1909.

Italians cautioned, the Sultan might interpret the gesture as an affirmation of his coastal rights of sovereignty, which the Italians wanted to
curb.[76]

Conclusion

In the course of a few short decades, Uthman and Yusuf 'Ali were set
against one another and reduced to the status of mutually antagonistic
military pawns in the realm of colonial chaos. It is thus a cruel irony
that this European export has come to be framed as a timeless fact of
Somali life. As the Somali anthropologist Ioan Lewis put it, Somalia
had 'no stable political units ... and an almost complete lack of
instituted [sic] government'. The roots of power in Somalia, Lewis
claimed, lay 'in man's search for security for his person'. 'Force is the
final sanction in political relations', he wrote, and 'the weak are always
more ready to come to terms than the strong.'[77] Late-nineteenth-cen-
tury officials and travellers likewise blamed tribalism and tribal custom
for attacks against ships along Somalia's shores. As one famous colonial geographer wrote, the whole population of the Guardafui peninsula '[a]ll claim the established rights of flotsam and jetsam ... [on the
occasion of a shipwreck] wreckers hasten to the spot from distances of
sixty or seventy miles round about'.[78]

   This anachronistic colonial view that Somali rulers are predisposed
towards violent solutions to their political problems and divisions has
filtered down to the present. In the more contemporary and global
language of Robert Kaplan, Somalia was a region where 'a pre-modern
formlessness governs the battlefield', where numerous small-scale
units – domestic and foreign, governmental and non-governmental –
all fought for pre-eminence. Violent anarchy evoked 'the wars in
medieval Europe prior to the 1648 Peace of Westphalia which ushered

---

[76] MAESS ASMAI Posizione 62/ Numero 1 – Somalia Settentrionale – Naufragi
sulle coste di Obbia e dei Migiurtini (1898–1909), Fasciolo 10, Letter, Signor
R. de Fontarce, Head of French Affairs, Rome, to Minister for Foreign Affairs,
27/09/1906.

[77] Ioan M. Lewis, 'Dualism in Somali notions of power', *Journal of the Royal
Anthropological Institute of Great Britain and Ireland* 93(1) (1963),
pp. 110–111; Ioan Lewis, *A Pastoral Democracy: A Study of Pastoralism and
Politics among the Northern Somali of the Horn of Africa* (Oxford: James
Currey, 1999), esp. pp. 6–8.

[78] Reclus, *Earth and Its Inhabitants*, p. 396.

in the era of organized nation states.'[79] As Kaplan concluded, the threat to the stability of Africa – and ultimately to the world – was of 'nature unchecked'.[80] The standard objection to such characterisations of Somali society are that they are essentialising, and that their reductionism dovetails with the imperialist world view about the primordial, even primitive character of African and Middle Eastern societies.[81] Misreading Somali society surely played a role in colonial authors' characterisation of the region, but as we have seen in Chapters 1 and 2, the creation of a fragmented and anarchic environment at the international level was a product of the way British and other officials exported a chaotic mode of international diplomacy, replacing regional treaties and law with a system of international brinkmanship in the nineteenth century.

Contemporary historians and International Relations scholars have argued that no 'state of nature' in the Hobbesian sense exists; the realms of anarchic lawlessness that Hobbes described were in practice zones of competition between rival orders.[82] Violence, in this view, is the by-product of plurality – or the coexistence of multiple approaches to law and diplomacy – in a social field or territory.[83] It is certainly true that the meeting of rival systems of law and contrasting cultures of diplomacy created conflict. But as I have outlined in these chapters, there was nothing inevitable about these conflicts. A local system of diplomacy offered another alternative to chaos and division, rooted in cooperation and mutual recognition. The Mukalla treaty, for example, might have served as a model for Anglo-Majerteen salvage agreements, whereby the two parties promised mutual support for their ships stranded along one another's shores. Instead, colonial actors and

---

[79] Robert D. Kaplan, 'The coming anarchy: How scarcity, crime, overpopulation, tribalism, and disease are rapidly destroying the social fabric of the planet', *The Atlantic* (February, 1994). Available at: www.theatlantic.com/magazine/archive/1994/02/the-coming-anarchy/304670/.

[80] Ibid.

[81] Ahmed I. Samatar, 'Review of Lewis, I. M., *A Modern History of the Somali: Nation and State in the Horn of Africa*', H-Africa, H-Net Reviews (December, 2003). Available at: www/h-net.org/reviews/showrev.php?id=8552.

[82] Benton, *A Search for Sovereignty*; Lauren Benton, *Law and Colonial Cultures: Legal Regimes in World History, 1400–1900* (Cambridge: Cambridge University Press, 2001).

[83] John Griffiths, 'What is Legal Pluralism', *The Journal of Legal Pluralism and Unofficial Law*, 18(24) (1986), pp. 36–39. See also Thomas W. Pogge, 'Sovereignty and cosmopolitanism', *Ethics*, 103(1) (1992), pp. 48–75.

regional upstarts purposely unravelled systems of diplomacy to create a more fractious, competitive and warlike international arena. Dissatisfied with mutual recognition, British and Italian officials sought to extract more from the system – specifically more advantageous treaty terms and more control over the maritime arena. To this end, they deployed a toolkit of diplomacy including brinkmanship, countervailing, leveraging and realpolitik.

Realpolitik became the norm right across the southern Red Sea region in the first few decades of the twentieth century. As diplomacy became more strategic, more focused on gaining a comparative advantage over other actors, so international actors' attitudes to treaties became more transactional. International relations scholars Alexander Cooley and Hendrick Spruyt characterise contemporary sovereignty as 'bundle[s] of rights and obligations that are dynamically exchanged and transferred between states'. In this market for sovereignty, rule-breaking, duplicity, countervailing – creating pressure on others by asserting one's power – as well as playing rivals off against one another became commonplace.[84] The pattern of using gunboat diplomacy, military patronage and competitive diplomacy to displace an existing network of royal international relations was echoed around the southern Red Sea basin throughout the late nineteenth and early twentieth centuries. As we see in Chapter 3, the new diplomatic norms gave rise to a more fluid group of international actors in the region. A staggering range of characters, who each resembled Yusuf 'Ali insofar as they were previously marginal to the system of international relations and government in the region, intruded on the international scene in the early twentieth century. They surfaced throughout the region, including along the coast of the Arabian Peninsula, where we head in Chapter 3. Each was united in their willingness to adopt the violent logic and tactics of the new era to increase their fortunes and followings.

---

[84] Alexander Cooley and Hendrik Spruyt, *Contracting States: Sovereign Transfers in International Relations* (Princeton University Press, 2009), pp. 4–8.

3 | The New Rules of International Engagement

The Tihamat Yemen is an arid coastal plain, often no wider than twenty miles across between the sea and mountains. The region is flanked by the Red Sea to the west, and to the east, a high mountain escarpment, rising sharply towards the Yemeni highlands. To the south of the Tihamat Yemen lies the isthmus of Shaykh Said. The northern boundary of the Yemeni coast lies roughly around the port of Hodeida (see Map 3.1). Beyond Hodeida lies 'Asir, and beyond 'Asir, the Hejaz.[1] Geologically speaking, the region is the far northern ridge in the Great Rift Valley, which stretches as far south as contemporary Mozambique, and once joined the whole of Africa with Eurasia. Indeed, the two sides of the Red Sea have much in common. As in Majerteenia, so along the eastern shores of the southern Red Sea, wadis carve their way through the mountains to the sea, enabling agriculture in the lower reaches of the mountains. But the region is in essence dry. In the nineteenth century, its population relied on a mix of transhumant animal husbandry, limited agriculture, and above all, maritime trade. Trade was no less precarious than agriculture and animal husbandry: the same geology that creates the precipitous rise of the land to the east of the Tihamat Yemen also shapes the shallow, reef-strewn shoreline. The Red Sea's high salinity and warmth nurtures coral reefs and creates erratic and powerful underwater currents. Such challenging conditions are aggravated by the erratic wind patterns, where the mountains have broken the monsoon wind patterns.

---

[1] See Johann Ludwig Burckhardt, *Travels in Arabia an Account of Those Territories in Hedjaz Which the Mohammedans Regard as Sacred* (London: Henry Colburn, 1829), pp. ix–x; Edme-François Jomard, *Études géographiques et historiques sur l'Arabie, accompagnées d'une carte de l'Asyr et d'une carte générale de L'Arabie* (Paris: Didot Frères, 1839), pp. 5–45. See also Wilfred Thesiger, 'A Journey through the Tihama, the 'Asir, and the Hijaz Mountains', *The Geographical Journal*, 110(4/6) (1947), pp. 188–200.

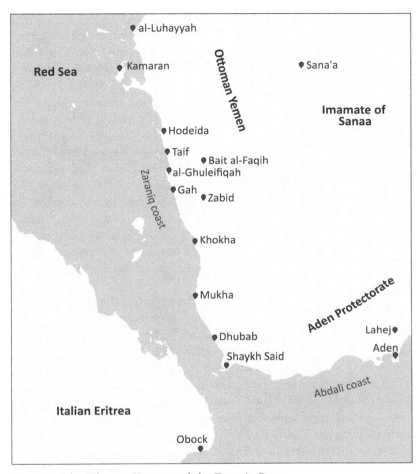

Map 3.1 The Tihamat Yemen and the Zaraniq Ports
(© 2021 Nicholas W. Stephenson Smith. All rights reserved)

The Tihamat Yemen's history was also subject to many of the same processes of imperial conquest, of Islamic government and regional diplomatic and commercial entanglement as was northeast Africa. For example, in the first century CE, the *The Periplus of the Erythrean Sea* recorded that the Tihamat Yemen was inhabited 'by rascally men speaking two languages ... by whom those sailing off the middle course [through the Red Sea] are plundered, and those surviving shipwrecks are taken for slaves'. However, the *Periplus* continued, the

Yemeni port of Mukha was safe and prosperous.[2] In fact, in ancient times, the Tihamat Yemen was the historical home of the Sabaeans, whose commercial and diplomatic influences reached across the Red Sea to Africa, and even into the Abyssinian highlands. In turn, following the retreat of the Kingdom of Saba in the first century CE, the Abyssinian Kingdom of Aksum established outposts along the Tihamat Yemen. While little is known about the nature of the relationship between the Kingdoms of Saba and Aksum, the dynamic was more likely one of entanglement and interpenetration than of conquest. As in northeast Africa, shipwrecks were likely events that cemented, rather than challenged, external bonds. Aksum's influence waned in the seventh century, when Yemen is said to have been converted to Islam by 'Ali, fourth Caliph and son-in-law of the Prophet Muhammad. A century or so later, in the early ninth century CE, Zayd ibn 'Ali, the Prophet Muhammad's great-great-grandson, established the Imamate of Sanaa, which split from the rule of the Caliphs; the Zaydi Imams ruled until 1962.

Since ancient times, the Tihamayin, the people of the Yemeni coastal plain, were caught between the large empires of the surrounding African and Arabian highlands, such as the Sabaeans, Aksumites and Zaydis. This chapter first explores their coastal culture of diplomacy, the webs of commerce and the mood of international relations in the Tihamat 'Asir prior to the nineteenth century. We see that as in northeastern Somalia, so in coastal Yemen the tradition of treaties, of *dar al-'ahd* and Islamic interconnections predominated in the region in the early modern era. We then survey the response of the Tihamayin to the unfurling of Ottoman and British colonial conquest in the Tihamat Yemen and Aden respectively. As in Majerteenia, so along the coast of Yemen, the nineteenth century dislodged historical rulers, disrupted local traditions of interstate peacemaking and created space for upstarts and military to insert themselves into a culture of maritime violence and colonial chaos. In the careers of two men, Shaykh Nasr Ambari and his lieutenant and successor Ahmad Fatini, we see not only

---

[2] *The Periplus*, pp. 29–30. See also Philemon Holland (trans.), *Pliny's Natural History: in Thirty-Seven Books* (London: George Barclay, 1847–1848); H. C. Hamilton, W. Falconer (trans.), *The Geography of Strabo: In Three Volumes* (London: Henry G. Bohn, 1857); Agatharchides, 'On the Erythraean Sea', in Karl Müller, *Geographi Graeci Minore: Vol. 1* (Paris: Instituti Franci Typographi, 1882).

the division of existing polities, but the emergence of entirely new sociopolitical groupings, in this case in the form of the Zaraniq, a band of mercenaries and sea raiders which at its peak in the 1910s numbered some 10,000 men and their families. Yet the culture of colonial chaos was inherently unstable. Colonial forms of recognition hinged on cold, geopolitical and strategic decision-making. The Zaraniq existed only as long as they could force their way into the colonial treaty system. The strategic agreements and alliances that underpinned their status in the international realm were ephemeral, extant only so long as they were expedient to the ruling coalition of the moment. After the collapse of the Ottoman Empire following World War I, the disparate band of local merchants, tribal agriculturalists and disaffected Ottoman troops dissipated. By the late 1920s, their leadership was dislodged. Their following disappeared, absorbed under the structures of other local military and religious leaders, notably Ibn Saud.

Connections and Conquests

By the 1500s, the Tihamat Yemen coast had long played a part in regional trade and international relations. It was a well-established province of the southern Red Sea's empires from the Sabaeans to the Aksumites and the Zaydi Imams. In the early modern period, the Tihamat Yemen's horizons broadened further still under the aegis of the coffee trade. While coffee grew wild in the Abyssinian highlands, it probably arrived in the Arabian Peninsula as a cultivated crop in the 1400s. Thereafter it became a popular regional commodity. For example, it entered wide use among Sufi brotherhoods of the region, consumed in order to inspire longer periods of devotion. It was subsequently discovered by the Ottomans, who spread the drink across the expanding Ottoman Empire thereafter. It was during this period of commercial expansion in the southern Red Sea, as the historian Alexis Wick writes, that the Ottomans began to perceive protecting the Red Sea as a whole – and not just the Holy Lands of the Hejaz – as one of their 'noble responsibilities'.[3] The Ottomans expanded their naval

---

[3] Wick, 'Self-portrait of the Ottoman Red Sea', p. 431. See also, Casale, 'Global politics', pp. 267–296; Rene J. Barendse, *The Arabian Seas: The Indian Ocean World of the Seventeenth Century* (Abingdon: Routledge, 2015, first published 2002), esp. pp. 126–151; Barendse, 'Trade and state', pp. 173–225.

forces in the region, and in the 1520s, sent a land force to conquer Yemen. They remained in Yemen until their retreat in 1635.[4]

The rise in trade and the arrival of the Ottomans spurred a significant regional expansion. By 1600, the port of Mukha had become a major entrepôt, both for coffee and other highland goods, including incense and horses, destined for markets in Egypt, South Asia and from there to Europe.[5] While the EIC established a trading factory in Mukha in the early seventeenth century, they remained under the writ of Muslim sultans, operating on licence – akin to the Somali *aban* system – from the Ottomans and later the regional representatives of the Imams of Yemen, the Sharifs of the city of Abu 'Arish, so called after the port in which they had served as governors. Not only did the EIC rely on the consent of local rulers for access to local markets; they accessed the Mukha coffee market via Gujarati contacts in the port of Surat, where the EIC had a base.[6] Not until James Bruce's mission to Egypt in 1768 did the rulers of Egypt agree with EIC officials to allow the latter's vessels to sail from India to Suez – and shortly thereafter began discussing with the Khedive of Egypt the idea of 'an aqueduct from the Nile to Suez' which would a century later become the Suez Canal.[7] Indeed, this eighteenth-century mission revealed the Ottomans' strength, not their weakness. As historian Lein Schuman and others have observed, the Red Sea could be controlled, and outsiders' access regulated, via control of the Bab al-Mandab straits. The Red Sea, unlike the wider Indian Ocean, could be sealed off from outsiders by

---

[4] Bruce Masters, *The Arabs of the Ottoman Empire, 1516–1918: A Social and Cultural History* (Cambridge: Cambridge University Press, 2013), pp. 33–35.

[5] Jane Hathaway, Karl K. Barbir (contrb.), *The Arab Lands under Ottoman Rule, 1516–1800* (Harlow, England: Pearson, 2008), pp. 162–165. See also Enseng Ho, *The Graves of Tarim: Genealogy and Mobility across the Indian Ocean* (Berkley: University of California Press, 2006), p. 112, note 13.

[6] Ho, *The Graves of Tarim*, p. 99; Ashin Das Gupta, *Indian Merchants and the Decline of Surat, c. 1700–1750* (Wiesbaden: Franz Steiner Verlag, 1979), pp. 20–93; David Washbrook, 'South Asia, the world system and world capitalism', *Journal of Asian Studies*, 49(3) (1990), pp. 479–508. See also Nancy Um, 'Spatial negotiations in a commercial city: The Red Sea port of Mocha, Yemen, during the first half of the eighteenth century', *Journal of the Society of Architectural Historians*, 62(2) (2003), pp. 178–193.

[7] John Baldry, 'The Yamani island of Kamaran during the Napoleonic Wars', *Middle Eastern Studies*, 16(3) (1980), p. 248.

regional empires with the naval capabilities to defend a very narrow
stretch of sea.[8]

But as we saw in Chapter 1, the EIC became increasingly aggressive
in the western Indian Ocean in the eighteenth century. Since the
eighteenth century, the EIC had perpetrated harassing attacks against
ships from the port of Surat in Gujarat, which EIC merchants justified
on the basis that the Marathas monopolised trade – a monopoly that
was, in reality, simply a measure of the Maratha Confederacy's commercial vigorousness.[9] Around the turn of the nineteenth century, the
Napoleonic Wars between France, Britain and their regional allies
expanded the Indian Ocean sea wars until the peace of 1815.
Thereafter, the EIC fought various battles against large maritime states
in the western Indian Ocean, culminating in the defeat of the
Marathas, who ruled much of the eastern coast of the Indian
subcontinent, in battle in 1818 and the Qawasim rulers in the Persian
Gulf, or contemporary Ra's al-Khayma in UAE, in the Persian Gulf
'General Peace' Treaty of 1820. In the same year, the EIC's Navy
bombarded Mukha in response to an attack on their trading post. In
the wake of the attack, the EIC renegotiated their commercial treaty
with the local ruler, the Imam of Sanaa, which provided for cheaper
anchorage for Anglo-Indian traders; the lowering of customs duties;
some ceremonial privileges for the British Resident – such as his right
to ride on horseback through the city gates – and the recognition of the
right of the British Resident in Mukha to preside over trials of merchants under his protection.[10]

---

[8] Lein Oebele Schuman, *Political History of the Yemen at the Beginning of the
16th Century: Abu Makhrama's Account of the Years 906–927 (1500–1521
A.D.)* (Groningen: Druk V. R. B. Kleine, 1960), esp. pp. 12–14, 69; Edward
Ingram, 'A preview of the great game in Asia: 1: The British of Perim and Aden
in 1799', *Middle Eastern Studies*, 9(1) (1973), pp. 11–12. A first-hand account
of the Ottomans shutting off the Red Sea to foreign explorers can be found in
Eyles Irwin, *A Series of Adventures in the Course of a Voyage up the Red Sea, on
the Coasts of Arabia and Egypt ... in the Years 1780 and 1781* (London:
J. Dodsley, 1787), pp. 3–20.

[9] Das Gupta, 'Trade and politics in eighteenth century India', in Muzaffar Alam
and Sanjay Subrahmanyam (eds.), *The Mughal State, 1526–1750* (Delhi:
Oxford University Press, 1998), pp. 374–381. See also James de Vere Allen,
'Habash, Habshi, Sidi, Sayyid', in Jeffrey C. Stone (ed.), *Africa and the Sea:
Proceedings of a Colloquium at the University of Aberdeen, March 1984*
(Aberdeen: Aberdeen University, 1985), pp. 132–133.

[10] Caesar E. Farah, *The Sultan's Yemen: Nineteenth-Century Challenges to
Ottoman Rule* (London: I.B. Tauris, 2002), pp. 2–13.

In the late 1830s, the EIC trained their violent inclinations on the port of Aden, just outside the Bab al-Mandab, in the far west of the southern littoral of the Arabian Peninsula. The urban settlement of Aden concentrates around a short peninsula; another peninsula just to the west – which the British called 'little Aden' – creates a naturally sheltered harbour. The bay's distinctive semicircular shape is formed by the rim of an extinct volcano. The area has long been the object of absorption into regional empires – including by the Sabaeans, Romans, Persians, Himyarites, Ayyubids, Rasulids, Portuguese and Ottomans – because of its natural advantages as a shipping port as well as its position on the way to Egypt. It is mentioned in the *Periplus*, and later as an important centre for Jewish merchants in the twelfth century in the Cairo Geniza and by Arab writers including Ibn al-Mujawir. It was visited by the Chinese Ming dynasty fleet led by the Muslim admiral Zheng He in the 1410s and early 1420s, as well as by the Portuguese navigator Albuquerque in the early 1500s. The nature of these conquests – or perhaps more accurately absorptions – of Aden into larger empires is a source of historical debate.[11] As we saw in the Introduction to this study, scholars contest whether these events were violent; which aspects of life under different regimes changed, and which stayed the same; whether Zheng He sought to exact tribute or laid siege to any of the western Indian Ocean ports; and whether the arrival of the Portuguese disrupted the precolonial peace.

There was likely some discontinuity and even some violence involved in these pre- and early-modern transfers of power in the region. But it is also clear there was a deep-rooted strata of social, ethnic, religious and commercial continuity – as well as a long tradition of treaty making and regional diplomacy – in ports such as Aden.[12] And while the Portuguese episode in places like Aden – where they had a fort in the early 1500s – was brief, and likely manageable for local Islamic rulers with concepts such as *aman*, *dhimmi* and the protection of foreigners – the British and the EIC tested the principles and frameworks to breaking point. The regional powers EIC officials

---

[11] See the introduction to this study. See also, Erik Gilbert, 'Review: Abdul Sheriff, dhow cultures and the Indian Ocean: Cosmopolitanism, commerce and Islam', *Journal of the Economic and Social History of the Orient*, 54(2) (2011), pp. 278–280.

[12] Margariti, *Aden*, pp. 109–205, and Margariti, 'Mercantile Networks', pp. 542–577.

encountered in Aden were the Abdali family. Originally from Sanaa, connected to the Imamate and highland markets, in the 1740s they declared independence from the Imamate and collected taxes on some of the smaller trade routes between highland Yemen and the Indian Ocean via Taif. Britain's early encounter with the Abdalis was ambivalent. Aden's position halfway between India and Egypt has led some historians to conclude the port was a strategic acquisition on part of the EIC, but the reality was more complex.[13] In practice the EIC was reluctant to make any territorial claims to the Arabian Peninsula, keen to avoid the perception they were a threat to the Muslim Holy Lands, or the Ottoman Empire.

However, circumstances reeled the British into the region. As in northeastern Somalia, so in Aden a series of shipwrecks and perceived attacks against British-flagged ships were the precipitate cause of contact between the EIC and the Abdali rulers. In the 1830s, a series of British-flagged South Asian ships from Bombay were wrecked in the vicinity of Aden, notably the *Daria Dowlut*. Rumours in Bombay suggested that the circumstances of the wreck of the *Daria Dowlut* was suspicious; the ship's financiers and insurers apparently suspected barratry – the deliberate sabotage of a ship for insurance purposes – between the Abdali owner and the ship's captain, perhaps as a result of a poor commercial haul. Whether or not those suspicions were founded, some of the South Asian ship's passengers accused local wreckers of assault, including sexual assault.[14] In response, the EIC sent an officer to secure compensation for the *Daria Dowlut's* ship-owners. The leader of the mission, Captain Haines, returned to India believing he had leased the port to the Company for $8,700 MT,

---

[13] See R. J. Gavin, *Aden under British Rule 1839–1967* (London: C. Hurst & Company, 1975); Thomas E. Marston, *Britain's Imperial Role in the Red Sea Area, 1800–1878* (Hamden, CT: The Shoe String Press, Inc., 1961); Gillian King, *Imperial Outpost – Aden: Its Place in British Strategic Policy* (London: Oxford University Press, 1964); Gerald S. Graham, *Britain in the Indian Ocean: A Study of Maritime Enterprise, 1810–1850* (Oxford: The Clarendon Press, 1967), p. 295. For a more critical interpretation of this literature, see Harvey Sicherman, *Aden and British Strategy, 1839–1968* (Philadelphia, PA: Foreign Policy Research Institute, 1972), esp. p. 15.

[14] See IOR R/20/E/2, Minutes, Secret Council, Bombay Government, 4/04/1838. See also Scott Reese, *Imperial Muslims: Islam, Community and Authority in the Indian Ocean, 1839–1937* (Edinburgh: Edinburgh University Press, 2018), pp. 48–56.

having established a relationship 'on the same terms' as existed between Mukha and the ruler of Surat.[15]

But Haines fundamentally misunderstood the nature of agreements and alliances in the *dar al-'ahd*. The permissive, mutually reaffirming character of relations between local representatives of the Imam of Sanaa and the Mughal-linked rulers of Surat afforded neither party any territorial rights. Nor did the agreement confer any inalienable rights to transact in the port. The relationship between Mukha and Surat was not a transactional one, in which money could be exchanged for access to markets or land. The terms of their relationship was, on the contrary, permissive, a supra-legal memorandum of friendship and a promise of assistance and mutual aid. But Haines' interpretation of the treaty system was adversarial; he had extracted 'terms' from the Abdali rulers, in exchange for money.

When Haines returned to Aden in 1839 with a contingent of EIC soldiers, the misapprehension became clear. The local ruler Muhsin al-Abdali refused them entry, in spite of the agreement. Haines sent for reinforcements, instigating a maritime siege and invasion of Aden, which marked a shift towards a deeply adversarial relationship between al-Abdali and the British, unlike anything that existed between the rulers of Mukha and Surat. Indeed, Anglo-Indian troops blockaded the port for six months, before launching an invasion with a ground force of 2,000 European and Indian troops (see Figure 3.1).[16] Only in 1843 did Muhsin al-Abdali sign a new treaty with the British, accepting the inevitable fact of their presence. And still in this treaty, al-Abdali refused to concede any territorial rights to the EIC, instead moving his capital to the nearby mountain settlement of Lahej. Indeed, al-Abdali and other local rulers never fully recognised Britain's sovereignty; Aden remained a 'protectorate', in which sovereignty continued to reside in local rulers until it was made into a 'colony', in which British exercised exclusive sovereignty in 1937, and then only in the geographical region of the port itself. Moreover, local people did not think of the British in Aden as a distinct entity. Rather, they were known locally as the 'Banu Haines', or the people of

[15] Willis, 'Making Yemen Indian', p. 23.
[16] Low, *History of the Indian Navy*, pp. 120–138.

Figure 3.1 Postcard showing the British capture of Aden, January 1839, from a painting by Captain R. N. Rundle, 'Preparation for the landing'.
(© The Trustees of the British Museum)

Captain Haines, an exotic group perceived in the framework of local political structures.[17]

Haines' conquest initiated a chain of competitive geopolitical violence in the region. Alarmed at the European presence close to the Hejaz, the Ottomans responded to the EIC's expansion into the Arabian Peninsula with violence of their own. In 1849, the Porte set about reconquering the Tihamat Yemen, re-establishing the historic sanjaks in the ports of Hodeida, Mukha, Luhayyah and Abu 'Arish, as well as creating a new regional vilayet in Zabid.[18] In the embassies of

---

[17] The journalist Gordon Waterfield quotes the colonial administrator based in Hadhramaut, Harold Ingrams, as writing in the 1930s that the people of Aden perceived and referred to the British as 'the children of Haines', or 'Banu Haines'. More recently, the writer Tim Mackintosh Smith suggests that Yemenis from the region of Aden continued to refer to the British as the 'banu' or 'sons of Haines' in the late twentieth century. Ingrams is cited in Gordon Waterfield, *Sultans of Aden* (London: John Murray, 1968), p. 8. See also Tim Mackintosh Smith, *Yemen: Travels in Dictionary Land* (London: John Murray, 1997), pp. 148–149.

[18] Farah, *The Sultan's Yemen*, p. 60; Thomas Kühn, 'Shaping and reshaping colonial Ottomanism: Contesting boundaries of difference and integration in Ottoman Yemen, 1872–1919', *Comparative Studies of South Asia, Africa and*

Europe and the meetings rooms of the Foreign Office and the Ottoman Porte, Britain acquiesced in the Ottoman Empire's (re)assertion of their sovereignty in the Tihamat Yemen. As we saw in northeast Somalia in the early 1880s, Britain's policy was to preserve the Ottoman and Ottoman-Egyptian Empires in the region, on the one hand because their control over the Ottoman Empire was an expedient way to influence the region, and on the other because the preservation of the Ottoman Empire discouraged Britain's European rivals from seeking to acquire colonial possessions in the Ottoman Empire's sprawling periphery.

But beneath the surface, British officials cultivated allies and signed defensive, quasi-military alliances with several populations bordering the EIC's outpost. Indeed, throughout the 1860s, 1870s and 1880s the British signed tens of treaties of friendship, military alliances, and salvage agreements with the population surrounding Aden.[19] As in Somalia, so in Yemen, historians often dismiss these treaties and alliances. The historian Caesar Farah derided the Anglo-Yemeni contracts signed between about 1860 and 1880 as 'forced "treaty" arrangements with hapless native chiefs'.[20] But the reality was more complex. The British signed the nine treaties with the various populations and political groups surrounding the port of Aden; this set of treaties formed the legal basis of the Aden Protectorate. But, as the historian John Willis points out, each of the signatories of the treaties was a known opponent of the Zaydi Imams of the highlands. The treaties were thus less a comprehensive set of agreements with each and every one of the regional political powers than an alliance between the British in Aden and opponents of highland rule.[21] As in Majerteenia, so in the immediate vicinity of Aden, the availability of British patronage, the proliferation of arms and the extension of British protection to shipwrecks on Yemeni shores created a competitive political atmosphere and empowered new, ambitious and opportunistic political leaders to

---

the *Middle East*, 27(2) (2007), p. 316; John Baldry, 'al-Yaman and the Turkish Occupation 1849–1914', *Arabica*, 23(2) (1976), p. 158.

[19] IOR R/20/E/176, Letter, Brigadier General Adam Hogg, Resident, Aden, to Secretary to Government, Bombay, 7/10/1889; IOR R/20/E/297, Letter, Brigadier General James Bell, Political Resident, Aden, to Secretary to the Government, Bombay, 13/1/1911.

[20] Farah, *The Sultan's Yemen*, p. 133.

[21] Willis, 'Making Yemen Indian', pp. 27–28.

rise to power. The EIC's approach to politics turned treaty and alliance making into a legalistic, transactional and at times even trivial process, devoid of the cultural references and nuances of earlier traditions of treaty making. In this new era, force, misrepresentation and duress were not only permitted but integral to the action of lawmaking.

Coastal Insurgents

By the late nineteenth century, the stage was set for the rise of Shaykh Nasr Ambari and his successor, Ahmad Fatini. The EIC's conquest of Aden, combined with the EIC's spiralling bellicosity in the region, created a culture of international retaliation, of competition, brinkmanship and zero-sum international politicking which displaced the culture of permissiveness that had prevailed under the Ottoman ascendancy. Not only did the EIC seek territorial conquests – rather than trading partners, as before – they also sought to pit regional rulers against one another, setting the patchwork of rulers, who previously coexisted peacefully, into fierce competition for patronage. The protagonists of this chapter were two political-military Tihamayin leaders from the Shaykh Said peninsula, roughly 150 miles east of Aden port, in the far south of the Tihamat Yemen. Both Ambari and Fatini rose to power, like Yusuf 'Ali in Chapter 2, as military-political leaders who profited from the tumult in the international sphere unleashed by colonial conquest. Moving north from Shaykh Said in the late nineteenth century, the two men established strongholds and a following known as the 'Zaraniq' throughout the Tihamat Yemen.

Focusing on the example of these two strongmen is not to conflate the whole late-nineteenth- and early-twentieth-century history of the Tihamat Yemen with the fortunes of the Zaraniq. Rather, their example underscores the diversity of social and political forms beyond 'tribalism' in precolonial Yemen, as well as the ways in which colonial chaos in the international realm incubated a form of leadership rooted in the perpetration of violence along the southern Red Sea littoral. Scholars such as Isa Blumi, Thomas Kuehn, Shelagh Weir and John Willis have already indicated both the diversity and fluidity of social forms existing in Yemen in history, as well as indicating the ways in which British colonial rule remoulded Yemeni society.[22]

---

[22] Isa Blumi, *Rethinking the Late Ottoman Empire: A Comparative Social and Political History of Albania and Yemen, 1878–1918* (Istanbul: The Isis Press,

Drawing on these insights, this chapter suggests that the argument may be pushed even further: at least some of the political entities that emerged in Yemen were forged in the crucible of European and Ottoman colonial conquest, and more especially in the climate of international chaos and competition that unfolded in the region during the second half of the nineteenth century. The Zaraniq's story thus chimes not only with the story of the Majerteen and with the evidence presented in this volume about the pernicious effects of international chaos on the littoral region, but also with recent historians' revision of the relevance of the concept of historically stable, purely lineage-based 'tribes' in the Arabian Peninsula. As we saw in Majerteenia, tribalism and lineage-identification became a problematic source of conflict in the colonial period not because lineage societies are inherently disposed to fracture and divide into mutually antagonistic groups; on the contrary, these regions have long histories of stable imperial rule bolstered by a cooperative climate of international relations. Rather, colonial geopolitical rivalries helped dissolve the international relationships that had strengthened local ruling structures, and encouraged upstarts such as Ambari and Fatini to compete for patronage and recognition, powerfully undermining the regional political fabric.

As part of their reconquest of the Tihamat Yemen in the mid-nineteenth century the Ottomans garrisoned Shaykh Said in 1849. However, the Ottomans' military presence on the peninsula was small and remote, numbering in the dozens, rather than hundreds, of armed men. Shakyk Said's closest large administrative outpost was in Mukha, more than 100 miles to the north. The Ottomans' influence in the far south of the Tihamat Yemen was thus fragile, heavily dependent on local alliances and regional consent. Recognising this, the EIC in Aden competed for allies to prevent a strong Ottoman presence which might threaten their outpost.

In 1870, for example, rumours circulated that a local chief had sold a French merchant rights to settle the peninsula.[23] In response, the Ottomans sent a company of soldiers to occupy the peninsula and

---

2003); Thomas Kuehn, *Empire, Islam, and Politics of Difference: Ottoman Rule in Yemen, 1849–1919* (Leiden: Brill, 2011); Shelagh Weir, *A Tribal Order: Politics and Law in the Mountains of Yemen* (Austin: University of Texas Press, 2007); John Willis, 'Making Yemen Indian', pp. 23–38.

[23] IOR R/20/E/134, Regarding the establishment of French Settlement at Sheikh Syed at the entrance of the strait of Bab-el-Mandeb, 1882; IOR R/20/E/143,

redouble the dwindling garrison. The British in Aden responded to the imperial intrigue so close to the port of Aden by instructing their local ally the Abdali Sultan to find a local accomplice with whom the EIC might establish an alliance. The Abdali Sultan selected Shaykh Nasr Ambari. The resulting agreement, which was either made orally or the written record of which remained with the Abdali Sultan, was somewhere between a salvage treaty and a military alliance, whereby Ambari promised to protect shipping and repel the Ottomans and any other interlopers on the peninsula in exchange for money and arms. Ambari duly attacked Ottoman engineers building a telegraph post to link the Bab al-Mandab straits with Mukha, Hodeida and Istanbul.[24]

As in Majerteenia, so in the Tihamat Yemen, colonial chaos corroded the bonds of royal, imperial and intercommunal loyalty which historically underpinned stability in the region. The result was increased intercommunal warfare as littoral groups competed for patronage, for the rights to claim the benefits accruing from controlling shipping salvage along the shoreline, and the proliferation of armed conflict. As in Majerteenia, British officials blamed the local population for the upheavals of Britain's and the Ottomans' making. In 1881, the Sultan of Lahej, as the Abdali rulers became known, branded the population of Shaykh Said as 'outlaws'. Operating through their key regional ally and representative, the British garrisoned the coast west of Aden in an effort to stem the upsurge in intercommunal violence, the proliferation of arms and the rise in attacks against ships stranded along the coast. Just as Yusuf 'Ali had fled Alula and established himself in Hobyo, so a number of the Sultan of Lahej's regional opponents, including Ambari, fled to neighbouring regions. In the early 1880s, Ambari led small columns of followers from Shaykh Said north into the Tihamat Yemen, where they encamped around natural anchorages such as Taif and Dhubab.[25] As well as in Shaykh Said, the Zaraniq now had a presence in Taif and Dhubab, in the immediate vicinity of Mukha, the Ottoman sanjak.

Increasingly, the Ottomans responded to Britain and the Sultan of Lahej's machinations by more intensively recruiting local military allies

Offer made by M. Sautereau to sell the site of a coaling station at Shaikh Sa'id to Her Majesty's Government.
[24] IOR R/20/E/142, The Subjection of the Subaihi Country to the authority of the Sultan of Lahej, Memo. No. 6518, Resident, Aden.
[25] Farah, *The Sultan's Yemen*, pp. 68–78.

such as Ambari. Throughout the Tihamat 'Asir, and especially in the hinterlands of their administrative outposts, the Ottomans conducted ornate ceremonies involving oaths and pledges of loyalty oaths to mark the transfer of arms to regional leaders professing loyalty, mimicking the older ceremonialism of the *dar al-'ahd*.[26] But these ceremonies could not achieve the same effect of mutual recognition and mutual aggrandizement as did older treaty making: the Zaraniq was a military movement, not a royalty. The bulk of Ambari's followers hailed from a subgroup of the Akk – sometimes rendered as Azd – lineage, one of the four ancient Sabaean tribes of Yemen, the other three being the Hashid, the Bakil and the Madhaj.[27] But Ambari's was not a tribal movement: his Akk followers were joined in the 1890s by a whole range of communities alienated by the Ottoman conquest of the coast, including increasing numbers of disaffected and frequently unpaid Ottoman soldiers from Hodeida, Mukha and Luhayya.[28] Thus Ambari's movement grew considerably in the 1890s and early 1900s. By 1900, Ambari marshalled in the region of 5,000 fighting men. By 1910, this number would swell to as many as 10,000.[29]

French and British counter-insurgency efforts further complicated this increasingly militarised, fractious political landscape along the coast. French officials had nursed colonial designs on Shaykh Said dating back to the Napoleonic wars, aiming to create a French 'Gibraltar' in the southern Red Sea with complete control of the southern entrance to the Red Sea via the Bab al-Mandab straits.[30] Ambari's strongholds in the ports of Taif and Dhubab were less than

[26] See Farah, *The Sultan's Yemen*, esp. p. 122; Selim Deringil, "They live in a state of nomadism and savagery': The Late Ottoman Empire and the post-colonial debate', *Comparative Studies in Society and History*, 45(2) (2003), p. 322. See also, Emrys Chew, *Arming the Periphery: The Arms Trade in the Indian Ocean during the Age of Global Empire* (London: Palgrave Macmillan, 2012), pp. 104–160.

[27] See J. E. Peterson, *Yemen: The Search for a Modern State* (Abingdon: Routledge, 2016, first published 1982), p. 58; Francine Stone, 'The Ma'azibah and the Zaraniq of Tihama', *New Arabian Studies*, 6 (2004), pp. 132–155.

[28] Baldry, 'al-Yaman and the Turkish Occupation', p. 179.

[29] Paul Dresch, *A History of Modern Yemen* (Cambridge: Cambridge University Press, 2002), p. 16. See also Jeffrey S. Dixon and Meredith Reid Sarkees, *A Guide to Intra-State Wars: An Examination of Civil Wars, 1816–2014*. Correlates of War Series (Thousand Oaks: SAGE Publications, 2016), pp. 343, 351–352; Farah, *The Sultan's Yemen*, pp. 204–208.

[30] IOR R/20/E/134, Letter, Major General Loch, Resident, Aden, to Chief Secretary to the Government, Bombay, 17/2/1882; IOR R/20/E/143, Letter,

a single night's sail from France's ports on the northern lip of the Gulf of Tadjoura; the French regularly sold arms to Ambari and his lieutenants in an effort to cultivate an alliance of their own with the Zaraniq. The British were naturally opposed to France's designs, repeatedly blocking French efforts to establish either a trading company or a garrison on the peninsula.[31] Britain likewise competed for Ambari's favour with their own gifts of arms and offers of treaties.[32]

Ottoman, French and British meddling benefited Ambari and the Zaraniq, but had a profoundly deleterious effect on the stability of the Tihamat Yemen. It was against this backdrop of hostility and competition that Ambari sponsored attacks against regional merchant shipping as well as the pilgrim traffic between Eritrean ports and the Hejaz. Officials estimated that attacks against ships off the coast of the southern Tihama rose to the rate of one per day and occurred as far afield as the Dahlak Islands close to the coast of Italian Eritrea. By the middle of the first decade of the twentieth century the situation at sea around the Tihamat Yemen and the southern part of the Tihamat 'Asir had grown so dangerous for the Red Sea's merchants – especially those using sail-driven ships, which were vulnerable to the vicissitudes of the wind – that Aden, the Foreign Office and the Government of India proposed that individual merchants be allowed to arm themselves under government license to guard against attack.[33]

Britain also demanded the Ottomans take military action against the Zaraniq menace at sea, but the Ottomans' response was tepid. Having once considered the protection of the safety of the Red Sea their 'noble

---

James Blair, Resident, Aden, to John Wodehouse, Secretary of State for India, London, 25/11/1884.
[31] See John Baldry, 'The French claim to Saykh Sa'id (Yaman) and its international repercussions, 1868–1939', *Zeitschrift der Deutschen Morgenlandischen Gesellschaft*, 133(1) (1983), pp. 93–133.
[32] IOR R/20/E/142, Memo. No. 6518, Resident, Aden; IOR R/20/E/245, Telegram, Brigadier-General P. J. Maitland, Political Resident, Aden, to the Secretary of State for India, Bombay, 9/07/1903, and Letter J. A. Sanderson, Under Secretary, Foreign Office, London, to India Office, London, 22/12/1902, and Office notes, Aden Residency, 23/5/1903; NA FO 367/34/102, Letter, Major General Mason, Political Resident, Aden, to Mr. Morley, Berbera, 17/1/1906.
[33] IOR R/20/A/1300, Letter, Commissioner's Office, Somaliland, to Secretary of State for the Colonies, 10/04/1906, and Letter, SNO, Aden Division, to the Commander-in-Chief, East Indies, 01/09/1905, and Letter, Government of India, Foreign Department, to Secretary of State for India, 05/09/1907.

responsibility', by the early 1910s the Porte was barely able to muster a single functioning navy ship. In response to British requests for the Ottomans to patrol the region, Istanbul sent five warships to patrol the coast, but four were declared unseaworthy on arrival in Hodeida, while another sank before it had left the Black Sea.[34] As a result of these naval failures, the Ottomans gave their consent to the British and Italians to patrol the southern Red Sea with one steamer each and a further two lighter surveillance dhows – a wholly inadequate patrol for an expansive, reef-and-island-strewn stretch of sea measuring some thirty thousand square kilometres.[35] The Italians duly bombarded Ambari's strongholds in retribution for attacks against Italian-Eritrean merchant shipping, forcing Ambari and his men to abandon their coastal positions closer to the Ottoman port of Hodeida.[36] In early 1912, consequently, Zaraniq forces retreated to their old anchorages in Dhubab, Midi and Taif.[37]

Warlord Diplomacy

The arrival of the Italians into the geopolitical scene along the Tihamat Yemen undermined the Zaraniq's fortunes, and aggravated the unrest

---

[34] NA ADM 116/928A, Letter, Thomas Sanderson, under Secretary of State for Foreign Affairs, Foreign Office, London, to the Admiralty, 22/10/190; NA FO 78/5484, Letter, J. R. Mannsell, Military attaché, British Embassy, Constantinople, to Sir Nicholas O'Connor, British Ambassador, Constantinople, 9/06/1902, and Telegraph, Sir Rennell Rodd, British Ambassador, Rome to Marquess of Lansdowne, Secretary of State for War, London, 11/11/1902.

[35] IOR R/20/A/1300, Letter, Commissioner's Office, Somaliland, to Secretary of State for the Colonies, 10/04/1906, and Letter, SNO, Aden Division, to the Commander-in-Chief, East Indies, 01/09/1905, and Letter, Government of India, Foreign Department, to Secretary of State for India, 05/09/1907.

[36] MAESS ASMAI Posizione 91/ Numero 3 – Pirateria e Insurrezione – Avvenimenti (III Trimestre) & (IV Trimestre) – 1904 & Avvenimenti (I Trimestre) – 1905 – Yemen. Letter, Tommaso Tittoni, Minister for Foreign Affairs, Rome, to Ferdinando Martini, Governor, Eritrea, 23/9/1904; Letter, M. Sola, Italian Consul, Hodeida to Tommaso Tattino, Minister for Foreign Affairs, Rome, 19/10/1904; Letter, Pecori Grimaldi, Civil Commissioner, Eritrea, to M. Tittoni, Minister for Foreign Affairs, Rome, 11/2/1905. See also IOR/R/20/A/1300, Memorandum communicated to Ministry for Foreign Affairs, London, by the Italian Embassy, London, 7/6/1906.

[37] AS Colonia Eritrea Somalia Italiana, File No. 1/3/262 – Buste 454 – Presidenza del Consiglio dei Ministri, 1913. Letter, Pietro Bertolini, Minister for the Colonies, Rome, to Giovani Giolitti, Prime Minister, Rome, 23/6/1913.

along the coast. One of Nasr Ambari's lieutenants, a man named Ahmad Fatini, boarded an Italian warship. In an echo of the old, consensual style of regional diplomacy, Fatini declared that the Zaraniq were a 'commercial people' who 'preferred Italian goods to all others'. Fatini claimed his men were in rebellion against Ottoman rule, obfuscating his older relationship with the Ottomans, recognising that the Italian approach was zero-sum. If he revealed his links to the Ottomans, Fatini knew the Italians would reject his advances. Having persuaded the Italians that he could be a useful military ally to them in their fight with the Ottomans, Fatini demanded the Italians relax the blockade of their coast. If the Italians refused, Fatini warned, he would be forced to make peace with the Ottomans and join with Ottoman forces to oppose the Italians. The classical, peacemaking diplomacy morphed abruptly into threats and brinkmanship, evincing Fatini's astute understanding of the geopolitical exigencies of colonial international politics. Fatini's advances met with a mixed response by Italian officials. At first the Italians sent Fatini arms and lifted the blockade of his port-stronghold in Taif. But when Fatini wrote to the Governor of Eritrea in the summer of 1912 warning him that if he refused to send more arms, his forces would settle with the Ottomans – or turn back to trading arms and looting the high seas – the Governor dismissed his claim out of hand. The Italians were no longer at war with the Ottomans and they had no need of Fatini's services.[38]

Ambari and Fatini smartly returned to attacking commercial shipping between the Dahlak archipelago off the African coast and the Farasan Islands close to Kamaran. In 1913–1914, the attacks became a near-daily occurrence for European-flagged merchant ships trading under sail in the region.[39] Between July and August of 1914, for example, Ambari and Fatini's sailors captured at least five British merchant ships between Kamaran Island and Lohayya, including one ship lying just outside the harbour in Hodeida. Indeed, violence in the maritime realm became so severe that trade between Eritrea and the

---

[38] MAESS ASMAI – Archivio Eritrea – Pacco 614 – 1912, Costa Araba, Vecchio. Informazioni – 10, 15 & 16 June, 4 & 18 July. See also, in the same file, Letter, Ahmad Fatini to Giuseppe Raggi, Governor of Eritrea, Asmara, 24/8/1912.

[39] Henry de Monfreid, Helen Buchanan Bell (trans.), *Sea Adventures* (Harmondsworth, England: Penguin Books, 1946, first translated 1937), pp. 16–17.

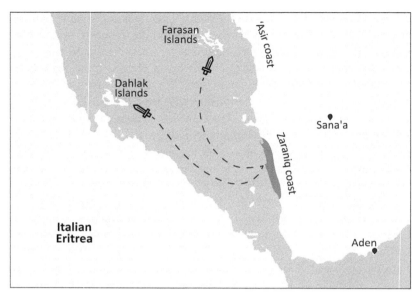

Map 3.2 The locations of Zaraniq attacks against Red Sea shipping
(© 2021 Nicholas W. Stephenson Smith. All rights reserved)

rest of the Red Sea coast came to a virtual standstill (see Map 3.2).[40] The cause of the violence was Ambari and Fatini's quest for recognition. By stoking chaos in the maritime realm, Ambari and Fatini knew from the past three decades that they could leverage more military support, renewing their alliances with the highest bidder, promising to advance some more or less ephemeral geopolitical aim. Yet both British and Italian imperial officials continued to blame the Zaraniq themselves for creating chaos. As the British Resident in Aden observed in the late nineteenth century, Ambari and his supporters became locked in a 'constant struggle for their existence'.[41]

Before Ambari and Fatini could translate their maritime reign of terror in the Red Sea into renewed alliances with either the Italians or the British, however, World War I transformed the geopolitical

---

[40] NA L/PS/11/81, Telegram, Mr. Richardson, British Consul, Hodeida, to Sir Louis Mallet, British Ambassador, Constantinople, 6/8/1914, and Telegram, Mr. Richardson, British Consul, Hodeida, to Sir Louis Mallet, British Ambassador, Constantinople, 24/7/1914.

[41] IOR R/20/E/176, Letter, Brigadier-General Adam Hogg, Resident, Aden, to Secretary to the Government of Bombay, Bombay, 15/1/1889.

situation. With the Ottomans' entry to the war on the side of Germany in November 1914, Britain, France and Italy discussed the introduction of a general blockade of the Ottoman coast to prevent the proliferation of arms in the region. Allied efforts focused on preventing arms from leaving the African coast,[42] as well as redoubling their efforts to cultivate allies along the coastline. The British, for their part, formed an alliance with Sayyid Muhammad Ibn Ali al-Idrissi (also referred to more simply as Sayyid al-Idrissi), a military and religious ruler from the Hodeida region who had been leading a military-religious polity opposed to Ottoman rule since around the middle of the first decade of the twentieth century.[43] Ambari and Fatini, by contrast, sought support from France. A few months prior to the outbreak of World War I, Fatini again offered to lease land on the Shaykh Said peninsula to French officials in Djibouti.[44] In the first years of the war, delegations from the ports of Taif and Dhubab travelled several times to Djibouti, where they met the Governor of French Somaliland, requested permission to fly the French flag on their boats – which enabled them to avoid inspection by the British Naval Red Sea patrol – and negotiated gifts of arms and ammunition in exchange for the promise of influence in the Tihama when the war ended.[45] The French did the same for mariners from the Omani port of Sur.[46]

While Britain, France and Italy cooperated on the battlefields in Europe, they remained competitors in the southern Red Sea. After the last Turkish garrison on the Arabian Peninsula surrendered to British forces in April 1919, a new window of opportunity opened for Ambari and Fatini to compete for influence and international

[42] IOR R/20/A/2965, Letter, E. Allenby, High Commissioner of Cairo, to Arab Bureau, Rear Admiral Egypt and the Red Sea; General Clayton; B. A., Jeddah and Political Resident, Aden, 08/05/1919.

[43] IOR R/20/A/4077, Letter, Charles Price, Political Resident, Aden, to Captain Thomson, SNO, Aden, 11/10/1915, and 'Report on the Trade Policy Authorised by the Political Resident, Aden, and General Remarks on Trade to Southern Yemen, 1915'.

[44] AOM FM 1/AFFPOL/93 – Sheikh Said – 1907–1938 – Schaik Said – divers, Letter, Adrien Bonhoure, Governor, French Somaliland, to Gaston Doumergue, Minister for the Colonies, Paris, 27/2/1914.

[45] IOR R/20/A/4077, Letter, SNO, Southern Red Sea patrol, HMS 'Empress of Asia' to General Officer Commanding, Aden Division, 9/10/1915.

[46] Fahad Bishara, '"No country but the ocean": Reading international law from the deck of an Indian Ocean dhow, ca. 1900', *Comparative Studies in Society and History*, 60(2) (2018), pp. 338–366.

patronage. Indeed, Hodeida and the whole surrounding coastline, once Ottoman, was now open to formal claims to sovereignty.[47] In the months immediately following the peace of November 1918, Nasr Ambari wrote repeatedly to British representatives on the island of Perim and in Aden of the famine prevailing in his lands on account of the blockade's inflationary effect on local prices. Without the British government's assistance, Ambari wrote, his people would soon be 'dead and wrapped in shrouds'. In an arch appeal to Britain's wartime foreign policy of supporting the so-called Arab Revolt against the Ottomans on the Arabian Peninsula, Ambari implored the British to lift the blockade. 'Knowing of your affection for the Arabs', he wrote, 'the dignity of the British government should not agree to let us die.' The British government, Ambari continued, was the guardian of these rights to rent and recompense. 'Whilst ever the British government exists', wrote Ambari, 'I will not be deprived of my rights'. However, as for the leaders of Arab Revolt from Mecca, so for Ambari and Fatini, faith in Britain's willingness to reward wartime loyalties soon faded. Officials in Aden refused to lift the blockade on his coastline, or to recognise Fatini's claims to rule the coast.[48]

When their negotiations with the British stalled, Ambari and Fatini restarted attacks against regional merchant shipping. In one notable episode in late 1919, the Zaraniq leaders ordered ten boats to take to the seas around the Tihamat Yemen. The Zaraniq vessels first looted a ship belonging to an Aden merchant anchored off Shaykh Said before proceeding to loot the cargoes of four further ships, including two belonging to merchants from Aden. Ambari claimed that as a coastal ruler he had the right to commandeer shipping passing through his waters and that, since the ships were registered in Aden, he was claiming by proxy debts incurred by the British for the use of Perim Island during the War.[49] In the meantime, Britain signed agreements

---

[47] See John Baldry, 'British naval operations against Turkish Yaman, 1914–1919', *Arabica*, 25(2) (1978), pp. 192–193.

[48] IOR R/20/A/2962, Letter, Sheikh Nasser Ambari to Colonel Cockayne, First Assistant Resident, Aden, 6/10/1919, and Letter, Sheikh Nasser Ambari to Captain Hume, Assistant Resident, Perim, 9/9/1919.

[49] IOR R/20/A/2716, Letter, Sheikh Bakr bin Salam Sharahil to Captain J. Gordon, British Consul, Hodeida, undated, c. May 1920, and Letter, Sheikh Nasr ali Ambari, Sheikh Said, to Colonel Hume, Assistant Resident, Perim, undated translation, probably 10/5/1920. See also IOR R/20/A/1301, Memo, Captain J. Gordon, British Consul, Hodeida, to Colonel Cockayne, First Assistant

with a military-spiritual ruler and fierce opponent of the Ottomans, Sayyid Muhammad Ibn Ali al-Idrissi. Al-Idrissi's family were originally spiritual leaders from north Africa who moved to the Hejaz in the nineteenth century and became influential in Mecca, where they also came into conflict with the Ottomans. After a period of teaching in the Sudan in the early twentieth century, the Sayyid himself moved to the 'Asir coast around Jizan in the middle of the first decade of the twentieth century, carving out an independent polity on the coast and contesting Ottoman rule in the region.

The Sayyid's deep-rooted hostility to Ottoman rule created the conditions for his alliance with the British during World War I. In late 1918, Sayyid Muhammad al-Idrissi covenanted with the British in Aden not to cede any of the coastal territory that fell under his control to any other power, in exchange for British patronage.[50] Yet for Ambari and Fatini, the British alliance with Sayyid al-Idrissi had the effect of undercutting their value as military clients. Instead of dealing directly with the Zaraniq rulers, the British in Aden began referring merchants' complaints of violence perpetrated by Ambari and Fatini in the waters of the Tihamat Yemen to Sayyid Muhammad al-Idrissi. Without ever expressing as much in a written treaty, Britain's alliance with Sayyid Muhammad al-Idrissi excluded Fatini and Ambari from the international sphere. But Fatini was not deterred by such technicalities; one of the hallmarks of the political economy of violence in the international realm was that the bar to entry was extremely low – as little as the cost of a crew of sailors willing to take risks. In 1921, Fatini led three dhows to Hodeida harbour to attack Sayyid Muhammad al-Idrissi's ships lying at anchor as well as other Idrissi ships in the port of Taif.[51] Sayyid Muhammad al-Idrissi responded by demanding the British send naval forces to suppress the threat Fatini posed to his shipping, just as they had sent warships in support of his military

Resident, Aden, 20/4/1920, and Précis of Arabic correspondence, Sheikh Admad Fitini of Taif in his letter of 29th Rajab, 1338, or 19/4/1920.

[50] Baldry, 'British naval operations', pp. 184–185; Robert L. Hess, 'Italy and Africa: Colonial ambitions in the First World War', *Journal of African History*, 4(1) (1963), pp. 105–126.

[51] IOR R/20/A/4923, Memo, Captain Fazluddin, British Political Officer, Hodeida, to First Assistant Resident, Aden, 6/2/1921. See also IOR/R/20/A/1300, Telegram, Captain Fazludin, Hodeida, to Sir James Stewart, Resident, Aden, 6/2/1921, and Telegram, Captain Fazludin, Hodeida, to Sir James Stewart, Resident, Aden, 10/2/1921.

actions against the Ottomans during the war.[52] The British agreed to
send patrol ships to Hodeida harbour, but – wary of becoming
embroiled in military action so close to the Hejaz – refused to authorise
their naval ships to engage in any fighting.[53]

Fatini abandoned his designs on Hodeida for the strategic town of
Bait al-Faqih, a day or two's march from the coast in the foothills of
the Yemeni highlands. Yet the loss of external military support undermined the Zaraniq leader's entire political currency; he was rapidly
losing followers. In desperation, Fatini sought to invoke a religious,
rather than military, authority, cultivating a rather dubious image as
an old-style religious leader. Bait al-Faqih's name translates roughly as
'the house of the sage'. It had been a waypoint on the pilgrimage route
from Southern Yemen to Mecca and a centre of religious learning for
centuries. It also lay just north of the Ottomans' extinct administrative
centre in Zabid. But the challenge Fatini faced in establishing his
control over Bait al-Faqih and transforming himself into a religious
authority was enormous. Bait al-Faqih had always played host to a
variety of religious convictions prevailing in Yemen, both Shafi'i and
Zaydi.[54] Indeed, the Zaydi Imams controlled – and even lived part of
the year – in the town during the seventeenth and eighteenth centuries.
Yet by the late nineteenth and early twentieth centuries, the town also
played host to some of Sayyid Muhammad al-Idrissi's followers, as
well as a number of preachers who were adherents of the eighteenth-
century Islamic reform movement led by Muhammad ibn 'Abd al-
Wahhab and promoted by the Saudi dynasty.

After only a few months, the Wahhabist quarter of Bait al-Faqih rose
against Fatini, followed in short order by protest from other quarters
of the town.[55] But keeping control of the town soon devoured Fatini's
resources. Indeed, Fatini became so desperate for munitions he ordered
his men to collect unexploded shells from the Italian war and to

---

[52] Baldry, 'British naval operations', pp. 179–183.
[53] IOR/R/20/A/1300, Letter, British Military Administrator, Hodeida, to Cyril
Barret, First Assistant Resident, Aden, 1/1/1921.
[54] See Brinkley Messick, *The Calligraphic State: Textual Domination and History
in a Muslim Society* (Berkeley: University of California Press, 1996), esp. p. 37;
Kühn, 'Shaping and reshaping colonial Ottomanism', pp. 323–324.
[55] IOR/R/20/A/1300, Letter, Zabeed Agent, Zabeed, to Captain Fazluddin, British
Political Officer, Hodeida, 16/ 11/21, and Letters, Zabeed Agent, Zabeed, to
Captain Fazluddin, British Political Officer, Hodeida, 9/12/21 and 25/1/22.

recondition nineteenth-century Ottoman cannons.[56] In July 1922, in the hope of securing reinforcements, Fatini sent an envoy to Aden carrying a letter 'offering the whole country from Bait al-Faqih to the Jabel Raimah to come under the protection of the Aden Government authorities'. In exchange, the delegation of Zaraniq notables – Fatini's counsellors – asked for British assistance in their fight against the Imam's forces, with whom the Anglo-Adenis were in a state of periodic war over the Protectorate's eastern Hadhrami districts. But the British distrusted Fatini and had less strategic need for allies along the coast since the end of the World War. They declined the offer to incorporate Fatini's coast into the Aden protectorate.[57]

Having failed to win the town's inhabitants around to his cause, Fatini returned to the coast. In addition to attacking ships himself, Fatini now began to assert that he protected shipping. In late 1922, Fatini dispatched a dhow to visit the Aden government and inform them that his ship had been 'pirated by outlaws', but that Fatini's men had secured the boat's release. Fatini should be supported in his efforts to maintain the peace of the sea, the merchant argued, and the British should send a steamer to the 'pirate' port of Gah.[58] Fatini knew the owner, in fact, and staged the attack to prove to the British authorities that he could act as an effective force against such acts of 'piracy' in the region, which he claimed emanated from 'renegade' regions, notably the port of Gah, in fact held by Sayyid al-Idrissi.[59]

Stalemate

In the months that followed, Fatini returned to his habitual diplomatic strategies. He accused almost every major regional leader of perpetrating acts of piracy against his own or one of his purported allies' ships.

---

[56] IOR/R/20/A/1300, Letter, Zabeed Agent, Zabeed, to Captain Fazluddin, British Political Officer, Hodeida, 16/3/22, and Letter, Captain Fazluddin, British Political Officer, Hodeida, to Cyril Barret, First Assistant Resident, Aden, 1/2/22.

[57] IOR R/20/A/3038, Letter, Mohamed Saeed Salah Sinan Laheji to Cyril Barret, First Assistant Resident, Aden, 27/7/22, and Letter, Cyril Barret, First Assistant Resident, to Mohamed Said Saleh Sinan Laheji, 31/7/22.

[58] IOR R/20/A/2716, Letter, Faraj Saleh, Nakhuda, 'Alawi', to Sayyid Ahmed bin Taha Assafi, merchant, 25/9/22; Telegram, Captain Fazluddin, Political Officer, Hodeida, to Cyril Barret, Political Resident, Aden, 24/10/1922, and Letter, Sayyid Assafi, merchant and owner of the 'Alawi', to Cyril Barret, First Assistant Resident, Aden, 11/10/1922.

[59] IOR R/20/A/2716, Letter, Ahmad Fitini Gunaid, Zaranik Sheikh, to Political Resident, Aden, 8/10/1922, and Letter, Ahmad Fatini, principal sheikh of the Zaraniq and sheikh of Taif, to Cyril Barret, First Assistant Resident, 28/12/22.

In late 1922, for example, Fatini accused the Abdali Sultan, Britain's most important local ally in the Aden Protectorate, of being a 'notorious pirate'. The accusation prompted the Resident in Aden to send a junior member of staff to conduct a search of the records of the Sultan's past, which indeed revealed that Muhsin al-Abdali, the present Sultan's ancestor, had attacked the *Daria Dowlut*. But the clerk who unearthed the *Daria Dowlut* incident unsurprisingly identified other more recent episodes – including incidents perpetrated by Fatini's own predecessor, Shaykh Nasr Ambari, in the late nineteenth century.[60] When his efforts to embroil the Abdali Sultan in accusations of piracy backfired, Fatini blamed the current Imam of Sanaa, Imam Yahya, of being behind the attacks. The Imam, Fatini claimed, forced him to attack commercial vessels on the Red Sea.[61] The British called Fatini's bluff. Instead of supporting Fatini, the British responded by encouraging the Imam, with whom they were engaged in a border war to the east of Aden, to attack Fatini's ports between Gah and Taif. At Britain's instigation, the Imam vowed to subject Fatini and his followers to his rule and launched a series of destructive raids against the Fatini's strongholds.[62]

But Fatini was not easily deterred. Violence and brinkmanship were the international politics he knew; without competition and chaos and the military patronage that came with it, Fatini knew the Zaraniq movement would collapse. Colonial chaos was the only geopolitical system the Zaraniq knew; it was better to maintain it and risk losing than face certain extinction in the absence of inter-imperial competition. In 1923, Fatini's soldiers attacked an Aden merchant's dhow close to the port of Dhubab, took the crew hostage, and transported them to Shaykh Said. Here the ageing Nasr Ambari instructed the crew to proceed to Aden to inform the dhow owner and the Aden authorities of the attack, which he insisted had been instigated by the Imam's

[60] IOR R/20/A/2716, Letter, Ahmad Fetini to FAR, Aden, 28/12/1922; Office Notes, 12/1922.

[61] IOR R/20/A/2716, Complaint of Sheikh Ahmed Fetini Gunaid to the effect that his sambook was attacked and looted by the Imamic soldiers at Salif, 5/12/1925; Letter, Ahmed Fetini Gunaid, Sheikh Maskayh of al-Zaranik, to Major B. R. Reilly, FAR, Aden, 05/12/1925.

[62] IOR R/20/A/2716, Office notes, 27/9/1922; Letter, Cyril Barret, First Assistant Resident, Aden, to Imam Yahya, Sanaa, 30/9/22; Letter, Imam Yahya to Cyril Barret, First Assistant Resident, Aden, 28/12/1922.

forces and not by Fatini's followers as the crew believed.[63] Suspicious of Ambari's claims, British officials warned Imam Yahya that Fatini and Ambari's ports were in rebellion against his rule. In early 1924, the Imam sent a force to occupy the port of Lohaya. The Imam's troops forced Ambari and Fatini, alongside a handful of their supporters, into hiding on the Farasan Islands.[64] Fatini, in turn, continued to denounce Imam Yahya's troops as pirates to officials in Aden, who continued to ignore his protestations.[65] In an astute, if futile, bid for international recognition, Fatini petitioned the League of Nations for recognition as an independent state in 1925.[66]

By 1925, Fatini had all but lost his military followers as well as his battle for international recognition and patronage. Meanwhile, to the north of the Tihamat Yemen, in the 'Asir and Hejaz, Ibn Saud had occupied Mecca and Jeddah and annexed the Idrissi ports and the Farasan Islands on which Fatini had taken shelter from the Imam's offensive in 1923. Fatini's followers found themselves, to quote a British observer, 'between the devil and the deep blue sea'.[67] To make matters worse for Fatini and his remaining followers, by late 1926 Imam Yahya's forces had garrisoned all the larger coastal ports between Lohaya in the north and Dhubab in the south, including the port of Hodeida.[68] There was, in short, only a narrow strip of coastal land separating Imam Yahya in the south and Ibn Saud's forces in the

---

[63] IOR R/20/A/2716, Deposition of nacouda Balgaith Hassan of Loheiha, undated, c. September, 1923, and Letter, Hassan Jaffer, merchant, to Cyril Barret, First Assistant Resident, Aden, 2/8/1923.

[64] IOR R/20/A/2716, Letter, Imam Yahya, Sanaa, to Major General Scott, Resident, Aden, 15/9/1923.

[65] IOR R/20/A/2716, Letter, Mr. Antone Chan, Trader, to British Civil Administrator, Kamaran, 19/10/1926, and Complaint of Sheikh Ahmad Fitini Gunaid to the effect that his Sambook was attacked and looted by the Imamic soldiers at Salif, 5/12/1925.

[66] Isam Ghanem, 'The legal history of 'Asir (al-Mikhlaf al-Sulaymani)', *The Arab Law Quarterly*, 5(3) (1990), p. 211.

[67] IOR R/20/A/2921, Letter, Sayyid al Hassan bin Ali bin Mohamed bin Ahmed bin Idris, the Idrissi Sultan, to FAR, Aden, 7/7/1926.

[68] Doc. 37, Capture of Hodeidah by the Imam of Yemen [despatch of US Consul, Aden, March 31, 1925] and Doc. 61, The Zeranik Rebellion; the Lahej's flight [despatch of US Consul, Aden, June 29, 1928], in Reginald Sinclair (ed.), *Documents of the History of Southwest Arabia: Tribal Warfare and Foreign Policy in Yemen, Aden and Adjacent Tribal Kingdoms, 1920–1929, Vol. 1* (Salisbury, NC: Documenting Publications, 1976), pp. 162–164 (Doc. 37) and 347–350 (Doc. 61) .

north. Surrounded, Fatini made a last, violent bid for British protection, sailing to Aden in search of a fresh agreement.[69] As soon as Fatini's dhows sailed into Aden harbour, the authorities detained them as an indemnity for their attacks against British ships, threatening to bombard Taif if they did not restore the goods of a ship they had recently attacked and looted.[70] Fatini protested that his followers were 'the sons of the British government'. 'Our dhows call weekly at Aden', wrote Fatini, 'we say that we are the subjects of the British government.' The British were unmoved, turning over Fatini's boats and followers to Imam Yahya.[71]

In 1928, Fatini not only lacked recognition of his control of the coast, he had no reliable means of accessing it. Fatini returned as a prisoner of the Imam to Bait al-Faqih with a handful of his followers. Fatini was taken from Bait al-Faqih to Sanaa; his fate thereafter is unclear, though journalist reports at the time had him attempting to escape by picking a fist fight with his captors.[72] As Joseph Kessel put it in a press article for the French daily *Le Matin*, 'Prince Ahmet (Fatini), a famous warrior … who his men described as invulnerable to bullets … fought to the last breath.'[73] The fate of the coast, by contrast, was clear. In late 1930, shortly after Imam Yahya signed a peace treaty with the British in Aden, Saudi forces launched a sudden assault on Yahya's strongholds along the coast south of Jizan near the Farasan islands. By September, the Saudis had control of the coast as far south as Hodeida.[74] In the ensuing peace negotiations Ibn Saud agreed to withdraw north of Lohaya, ceding Hodeida back to Imam Yahya and drawing the border of what would become North Yemen and Saudi Arabia.

---

[69] IOR R/20/A/2716, Letter, Commanding Officer, HMS Endeavour, Red Sea Patrol, to Port Officer, Aden, 14/2/1926.

[70] IOR R/20/A/2716, Letter, Wharf Manager, Aden, to Secretary, Port Trust, Aden, 16/2/1926, and Interview, Abdurrahman bin Ahmad bin Uthman, an agent of Ahmad Fatini, at Resident's Office, 17/2/1926.

[71] IOR R/20/A/2716, Letter, Shaikh Ahmad Fatini of Taif, to Bernard Reilly, First Assistant Resident, Aden, 28/2/1926.

[72] IOR R/20/A/4925, Letter, Hassan Ibrahim Kanjuni, Political Clerk, Hodeida, to Second Assistant Resident and Protectorate Secretary, Aden, 5/7/1929, 3/11/ 1929 and 12/11/1929.

[73] IOR/L/PS/12/4090, Slavery and the Slave Trade – Red Sea and Arabia (attitude of Ibn Saud), enclosing Joseph Kessel, 'The Slave Trade: Kessel's investigations into the countries close to where the trade continues', *Le Matin*, 11/06/1930.

[74] Ghanem, 'The legal history of 'Asir', pp. 212–214.

Conclusion

The anthropologist Ernest Gellner observed that the more developed a ruler's external relations, the more effective their domestic leadership would be.[75] This was true under the old system of the *dar al-'ahd*, of treaties, mutual recognition and cooperative international relations. However, from the mid-nineteenth century onwards, during the era of colonial chaos, the relationship between domestic power and external recognition became more complex. By engaging in the arms trade, soliciting military patronage from the British, the Ottomans, the French and the Italians, Shaykh Nasr Ambari and his successor, Ahmad Fatini, inserted themselves into the emerging system of sovereignty in the region. By exploiting the chaotic, competitive, violent and even anarchic system of international relations that European colonists created, Ambari and Fatini transformed themselves from local chiefs to regional leaders with international recognition. But their entanglement in colonial chaos came at a cost. Colonial rule embedded violence in the fabric of international relations in the region; it ushered in a form of sovereignty-sharing in the maritime and littoral region which was inherently adversarial, based on an anarchic political logic that put merchant, ruler, European, African and everyone in between in fierce competition with one another for political influence, territorial control and maritime economic resources. Ambari and Fatini ultimately fell prey to the system that had driven their earlier military and political successes. The Zaraniq movement was displaced first by Ibn Saud, then by the Imam's forces. The Zaraniq movement fell prey to the same unsettled environment that produced it.

As in Majerteenia, so in Yemen, colonial officials blamed the lawlessness and warlike character of the coastal populations for the upheaval, shifting blame away from the gunboat diplomacy of the Europeans. As one Aden official wrote in the early 1920s, the Zaraniq was 'divided into different groups of robbers and pirates [who], in consequence of their profession ... are naturally antagonistic to each other ... [and] do not seem to be amenable to any kind of

[75] Ernest Gellner, 'Tribalism and the state in the Middle East', in Philip S. Khoury and Joseph Kostiner (eds.), *Tribes and State Formation in the Middle East* (Berkley: California University Press, 1990), p. 111.

discipline or control.'[76] But such an assessment failed to account for the historical processes that led to the destruction of diplomatic conventions and their replacement with an increasingly violent and chaotic international politics. Indeed, while Fatini was styled as a 'pirate', in practice his attacks against regional shipping formed part of an interminable international maritime war, which the British had effectively begun with attacks against Gujarati ships in the eighteenth century, the destruction of the Qawasim navy in the 1810s, the bombardment of Mukha in 1820 and the conquest of Aden in 1839. War and brinkmanship – rather than reciprocal recognition, gift giving and permissive diplomacy – emerged as the core operational values of the international system in the southern Red Sea region. Tensions escalated rapidly, new actors emerged and disappeared as one warlord diplomat displaced another. The permanence and stability that old aristocratic modes of diplomacy had underpinned disappeared. The bar to entry into the international system fell lower and lower. In Chapter 4, even complete outsiders could compete for influence in the region by the 1910s and 1920s.

[76] IOR R/20/A/2716, Office Notes, undated, September 1922.

4 | *Undercover Colonialism, Coups and Chaos*

Part way between the Tihamat Yemen and Majerteenia, just south of the Bab al-Mandab strait, lies the Gulf of Tadjoura (see Map 4.1). While we now think of the whole region surrounding the Gulf as Djibouti, in fact both the country and the name were a French invention. Until the French established Djibouti port in 1888, the region was sparsely inhabited and largely dominated by the commercial networks of the Sultans of Tadjoura, based in the port of the same name, on the northern side of the Gulf. The name 'Tadjoura' is the Latinised version of the Somali-Afar word for 'water-wells', after the fresh water available in the area – a rarity in this exceptionally arid region of the world, drier than almost anywhere else on Earth and receiving even less rainfall than the Tihamat Yemen opposite. But this did not protect the area from the depredations of colonial rule. In Chapters 1–3 of this study we saw how Britain – and later the Ottoman Empire, France, Italy and Germany – insinuated themselves into and disrupted established networks of diplomacy and international relations in the north-western Indian Ocean from 1839 onwards.

By signing treaties, strong-arming coastal powers, and disbursing military patronage in the region, Europeans created anarchy and emboldened opportunistic power-seekers from the coast to muscle their way into the international community, nesting their claim to sovereignty under the wing of the colonial powers. In Chapters 1–3 of this study we saw that the colonial powers undermined African and Arab sovereignty in the region, disrupted the diplomatic alliances between royals in the region and stoked a competitive market for military proxies. As a result, the international arena was thrown open to upstarts and strong-men – such as Yusuf 'Ali, Shaykh Nasr Ambari and Ahmad Fatini – who used arms dealing and violence against shipping to win power, patronage and a place in the new international state system. In this chapter, we see the tentacles of this new,

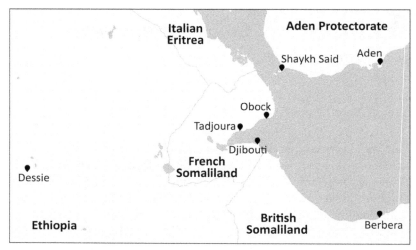

Map 4.1 The Gulf of Tadjoura and eastern Abyssinia
(© 2021 Nicholas W. Stephenson Smith. All rights reserved)

competitive, retributive, even anarchic regime of maritime law and international relations spread more widely still. The logic of chaos and war engulfed an even wider cast of actors, empowering foreign fortune-seekers and upstarts to participate in the realm of international diplomacy and geopolitics.

In this chapter, we follow the career of Henry de Monfreid, who arrived in French Somaliland as a novice merchant in 1911 and stayed until 1929, when he left as an influential and wealthy merchant who almost succeeding in launching a coup against the French colonial state in Djibouti. Far from being known as a wealthy businessman, however, Henry de Monfreid is most widely recognised for his writing, which he pursued after quitting the Red Sea for France in the 1930s. As a writer, de Monfreid told the stories of some of the southern Red Sea's most memorable and archetypal characters: the old men who manufactured pearls on remote uninhabited islands, where the poor and wretched fished sea snails, where blind Somali captains navigated treacherous reefs and rocky shores, where evil spirits spun the fortunes of grown men, and where pirates preyed on the unwitting.

De Monfreid styled himself in his books as an outsider, a man more at home among his Somali crew than the salons of Djibouti town. Colonial civilisation, wrote de Monfreid, was a 'form of slavery'.[1] 'Bandits', as he put it, did the 'real work' of government.[2] The business world, de Monfreid wrote, was populated by, 'swindlers disguised ... as honest men'.[3] Rejecting so-called colonial civilisation, de Monfreid converted to Islam and adopted the Muslim name Abd al-Hai – literally 'the servant of God, and none other' – at the behest of his Somali crew during a violent storm.[4] In his own words, the Frenchman was a 'good pirate', a maritime vigilante who threw off the racial and cultural constraints of civilisation and bridged the gap between European and African.[5] There is truth in de Monfreid's characterisation of political and commercial life in the colonial southern Red Sea as populated by tricksters, filibusters and charlatans, but de Monfreid's actual involvement in the political economy of the region was more complex than his novels suggest.

De Monfreid did not oppose colonial power; on the contrary, on several occasions outlined in this chapter he acted on behalf of the French colonial state, helping to further France's regional geostrategic ambitions. Far from being opposed to colonialism in the southern Red Sea, de Monfreid participated in the transformation of the international system in the early twentieth century. Like Yusuf 'Ali and others before him, de Monfreid helped upend an older idiom of international relations and the political order that supported it. As we saw in Chapter 1, the prevailing model of international relations before the arrival of European colonial conquerors in the nineteenth century was broadly one of *aman* (security for the sake of trade and treaties between Muslim and non-Muslim states alike). Foreign traders were

---

[1] Henry de Monfreid, *Hashish: A Smuggler's Tale* (London: Penguin Books, 2007, first published 1935), p. 37. See also Letter, Henri de Monfreid to George-Daniel de Monfreid, 15/04/1912 and Letter, Henri de Monfreid to Armgart Freudenfeld, 15/3/1915, in Henry de Monfreid, Guillaume de Monfreid (ed.), *Aventures extraordinaires (1911–1921): Lettres d'Abyssinie, Lettres de la Mer Rouge, Lettres d'Égypte, Arabie, Érythrée, Inde et autres lieux* (Paris: Arthaud, 2007), pp. 258; 135.

[2] Henry de Monfreid, *Journal de bord, 1913–1923* (Paris: Arthaud, 1983), p. 80.

[3] De Monfreid, *Sea Adventures*, pp. 33–36.

[4] Letter, Henry de Monfreid to George-Daniel de Monfreid, 5/5/1914, in de Monfreid, *Aventures extraordinaires*, pp. 362–363.

[5] Henry de Monfreid, *Secrets of the Red Sea* (London: Faber and Faber, 1934) pp. 136, 188. See also Wilfred Thesiger, *The Life of My Choice* (London: Collins, 1987), p. 167; Daniel Grandclément, *L'Incroyable Henry de Monfreid* (Paris: Grasset, 1998), esp. p. 121. Joseph Kessel provides another interpretation: that de Monfreid was vengeful. Joseph Kessel, *Fortune Carrée* (Paris: Julliard, 1955), p. 181.

integrated into local politics via institutions such as *aban*. But when the British arrived in Aden in the mid-nineteenth century, they brought a new approach, broadly rooted in the thinking of jurists such as Hugo Grotius. The new European colonial approach to foreign relations effectively transformed entire oceans into warzones. By invoking the rules of warfare in large swathes of the maritime realm, the new approach also empowered private merchants to take prizes of ships flying their enemies' flags. As we saw in Chapters 2 and 3, European and Ottoman colonists negotiated brand new treaty arrangements with coastal powers, as well as sponsoring military proxies where existing rulers refused assent to new terms in matters such as salvage. In the process, Eiuropeans created an anarchic, even Hobbesian scramble for influence and power in the southern Red Sea. Upstart actors such as de Monfreid took full advantage of the new rules to further their own commercial interests and the geostrategic goals of the French. In de Monfreid's career, we see the way private commercial interests and state geostrategy increasingly coalesced. In turn, we see that in the early decades of the twentieth century, the novel international culture of colonial chaos became firmly entrenched in the southern Red Sea region.

Frontiers

France's military and naval involvement in the southern Red Sea dates back to the French East India Company's presence in the coffee market at Mukha and the Napoleonic Wars in 1798. But France's participation in the region's politics increased significantly in the second half of the nineteenth century, following Britain's occupation of Aden. Explorers such as Charles Guillain (see Chapter 1) sought to identify a French harbour to rival Aden, including in the Gulf of Tadjoura. In response, British officials purchased their own rights to settle anchorages from local rulers in the Gulf of Tadjoura in the 1840s and insisted that the Gulf of Tadjoura fell within the Ottoman-Egyptian Empire. In spite of Britain's attempts to curtail their expansion, French naval commanders bought the rights to settle the tiny Gulf port of Obock in 1862 from the local ruler, the Sultan of Tadjoura, on the basis that it would serve as the staging point from which to acquire the peninsula of Shaykh Said opposite.[6] Those same rights were recognised by the

---

[6] IOR R/20/E/67, Letter, Major General R. W. Homer, First Assistant Resident, Aden, to Henry Anderson, Secretary to Government, Bombay, 23/5/1862; IOR

British when they negotiated with the Ottomans over the sovereignty of northern Somalia in the early 1880s.[7] Yet there was barely any official French presence in the region.

Instead of negotiating formal treaties, instead of acknowledging the *dar al-'ahd*, the French relied on a cursory settlement agreement with the Sultan of Tadjoura, who had ruled the mountains and natural harbour surrounding the town of Tadjoura since the collapse of the large regional Muslim Sultanates – namely Ifat and the Afar Sultanates. By the nineteenth century, the Sultan of Tadjoura was linked to the Sultanate of Aussa, which was in turn loyal to the Abyssinian ruler Tewodros II, who had brought much of what is today central and eastern Ethiopia, formerly part of the Adal Sultanate, under the northern Tigrayan-Amhara yoke. From the 1870s, a clandestine network of French traders funnelled arms from mainland France through the Sultan of Tadjoura to Abyssinians such as Tewodros to support his internal wars.[8] The closest colonial oversight was the French consul in Aden; French firearms traders operated as frontiersmen, on the sufferance of the Sultan of Tadjoura.

Only in the 1880s did the French government seek to formalise its presence by sending its first official representative to the area, in the form of the colonial diplomat Léonce Lagarde, who established a small governmental post in the port of Obock in 1882. Initially, Lagarde sought to transform the economy of the region, experimenting with the creation of a penal colony to boost the population and agricultural production in the region. But the experiment failed; the prisoners repeatedly conspired with French arms dealers and the Sultan of Tadjoura's troops to break free. Lagarde subsequently moved the colony's capital to the southern rim of the Gulf of Tadjoura, establishing the port of Djibouti, in part to distance himself and the French government from the arms dealers. But the traders simply followed Lagarde there, establishing a new trade route

---

R/20/E/69, Letter, William Coghlan, Political Resident, Aden, to Henry Anderson, Secretary to Government, Bombay, 29/4/1863. See also Henri Brunschwig, 'Une colonie inutile: Obock, 1862–1888', *Cahiers d'études africaines*, 8(29) (1968), pp. 34, 43.

[7] IOR R/20/E/133, Letter, Earl of Dufferin, British Ambassador, Constantinople, to Earl Granville, Secretary of State for Foreign Affairs, London, 14/3/1882.

[8] IOR R/20/E/143, Letter, Frederick Hunter, British Consul, Somali Coast, Aden, to Sir Evelyn Baring, HMS Consul General, Cairo, 20/11/1884.

running from Djibouti up the Awash river valley to the Abyssinian uplands.[9]

Lagarde soon gave up resisting the arms business. Instead, French Somaliland embraced its role as a transhipment point between highland Abyssinia and the coast. The creation of a railway line between Djibouti, Dire Dawa and ultimately Addis Ababa in the first decades of the 1900s helped diversify the trade.[10] But the port colony continued to rely on the trade in firearms, French firearms dealers and the relations they forged with local rulers for access to regional markets. Thus Lagarde and his successors were compelled to act as intermediaries between the international community and local interests. In response to a raft of anti–arms proliferation treaties that followed the Berlin Conference in 1884–1885, Lagarde insisted that French Somaliland remain exempt from restrictive treaty articles, for example negotiating Abyssinia's exemption from all anti-proliferation treaties.[11] Abyssinia was a sovereign state like any in Europe, France's representatives argued, and could control the proliferation of arms within its own borders. Likewise, in 1890, when some twenty European and regional powers signed the Brussels Act, the French refused to accede to various articles that they saw as damaging to French Somaliland's interests, including reciprocal rights of search for seaborne vessels, on the grounds that it infringed on the sovereignty of ships flying the French flag.

In practice, the argument for Abyssinian exceptionalism allowed the inward flow of arms from Europe to northeast Africa via Djibouti to continue, whilst – as we saw in Chapter 2 – French officials ignored re-exports to other destinations like the Somali regions. French officials used various methods of obfuscation to protect Abyssinia as an outlet for French firearms. For example, in treaty negotiations in the early 1900s the French argued a blanket ban on arms, slaves, liquor and narcotic drugs contravened the Abyssinian government's exclusive right to decide what did and did

---

[9] IOR R/20/E/167, Letter, Government of India, to John Wodehouse, Secretary of State for India, 16/5/1887.

[10] Simon Imbert-Vier, *Tracer des frontières à Djibouti: des territoires et des hommes au XIXe et XXe siècles* (Paris: Karthala, 2011).

[11] IOR R/20/E/170, Enclosing extract from a letter sent by Assistant Secretary, Political and Secret Department, India Office, London, 7/10/1887.

not cross its borders.[12] When forced to subscribe to international regulations, weak implementation rendered the laws ineffective within French Somaliland. For example, in 1904 Governor Adrien Bonhoure increased tenfold the penalties for trafficking illegally in arms in response to British reports of French arms filtering through to the leader of the anti-colonial religious movement in Somaliland, which we saw in Chapter 2. But the outcry against the strengthening of the law was so great that Bonhoure repealed the orders to avoid a coup.[13] Instead, French administrators exaggerated exports to legal destinations such as Abyssinia and sold the surplus covertly to Somalis and other African buyers.[14] Thus adventurous stories of smuggling, false containers, concealed holds and deception are overblown: evasion was unnecessary.[15] Customs officials routinely allowed the export of arms to other local rulers who opposed British rule in Somaliland, such as the Abu Bakrs in Zeila.[16] The extent of this clandestine, semi-licit arms trade is unknown, since much was conducted unofficially, meaning that customs receipts do not fully account it. However, historian Agnès Picquart estimated that French Somaliland derived between 35 and 55 per cent of its tax revenues from arms imports in the early 1900s.[17]

The extent of France's involvement in the arms trade caused a degree of disquiet among the French public, some officials, other nations and indeed the local population. But French personnel dismissed any humanitarian objections on the grounds that it was strategically necessary if France wanted to maintain a presence in Djibouti and

---

[12] NA FO 367/35, Correspondence re. a tripartite agreement between Britain, France and Italy to restrict the sale of arms to the Horn to King Menelik and a few designated chiefs in 1906. See also Valeska Huber, *Channelling Mobilities: Migration and Globalisation in the Suez Canal Region and Beyond, 1869–1914* (Cambridge: Cambridge University Press, 2015), esp. p. 199.

[13] IOR R/20/A/1288, Letter, Harry Cordeaux, Commissioner's Office, Somaliland, to Winston Churchill, Under Secretary of State for the Colonies, 10/4/1906.

[14] See Francis A. Waterhouse, *Gun Running in the Red Sea* (London: Sampson Low, 1936), pp. 22–23.

[15] See Beachey, 'The arms trade', p. 465.

[16] AOM FM 1/AFFPOL/689, Letter, Charles Chanel, head of indigenous affairs, to M. Bonhoure, Governor, French Somaliland, 13/1/1914; NA FO 403/83, Letter, Abu Bakr Ibrahim, Sultan of Zeila, to Frederick Hunter, British Consul, Berbera, 1/1/1885.

[17] Agnès Picquart, 'Le commerce des armes à Djibouti de 1888 à 1914', *Revue française d'histoire d'outre mer*, 58(213) (1971), pp. 415, 426.

counterbalance British influence in the region. The Suez Canal had, after all, been the project of a Frenchman – Ferdinand de Lesseps – even if it was paid for with British capital. Indeed, the government hierarchy prioritised geo-strategic concerns over humanitarian ones. When a junior administrator in French Somaliland complained – with good reason – about the prevalence of illicit arms dealing and corruption in the colony, including accusing the Governor of being a 'pirate', his concerns were widely ridiculed.[18] In the metropole, by contrast, patriotic newspapers reported the story as one of anti-French sentiment in the colonial ranks; the French Colonial Office eventually recalled the prosecutor from his position in French Somaliland to face retirement in disgrace. Bonhoure replied that the transgression of international law was justified on the grounds that France's continued presence in northeast Africa depended on satisfying Abyssinia's demand for arms.[19]

Imperial Designs

It was against this backdrop that de Monfreid, a former dairy farmer from southern France (see Figure 4.1), set sail for the port of Djibouti. Arriving in the summer of 1911, de Monfreid carried with him two letters of introduction – one to the Governor, Adrien Bonhoure, and the other to a major local arms merchant, Gabriel Guignuiony.[20] From the summer of 1911 to the summer of 1912, de Monfreid worked as a broker for Guignuiony in the booming railway town of Dire Dawa in Abyssinia, just over the border from French Somaliland. In early 1912, he turned his attentions to maritime commerce, moved back to Djibouti port and bought a six-ton skiff with a view to trading arms across the Red Sea.[21] Like numerous Frenchman before him, de

---

[18] AOM FM 1/AFFPOL/689, Letter, C. Chanel, Third Class Administrator, 11th Section of the aeronautical military, French Somaliland, to M. Maurice Raynaud, Minister for the Colonies, 7/8/1914 and 27/7/1914.

[19] AOM FM 1/AFFPOL/689, Letter, Adrien Bonhoure, Governor, French Somaliland, to Gaston Doumergue, Minister for Foreign Affairs, Indian Ocean Section, 27/2/1914, and Declaration, Said Ali, Government interpreter, made before Governor Fernand Deltel, 21/8/1914.

[20] de Monfreid, *Aventures extraordinaires*, p. 531, note 1.

[21] Letter, Henry de Monfreid to Georges-Daniel de Monfreid, 7/06/1912, in de Monfreid, *Aventures extraordinaires*, p. 144.

Figure 4.1 Portrait of Henry de Monfreid taken in 1935
(AFP/Stringer/Getty Images)

Monfreid moved into the arms trade. In 1912, he took delivery of his first shipment of weaponry, including some 600 firearms and a large quantity of ammunition. Sold through legal channels to Abyssinia or Muscat, de Monfreid noted in his diary, he would have taken a substantial loss. As contraband in Yemen, the same shipment promised a profit of some 5,000 French Francs.[22]

De Monfreid faced the same risks in violating international agreements to curtail the trade as any other merchant; his advantage was his astute assessment of the increasingly cut-throat, competitive international culture of the region and his connections to the colonial establishment. As we saw in Chapter 3, France had a long-standing interest in Shaykh Said on the opposite coast of the Red Sea. The realist, geopolitical case for annexing Shaykh Said was clear: a French outpost on the peninsula promised to place the whole Red Sea shipping lane – and thus the entire sea trade between Europe and Asia – under French control. Recognising that pursuing the goal of annexing Shaykh Said would benefit both his own commercial ambitions as well as France's geostrategic standing in the region, de Monfreid concocted a plan to cultivate local allies in the area. De Monfreid's approach echoed that of Britain and the Ottomans, which we saw in Chapter 3. By supplying arms to the population of Shaykh Said and to men such as Fatini and Ambari, de Monfreid made money and helped maintain the independence of local groups from British and Ottoman influence.[23]

De Monfreid's timing was opportune. Not only was the climate of diplomacy in the region radically different to what it had been even fifty years earlier, inter-European competition was on the rise. The Italian–Ottoman wars in the Mediterranean raised the perennial spectre of European war, while in France, perhaps unsurprisingly, this was attended by a spike in interest (in French colonial circles) in the establishment of a French colony on the Shaykh Said peninsula. From a Zanzibari merchant's offering to buy the land through his commercial contacts in the Arabian Peninsula to a Vice Admiral in the French Navy's offering to conquer it by force, Shaykh Said animated the French popular colonial imagination.[24] Only two months prior to de Monfreid's first meeting with Bonhoure, in December 1913, a French

---

[22] de Monfreid, *Journal de bord*, pp. 51–52.
[23] AOM FM 1/AFFPOL/93, Letter, Adrien Bonhoure, Governor, French Somaliland, to Gaston Doumergue, Minister for the Colonies, Paris, 27/2/1914. See also, Letter, Henry de Monfreid to George-Daniel de Monfreid, 25/7/1914, in de Monfreid, *Aventures extraordinaires*, p. 410.
[24] See AOM FM 1/AFFPOL/93 – Sheikh Said – 1907–1938 – Schaik Said – divers & IOR R/20/E/83.

soldier published an article in a popular French-language colonial journal repeating calls for France to conquer the peninsula.[25]

Moreover, de Monfreid knew the Governor, whom he had met on several occasions between 1911 and 1914. The Governor at the time, Adrien Bonhoure, was receptive to the idea, granting de Monfreid coded permissions to establish a depot to store firewood and cultivate pearls on Mascali and Mussah Islands, a couple of hours' sail off the coast from Djibouti port, within the insular, protected waters of the Gulf of Tadjoura. According to a British local intelligence agent, however, French colonial officials commonly referred to 'wood' as a euphemism for various illicit goods, such as slaves and arms. The convention had come about, it seems, because Afar traders who brought firewood to the coast from the mountains also brought information about impending deliveries of slaves to forewarn merchants to prepare their ships.[26] By July 1914, de Monfreid's cache on the islands of Mascali and Mussah amounted to thousands of rifles and upwards of 300,000 rounds of ammunition. He had also made rudimentary nautical charts of the Shaykh Said peninsula.[27]

De Monfreid's designs over Shaykh Said stalled, however, in the midst of rising tensions in Europe. In June 1914, Archduke Franz Ferdinand was assassinated in Sarajevo, threatening to create a chain reaction that would activate France's alliance with Britain. On 28 July 1914, Austria-Hungary declared war on Serbia; by the first week of August a full-scale inter-European war had erupted. The French Colonial Ministry recalled Bonhoure and replaced him with an interim governor, Governor Deltel, who took a more active interest in curbing illicit arms dealing, including monitoring various local traders' activities – and those of de Monfreid.[28]

In early 1915, the French Somaliland coastguard followed one of de Monfreid's ships on a trip between Djibouti port and Mascali Island. Realising they were being followed, de Monfreid's crew fired on the

[25] AOM FM 1/AFFPOL/93 – Sheikh Said – 1907–1938 – Demande de concession formée par M. Corbie.

[26] IOR R/20/A/1559, Letter, Major Stewart, Resident, Aden, to Leo Amery, Secretary of State for the Colonies, London, 1/2/1928.

[27] Letter, Henry de Monfreid to George-Daniel de Monfreid, 25/07/1914, in de Monfreid, *Aventures extraordinaires*, pp. 408–410.

[28] AOM FM 1/AFFPOL/689 – Note on the situation of M. Bonhoure, Governor of French Somaliland, by administrator, Ministry for the Colonies, 1/8/1914.

officials and made for the open seas, returning to Djibouti a few days later to find six customs officials and a brigadier searching Mascali Island. De Monfreid responded by upbraiding the stand-in governor for interfering in his affairs and visiting French Somaliland's chief prosecutor, who in turn ensured that the government dropped its case against de Monfreid and his men.[29] In response, and convinced that de Monfreid was a principal actor in the illicit arms trade,[30] Governor Deltel used his emergency wartime powers to conscript de Monfreid to the battlefield of France in September. But de Monfreid ignored the request and left on an arms-selling mission to British Somaliland.[31]

In de Monfreid's absence, customs officials again searched his settlement on Mascali Island, where they uncovered some 80 cases of ammunition buried in the sand. A local witness claimed to have bought some 250 rounds of ammunition from de Monfreid on Mascali Island, adding weight to the case that de Monfreid was trading arms to unauthorised groups even within the colony of French Somaliland itself.[32] For his part, de Monfreid dismissed Governor Deltel's accusations as fabricated, evidence of Deltel's pettiness, his inability to see the larger strategic picture and his parochial suspicions about de Monfreid's loyalties since his wife was Alsatian.[33]

While the British accused de Monfreid of criminality – of smuggling and perpetrating violence at sea for private ends – in reality his actions challenged the conventional division between state and non-state actor, between government-led war and illicit private acts of assault. Just as

---

[29] See Captain's log, '10, 13, 15 juillet, 1914', and '14 Janvier, '1915', de Monfried, *Journal de bord*, pp. 64–67, 82. See also, Letter, Henry de Monfreid to Armgart de Monfreid, 21/08/1914; Henry de Monfreid to George-Daniel de Monfreid, 31/08/1914 and Henry de Monfreid to Armgart de Monfreid, 26/09/1914, in de Monfreid, *Aventures extraordinaires*, pp. 424–425, 432.

[30] AOM FM 1/AFFPOL/689, Telegram, Governor Deltel, French Somaliland, to M. Brice, Chevalier, Ministre de France en Ethiopie, 9/9/1914.

[31] '18 Decembre', de Monfreid, *Journal de bord*, p. 75; Letter, Henry de Monfreid to George-Daniel de Monfreid, 30/11/1914; Letter, Henry de Monfreid to Armgart de Monfreid, 7/12/1914; Letter, Henry de Monfreid to Armgart de Monfreid, 24/12/1914, in de Monfreid, *Aventures extraordinaires*, pp. 444–448.

[32] See AOM FM 1/AFFPOL/696 – Monfreid, Kessel and Slave Trade – Dossier Judiciare de Henry de Monfreid.

[33] '26 Decembre', de Monfreid, *Journal de bord*, pp. 79–83; Letter, Henry de Monfreid to George-Daniel de Monfreid, 1/1/1915, in de Monfreid, *Aventures extraordinaires*, p. 470. See also, Henry de Monfreid, *L'escalade: l'envers de l'aventure* (Paris: Grasset, 1970), pp. 233–246.

Hugo Grotius argued that the VOC Captain was justified in his attack against the Portuguese merchant shipwreck the *Santa Catarina* on the basis of the Dutch war with the Spanish, so de Monfreid and certain officials in French Somaliland held their sale of arms to their allies out as the just actions of an imperial nation seeking to advance its interests against rival imperialists. After all, the Ottomans and British also armed the peoples of the coast of the western Arabian Peninsula, as we saw in Chapters 1–3. Whereas Grotius appealed to a more or less universal principle – freedom of trade – the justification of reason of state could, by definition, only appeal to the state whose reason the action served. For this reason, de Monfreid walked a fine line between official support and sanction, as well – as we will see – as risking international reprisals.

In February 1915, with war in Europe intensifying, de Monfreid was arrested for unlawful possession of firearms and non-payment of customs fines. In mid-January, he pleaded not guilty to the charges in Djibouti's European court. He could prove he had Governor Bonhoure's approval to withdraw the arms from customs, he pro-tested, and had paid Bonhoure the relevant duty directly. Unable to pursue the charge of non-payment without implicating the absent Bonhoure in the case, the court dropped the charges against de Monfreid, who returned to prison to await the more serious hearing of illegally re-exporting arms to unlicensed and unauthorised buyers. De Monfreid turned to his father to lobby the government in Paris on his behalf. The Colonial Ministry could not be seen to exonerate an arms trader – not least because it would expose the government's complicity in an industry worth hundreds of millions of francs in the southern Red Sea – but they might be persuaded to pressure the judiciary to overturn the case on a technicality.[34] De Monfreid's father appealed directly to the colonial minister, and future president, Gaston Doumergue, who likely knew of de Monfreid in connection with the Shaykh Said project. De Monfreid may also have been assisted by contacts in the Freemasons.[35] In due course, de Monfreid walked free

---

[34] Letter, Henry de Monfreid to George-Daniel de Monfreid, 7/2/1915, in de Monfreid, *Aventures extraordinaires*, p. 492.

[35] Lukian Prijac, 'Aperçus sur la franc-maçonnerie française à Djibouti de 1911 à 1940', *Pount: cahiers d'etudes: Corne de l'Afrique – Arabie du Sud*, (1) (2007), pp. 101–130.

with a lesser conviction of failing to store arms destined for export with the proper customs authorities; the offence carried a maximum penalty of a fine and six months in prison.[36]

Yet by the time of de Monfreid's trial, Governor Deltel had been found dead at his desk in an apparent suicide. The new incoming Governor of Djibouti, Paul Simoni, arrived in Djibouti the day after de Monfreid's hearing and was briefed to release de Monfreid. De Monfreid served only two days of his six-month sentence, on condition he return to France to face conscription to the army.[37] Back in France, de Monfreid avoided the draft to the battlefields of northern France on the grounds of an earlier, possibly feigned, bout of tuberculosis.[38] In Paris in April 1915, de Monfreid met with Colonial Minister Gaston Doumergue to make a fresh proposal for the advancement of the French cause in the southern Red Sea. De Monfreid pointed out that since the outbreak of World War I, Britain had supported the anti-Ottoman independence movement of Sayyid Muhammad al-Idrissi, whom we met in Chapter 3, on the 'Asir coast of the Arabian Peninsula. The relationship threatened to give Britain a claim to control the whole south-eastern shore of the Red Sea after the war, a geopolitical advantage over France that the French Somaliland government could not ignore. De Monfreid promised to improve France's standing in the region in much the same way as he had done in Shaykh Said, by channelling arms and patronage to local powers.[39] Doumergue encouraged de Monfreid to register a company called the 'Société des cultures perlières et pêcheries des îles Farsan (The Farasan Island Pearl Culture and Pearl Fishing Company)' and return to the region as soon as possible.[40]

---

[36] ADC 63 CPCOM 9 – dossier 1, Letter, Henry Simon, Minister for the Colonies to Stéphen Pichon, Minister for Foreign Affairs, 10/10/1918; AOM FM 1/ AFFPOL 698 – dossier 2, Letter, Léon Perrier, Minister for the Colonies, to Aristide Briand, the Minister for Foreign Affairs, 3/1/1928.

[37] Letter, Henry de Monfreid to George-Daniel de Monfreid, 19/03/1915, in de Monfreid, *Aventures extraordinaires*, pp. 521–524.

[38] Letter, Henry de Monfreid to Armgart de Monfreid, 20/04/1915, in de Monfreid, *Aventures extraordinaires*, pp. 531–533, esp. note 2.

[39] Letter, Henry de Monfreid to Armgart de Monfreid, 1/5/1915, in de Monfreid, *Aventures extraordinaires*, pp. 533–534, esp. notes 1 and 2. See also Grandclément, *L'incroyable*, pp. 172, 179–180.

[40] Letter, Henry de Monfreid to George-Daniel de Monfreid, 5/6/1915, in de Monfreid, *Aventures extraordinaires*, pp. 552–553.

Alliances

On his return to Djibouti, de Monfreid received a new passport and a note authorising him to fish for pearl and corals in the waters around the Farasan Islands.[41] The pass amounted to sanction from the French government to circumnavigate the British wartime blockade of the Ottoman Empire in the Arabian Peninsula, which took effect in the summer of 1915.[42] Indeed, Governor Simoni repeatedly exempted de Monfreid's ships sailing between Obock and Aden, ostensibly so his ships could run supplies of food between French Somaliland and Aden, but in practice to allow de Monfreid to cultivate local allies along the Arabian coast.[43] In 1915, for example, de Monfreid sailed to the Farasan archipelago, docking at the mainland port of Midi where he requested an audience with Sayyid Muhammad Ibn Ali al-Idrissi, the regional ruler, to negotiate his pearl farming concession. The timing was important: Britain had just entered formal negotiations with the Sayyid to discuss the terms of their post-war relationship and France, via de Monfreid, sought to better Britain's offer.[44] De Monfreid was granted an audience with Sayyid Muhammad al-Idrissi's lieutenant and military commander, Sayyid Mustapha, with whom he agreed to send arms to al-Idrissi's troops, who at the time were engaged in a struggle with the ruler of highland Yemen, the Imam Yahya. After a brief stop at Aden, de Monfreid returned to Djibouti and wrote to his father to request up to a million rounds of Gras rifle ammunition for export to the Arabian Peninsula.[45]

[41] Letter, Henry de Monfreid to Armgart de Monfreid, 28/6/1915 and Letter, Henry de Monfreid to Armgart de Monfreid, 8/7/1915, in de Monfreid, *Aventures extraordinaires*, pp. 565, 569.

[42] AOM FM 1/AFFPOL/696 – Monfreid, Kessel & Slave Trade – Dossier Judiciare de Henry de Monfreid.

[43] IOR R/20/A/4077, Letter, Adolphe Riès, Acting Consular Agent for France, Aden, to Harold Jacob, Resident, Aden, 27/11/1915; Letter, Charles Price, Political Resident, Aden, to Assistant Resident and Port Trust; Letter, Commander of the Red Sea Patrol and British Commissioner, Berbera, 5/1/1915.

[44] NA ADM 116/2291, Agreement concluded between Britain and the Idrisi, Aden 22/1/1917, updated 7/4/23; '30 novembre', in de Monfreid, *Journal de bord*, pp. 176–179.

[45] Letter, Henry de Monfreid to George-Daniel de Monfreid, 29/12/1915 and Letter, Henry de Monfreid to Armgart de Monfreid, 29/12/1915, in de Monfreid, *Aventures extraordinaires*, pp. 700–702.

De Monfreid's attempted alliance with Sayyid Muhammad al-Idrissi reveals the extent to which colonial chaos was embedded in the region as well as the more competitive side to Britain and France's military alliance. In 1916, de Monfreid returned to the islands and met directly with al-Idrissi, whom he gave some 10,000 francs in exchange for a French fishing concession on Dumsuk Island.[46] In exchange, al-Idrissi bought a consignment of Gras ammunition.[47] Believing he had secured a concession for France on the Farasan Islands to rival Britain's, de Monfreid left an eight-strong section of his crew to guard their outpost while he returned to France to obtain further instructions. But de Monfreid's retainers 'bragged right, left and centre' about his plans to build a fort and a town on the island, and the rumours of a European colony on the island sparked popular unrest.

Sayyid Muhammad al-Idrissi had little choice but to expel de Monfreid's crew or face a popular uprising against his rule, not to mention tensions with British officials in Aden. To make matters worse, as the crew made to depart, one of de Monfreid's men accidently set off a stick of dynamite, which severed his arm. The soldiers under al-Idrissi's control overseeing the crew's departure informed the Sultan that the crew planned to resist their eviction, prompting Sayyid Muhammad al-Idrissi to denounce de Monfreid's mission to the British for breaching the blockade by importing explosives.[48] In spite of this failure, de Monfreid returned to French Somaliland to be rewarded with the lease of a large house in Obock and a permit to run the government's passenger service between Djibouti and Aden.[49] De Monfreid capitalised on his favour with the French government by building and licensing a small fleet of boats, including two weighing

---

[46] IOR R/20/A/4085, Report, Captain Crawford, SNO, Aden division, to Commander in Chief, East Indies Section, 24/3/1918.

[47] Letter, Henry de Monfreid to Armgart de Monfreid, 25/1/1916, in de Monfreid, *Aventures extraordinaires*, pp. 708–709.

[48] Letter, Henry de Monfreid to Armgart de Monfreid, 27/4/1916, and Letter, Henry de Monfreid to Armgart de Monfreid, 21/8/1916, in de Monfreid, *Aventures extraordinaires*, p. 736.

[49] IOR R/20/A/4085, Telegram, Adolphe Riès, French Consul, Aden, to Major Wood, First Assistant Resident, Aden, 8/6/1916. See also Letter, Henry de Monfreid to Armgart de Monfreid, 19/6/1916, and Letter, Henry de Monfreid to Armgart de Monfreid, 7/7/1916, in de Monfreid, *Aventures extraordinaires*, p. 752.

more than one hundred tons, which he ran as the sole licensed passenger service between Aden and Djibouti during the war, conveying vital food supplies to the French colony.[50]

De Monfreid had by now placed himself squarely in the sights of suspicious British officials in Aden. For the British, de Monfreid's actions were not only in breach of wartime international agreements, they also threatened Britain's interests and local alliances in the Tihamat Yemen and 'Asir. In March 1918, British informants reported that a dhow captained by a Frenchman acting under the name of Abd al-Hai – de Monfreid's assumed Muslim name – had anchored off Kamaran. The dhow carried arms and ammunition, including a small machine gun intended for local dervishes – dissenting groups within Muhammad al-Idrissi's sphere who opposed their ruler's increasing closeness with the British.[51] The report confirmed the idea circulating in Aden for some time that de Monfreid was not only an arms smuggler but was also intent on disrupting Muhammad al-Idrissi's sovereignty in pursuit of France's interests along the littoral.

The Resident in Aden instructed one of Britain's naval patrol boats to search for de Monfreid's dhow, which they found some seven miles from the Somali coast carrying $13,000 MT in cash and manifests for Mukalla to buy 'wood'.[52] Given the common suspicion that 'wood' was code for either slaves or illicit arms, alongside the large sums of money in de Monfreid's possession, the British Resident reckoned the evidence against de Monfreid was sufficient to hold him as a prisoner of war. Worse still for de Monfreid, when a naval officer retraced the Frenchman's most recent journey, the officer reported that he had unloaded arms at the port of Xiis, just east of the Majerteen coast and a stronghold of Muhammad Abdille Hassan, who had recently taken up arms (again) against the British.[53] De Monfreid was duly

[50] Letter, Henry de Monfreid to George-Daniel de Monfreid, 5/6/1915, and Letter, Henry de Monfreid to Armgart de Monfreid, 13/9/1915, in de Monfreid, *Aventures extraordinaires*, pp. 552–553, 637. See also '26 Mai' and '16 août', in de Monfreid, *Journal de bord*, pp. 103–108, 158.
[51] IOR R/20/A/4085, Telephone message, Geoffrey Archer, British Commissioner, Berbera, for Major Wood, Resident, Aden, 4/3/18.
[52] '28 février–4 mars', in de Monfreid, *Aventures extraordinaires*, pp. 781–782.
[53] IOR R/20/A/4085, Translation, Interview of Nur 'Ali Hadji (Gadabursi), nacouda, residing in Zeila, conducted by Vernier Maurice, Commissioner of Police at Djibouti, 18/12/1917; Report by Captain Palmer, SNO, Aden division, Commander of HMS *Juno*, 5–11 March, 1918; Proclamation, G. H. Summers,

taken to a prison camp for anti-British insurgents and war criminals near Berbera in British Somaliland.

Governor Simoni responded to the news of de Monfreid's imprisonment with a volley of telegrams to the French Consul in Aden denouncing British machinations. Such was Simoni's fury at British officials' interference in de Monfreid's affairs that only the text of the eleventh telegraph, the Consul observed, was cordial enough to forward to the Resident's office. Even this telegraph threatened to 'arrest every British citizen in his passage through the colony' if the British would not release de Monfreid.[54]

Underlying this escalation of intercolonial tensions – a war within the War – was an anarchic culture of diplomacy and international relations in the region. Clandestine efforts to subvert sovereignty between the regions' rulers, and apoplectic threats of reprisals would have been all but unimaginable in the older treaty agreements between regional rulers such as the Sultan of Majerteenia and the Naqib of Mukalla, or between the Yemeni Imams and the Gujaratis. By contrast, the Europeans' transactional approach to alliance making embraced a whole cast of actors, including African and Arab chiefly upstarts, mercenaries, private foreign citizens and European colonial officials. Rather than recognising and reciprocating one another's authority, newcomers attempted to unseat one another through brinkmanship, countervailing, violence and power-politicking. Moreover, the destruction of indigenous royalties and their associated diplomatic networks opened the international arena not only to ambitious minor royals but also to global fortune-seekers.

Shortly after the end of World War I, de Monfreid met with yet another new governor of French Somaliland, this one named Jules Lauret. Following the meeting, Lauret wrote to the British in Aden demanding the end of the blockade and the exclusion orders that prevented de Monfreid from sailing in Aden and British Somaliland's waters. In August 1919, Aden officials lifted the wartime restrictions

Government Administrator, Berbera, 1st April, 1918; Letter, Major Wood, British Resident, Aden, to Adolphe Riès, French Consul, Aden, 4/4/1918.

[54] IOR R/20/A/4085, Transcript, Meeting, Adolphe Riès and Major Wood, Resident, Aden, 24/3/18, and Letter, Governor, French Somaliland, to Resident, Aden, 1/4/18. See also in the same file, Letters, Geoffrey Archer, British Commissioner, Berbera, and Major Wood, Resident, Aden, 8/3/1918, 9/3/1918 and 10/3/1918.

against sailing in the waters of the Arabian Peninsula but refused to repeal the banning orders against de Monfreid sailing in Aden or Somaliland waters.[55] The stand-off escalated rapidly. France threatened the British with reprisals against British subjects in French Somaliland if they would not lift the ban on de Monfreid's travel. Britain eventually backed down, reluctant to aggravate the French on a relatively peripheral issue with negotiations over the break-up of the Ottoman Empire going on in the background.[56]

After Britain lifted its restrictions against his travel, de Monfreid made for the coast of the Arabian Peninsula with two 'sand-bag sized bags' full of much sought-after Austro-Hungarian MT dollars. By now, however, Muhammad al-Idrissi's influence in the region was waning and France sought to court new allies. The money that de Monfreid transported to Yemen in 1920 was destined for highland Yemen, to support Imam Yahya, who was at war with the Aden Protectorate.[57] These French deliveries of arms and financial support to the inhabitants of the Tihamat Yemen, 'Asir and the northern Yemeni highlands continued throughout the period 1920–1921.[58] In early 1922, de Monfreid helped to land a delegation of Kemalist Turks at Mukha bound for the Imam's capital in Sanaa, destined to advise the Imam on questions around inspiring Yemeni nationalism and on modernising Yemen.[59] In return for this patronage, de Monfreid requested

[55] ADC 63 CPCOM 9 – dossier 1, Letter, M. Lauret, Governor of French Somaliland, Djibouti, to Stephan Pichon, Minister for Foreign Affairs, Paris, 16/8/1919; IOR R/20/A/4085, Complaint, Governor of Djibouti, 1919. See also '27 Juin, 1919', in de Monfreid, *Journal de bord*, pp. 193–194.

[56] IOR R/20/A/2965, Letter, James Stewart, Political Resident, Aden, to Edmund Allenby, High Commissioner, Cairo, 15/8/1919; AOM FM 1/AFFPOL 698 – dossier 2, Letter, Jules Lauret, Governor of French Somaliland, Djibouti, to Albert Sarraut, Minister for the Colonies, Paris, 24/2/1920, and Letter, Stephan Pichon, Council President, Minster of Foreign Affairs, Paris, to Albert Sarraut, the Minister for the Colonies, 10/2/1920.

[57] IOR R/20/A/4085, Letter, Officer Commanding, Perim, to Military Head Quarters, Aden, 15/9/20 and 17/9/20.

[58] IOR R/20/A/4085, Letter, Commanding Officer, HMS Clematis, to Major Barrett, FAR, Aden, et al, 6/11/1920 & Report made by the Naval Liason Officer, Cairo, that de Monfreid is engaged in gunrunning between Djibouti and Khokha.

[59] IOR R/20/A/3022, Letter, Ashoor Mohamed, Government Translator, Aden, to Senior Naval Officer, Aden Division, 3/4/22, 5/1/1922, and Resident's Notes, April, 1922.

of the Imam and his advisors that the French be allowed to occupy the Yemeni coast and facilitate the construction of telegraph lines as well as a railway between the coast and Sanaa.[60] In short, de Monfreid continued his efforts to establish a French outpost on the Tihamat Yemen, failing which he promoted the interests of Britain's adversaries, or attempted to turn Britain's allies into French proxies. The recruitment of political allies, and the subversion of others' alliances, were two sides of the same coin in the new geostrategic calculus; in both cases, the outcome was a chaotic and endless scramble for power along the coastline.

Alongside his efforts on the Arab coast, de Monfreid exercised progressively more police power on behalf of the French Somaliland government in the maritime neighbourhood of the Gulf of Tadjoura. During World War I de Monfreid had built up a fleet of dhows that plied the Obock–Aden route, which supplied French Somaliland during the blockade. From about the mid-1920s, after normal passenger and goods transport services resumed in the Red Sea after the war, de Monfreid won an informal contract to provide coastguard services to the French Somaliland government. In the service of policing shipping traffic in the Gulf of Tadjoura, from a base in the port of Obock, de Monfreid's ships taxed local merchants and policed which ships could sail in and out of the Gulf. In so doing, de Monfreid was in a position not only to extract customs dues, but also to facilitate or hinder the general trade in arms and even in slaves between Africa and the Arabian Peninsula.[61] Prior to 1925, French Somaliland's offi-

---

[60] IOR/R/20/A/1300, Letter, Zabeed Agent, to Captain Fazluddin, British Political Officer, Hodeida, March, 1922 and 3/7/22. See also AOM FM 1/AFFPOL 698 – dossier 2, Letter, Pierre-Amable Chapon-Baissac, Governor of French Somaliland, to Aristide Briand, Minister for the Colonies, Paris, and Edouard Herriot, Minister for Foreign Affairs, Paris, 17/12/1926. See also Letter, Henry de Monfreid to Armgart de Monfreid, 29/1/1920, and Letter, Henry de Monfreid to George-Daniel de Monfreid, 21/4/1921, in de Monfreid, *Aventures extraordinaires*, pp. 832, 837–838.

[61] AOM FM 1/AFFPOL/ 123 – dossier 2, Report made by M. Horès concerning the verification of the service led by M. Bouet, 2/3/1911; IOR R/20/A/4085, Report by British secret agent in Djibouti on subjects X and Y, 31/10/1920. See also Letter, Henry de Monfreid to Armgart Freudenfeld, 4/06/1912. See also Letter, Henry de Monfreid to George-Daniel de Monfreid, 29/05/1912, and Letter, Henry de Monfreid to Armgart Freudenfeld, 4/06/1912, in de Monfreid, *Aventures extraordinaires*, pp. 139, 141–143.

cial coastguard consisted of a single motor dhow to survey the Gulf's 200 miles of coastline – and had apprehended but a mere handful of illicit cargoes in its first few decades of existence. Thereafter, policing the northern portion of the Gulf appears to have fallen under de Monfreid's exclusive jurisdiction, in spite of the fact that he was in no way an official representative of the government.[62] Indeed, as historian Fahad Bishara suggests, shipping throughout the region increasingly used the French flag, granted by quasi-official French consuls, as cover from British patrols, so as to curtail the British Navy's propensity to search foreign-flagged ships without strong authority in the late-nineteenth and twentieth centuries in the north-western Indian Ocean.[63]

Outlawry

It was from this position of power, independence and even impunity that de Monfreid accomplished his most famous feats of outlawry. For example, in 1923, de Monfreid sent some ten tons of marijuana in a single shipment between India and Egypt via the British Seychelles and Djibouti. While de Monfreid fictionalised the feat as one of subterfuge and cunning in his most famous book, *Hashish: A Smuggler's Tale*, in reality he accomplished the act only because he won exemption from the normal laws governing such international crimes.[64] The French foreign minister wrote simply that France was under 'no obligation' to regulate the introduction of hashish to their territories since a new treaty regulating the international trade in hashish had yet to come into

---

[62] NA ADM 116/2291, Report on change in French Naval Organisation in the Red Sea, 8/9/1925.

[63] Fahad Ahmad Bishara, 'Paper routes: Inscribing Islamic law across the nineteenth-century western Indian Ocean', *Law and History Review*, 32(4) (2014), pp. 797–820.

[64] de Monfreid, *Hashish*, esp. pp. 117–217; de Monfreid, *La Poursuite du Kaïpan* (Paris: Grasset, 1934). The relevant archival sources in Britain are NA CO 323/973/9 & NA CO 530/111. In France: ADC 63 CPCOM 9 – dossier 2 – Agissements de M. de Monfreid, Mars 1923–Mars 1929, and AOM FM 1/AFFPOL/698 – dossier 2. See also Letter, Henry de Monfreid to George-Daniel de Monfreid, 21/4/1921 and Letter, Henry de Monfreid to George-Daniel de Monfreid, 11/5/1921 and Letter, Henry de Monfreid to Armgart de Monfreid, 17/8/1921, in de Monfreid, *Aventures extraordinaires*, pp. 837–842; '17 août à 9 novembre 1921', in de Monfreid, *Journal de bord*, pp. 197–226.

force.[65] The foreign minister's involvement in defence of de Monfreid is at odds with any claim of 'outlawry' in the sense of subversion of the state. Rather, as historian Johan Mathew argues, smuggling was a negotiation with the law.[66] As we see here, such negotiations took place against an increasingly cutthroat geopolitical backdrop. Arguments for and against the 'illegality' of de Monfreid's actions were, in other words, measured against their strategic necessity. And de Monfreid was a past master at inflating the value of his geostrategic stock. By the early 1920s, his influence appears to have been considerable. In 1922, for example, when the French government tried to install a representative in the port of Tadjoura, then being run by one of de Monfreid's associates and a Sultan whose principal interest was in slave dealing, local retainers repulsed the government's forces.[67] In the chaotic, competitive international climate of the southern Red Sea in the 1920s, de Monfreid not only persuaded the government to interpret the law in his favour, he helped shape the French Somaliland government's policy as well.

Alongside arms dealing and drugs smuggling, British and French colonial officials also implicated de Monfreid in slave trading. The port of Tadjoura on the northern shore of the Gulf had long been a major slave trading port in the southern Red Sea region, funnelling slaves captured or taken as prisoners of war from conflicts in Abyssinia and Sudanese southern Egypt to markets in the Arabian Peninsula. In 1888, French officials recorded that some 2,000 slaves left Tadjoura every year for the Arabian Peninsula and the Middle East.[68] Although the trade declined under French colonial rule, it nevertheless continued in quite substantial numbers. By the mid-1920s, some 40 to 50 slaves

---

[65] AOM FM 1/AFFPOL/698 – dossier 2, Letter, Edouard Herriot, Minister for Foreign Affairs, Paris, to Robert Milnes-Crewe, British Ambassador, Paris, 29/1/1925, and Letter, Robert Crewe-Milnes, British Embassy, Paris, to Edouard Herriot, Minister for Foreign Affairs, Paris, 17/11/1924.

[66] Johan Mathew, 'Smoke on the water: Cannabis smuggling, corruption and the Janus-faced colonial state', *History Workshop Journal*, 86 (2018), pp. 67–89.

[67] AOM FM 1/AFFPOL/696 – dossier 1, Letter, M. Tellier, Interim Governor, French Somaliland, to Léon Perrier, Minister for the Colonies, Paris, 9/10/1926.

[68] IOR R/20/A/1559, Letter, Robert Crew-Milnes, British Ambassador, Paris, to Aristide Briand, Ministry of Foreign Affairs, Paris, 9/11/1926. See also AOM FM/SG/CFS 6 – dossier 79, Letter, Léonce Lagarde, Governor, Colony of Obock, to Jules Krantz, Minister of the Marine and the Colonies, Paris, 25/12/1888.

left Tadjoura each month during the trading season between October and April, or between 400 and 500 slaves each year.[69] As Britain's agent in Hodeida observed, French-protected slave traders enjoyed virtual immunity from external interference throughout the Red Sea; their ability to circumnavigate the Red Sea patrol, he claimed, earned the indigenous population living around the port of Tadjoura the reputation of possessing 'magical powers of eluding the vigilance of ships, even though they may be right under their bows'.[70] French officials themselves estimated that human exports from the Gulf of Tadjoura to the Arabian Peninsula numbered in the hundreds or low thousands annually.[71]

Various colonial officials in the region suggested de Monfreid played a role in the commercial networks that shipped slaves across the southern Red Sea.[72] For example, in 1926, the British administration received complaints from the British Legation in Addis Ababa that de Monfreid was involved in the slave trade in the French Somaliland port of Tadjoura.[73] In early 1927, Governor Pierre-Amable Chapon-Baissac investigated the allegations of slave trading against de Monfreid and other European traders, hypothesising that the root of the issue lay not so much in the absence of laws, surveillance or policing – all of which were within the powers of the French Somaliland government – but in the symbiotic relationship between the colonial government and merchants. De Monfreid in particular, wrote Chapon-Baissac, was 'the king of his universe', and there was

---

[69] IOR R/20/A/1559, Memo, Mr. Philip Zaphiro, Oriental Secretary, Addis Ababa; Report, Abdullah Shaikh Ahmed, 5/1/1927, and Djibouti Agent's report, 5/3/1927. See also AOM FM 1/AFFPOL 696, Letter, Maurice Bokanowski, Minister for the Marine, to Lieutenant-Commander, Diana, Red Sea Division, 4/9/1923.

[70] IOR R/20/A/1559, Memo, Captain Fazluddin, Hodeida, to Bernard Reilly, First Assistant Resident, Aden, 6/12/1922.

[71] AOM 1/AFFPOL 696 – dossier 3, Letter, M. Tellier, Governor by Interim, French Somaliland, to Léon Perrier, Minister for the Colonies, Paris, 19/10/1926.

[72] IOR R/20/A/1559, Letter, Commanding Officer, HMS Weyneck, to Bernard Reilly, First Assistant Resident, Aden, 4/12/1927; Letter, Thomas Stewart, Resident, Aden, to Leo Amery, Secretary of State for Colonies, London, 1/2/1928. See also MAESS ASMAI Archivio Eritrea – Pacco 941 – Arabie Varie.

[73] ADC 63 CPCOM 9 – dossier 2, Letter, F. R. Hoyer Millar, British Embassy, Paris, to M. Doynel de Saint-Quentin, Africa Desk, Ministry for Foreign Affairs, Paris, 9/12/1926.

good evidence that he and his associates had very recently paid a large sum of money to a well-known slave trader in Tadjoura.[74] More generally, the slave trade spiked in the 1920s. Ibn Saud's rise to power in Nejd and the Hejaz created an uptick in demand – to between 2,000 and 5,000 annually – for African slaves to serve as soldiers, domestic servants and retainers.[75]

Whether de Monfreid was directly involved in slave transactions is unclear. It is more certain that as a customs agent, de Monfreid afforded local rulers and dealers protection from the international anti-slavery law the French government was bound to enforce. But unlike the *aban* of precolonial Majerteenia, de Monfreid's role as a broker in such transactions was about gatekeeping rather than alliance building; it was about mutual strategic benefit rather than mutual recognition. He was a middleman rather than an agent of reciprocity and diplomacy. This is not to hold de Monfreid accountable for the transformation of international relations in the region. De Monfreid was both the product of, and a protagonist in, the creation of the combative, chaotic maritime culture. The international tensions from which he benefited had been unfurling since the beginning of the colonial era in the early nineteenth century, particularly as a result of the actions of British officials from Aden. Nevertheless, de Monfreid's activities reveal the extent to which, in just over half a century, the culture of chaos and competition had embroiled northern Somalia, coastal Yemen and the Gulf of Tadjoura.

Mutiny

The final few years of de Monfreid's career in French Somaliland encapsulated all the anarchic, chaotic qualities forming in the international realm in the region in the preceding half-century. In response to reports of de Monfreid's involvement in the slave trade, Britain banned de Monfreid from the waters of Aden and British

---

[74] ADC 63 CPCOM 9 – dossier 2, Letter, Pierre-Amable Chapon Baissac, Governor, French Somaliland, to Léon Perrier, Minister for the Colonies, Paris, 2/6/1927.

[75] IOR R/20/A/1559, Memo, Captain Fazluddin, Hodeida, to Bernard Reilly, First Assistant Resident, Aden, 6/12/1922, and Letter, Thomas Scott, Political Resident, Aden, to Winston Churchill, Secretary of State for the Colonies, London, 3/1/1923.

Somaliland, and asked France to likewise withdraw de Monfreid's manifests, which allowed him to sail beyond the confines of French Somaliland's seas.[76] British Foreign Office officials also compiled a memorandum detailing de Monfreid's illicit activities, which they submitted to the newly-formed League of Nations Opium and Dangerous Drugs Section in Geneva.[77] Liaising with the Central Narcotics Intelligence Bureau of the Egyptian police, the League oversaw the investigation of a network of drugs dealers based in Vienna to which British – and some French – officials suspected de Monfreid was connected.[78] In 1928 and 1929 the Egyptian police arrested various members of the network throughout Egypt and central Europe, extradited them to Egypt and tried and sentenced them for drugs smuggling crimes.[79]

In an effort to subvert Britain and Italy's strategic counter-attack, in late 1927 de Monfreid travelled to Paris to meet Ministers and other high officials. In Paris, de Monfreid denounced the Governor of French Somaliland for promoting what he saw as a new French policy of political and legal reform designed to appease Britain and the League of Nations.[80] In making the case against reform, de Monfreid articulated the demands of a sizeable constituency in French Somaliland, and echoed the assertions of three generations of regional firearms

---

[76] ADC 63 CPCOM 9 – dossier 2, Letter, Robert Crewe-Milnes, British Ambassador, Paris, to Aristide Briand, Minister for Foreign Affairs, Paris, 10/9/1927.

[77] LN, Social and Opium Sections, 1928–1932, Registry File 773 – 12 A/ 61714/24297 – 'Illicit traffic in drugs by M. Henri de Monfreid', British Memorandum Regarding the Illicit Activities of Henri de Monfreid, 13/9/1927.

[78] AOM FM 1/AFFPOL/697, Letter, J. Taillo, merchant, Djibouti, to Gabriel Angoulvant, French delegate to the League of Nations anti-slavery committee, Paris, 5/4/1926.

[79] See LN, Social and Opium Sections – File No. O.C. 1118, Letter, M. Marc, sous-inspecteur of Police in Cairo, to the adjunct-commander of police, Cairo; LN, Social and Opium Sections – File No. O.C. 1118, Annexe D – Note du Central Narcotics Intelligency Bureau du Gouvernement Égyptien; LN, Registry Files, 1928–1932 – Registry File 3120 – 12/11391/157 – Illicit Traffic in Egypt by an Austrian Organisation – 1929–1938, Letter, Directorate of Political and Commercial Affairs, Ministry for Foreign Affairs, Cairo, to Malcolm Delevingne, Secretary-General, Advisory Committee on the Traffic in Opium, 7/12/1929.

[80] AOM FM 1/AFFPOL 698 – dossier 2, Letter, Léon Perrier, Minister for the Colonies, Paris, to Pierre-Amable Chapon-Baissac, Governor, French Somaliland, 17/1/1928.

merchants, who had long fought against official efforts to diversify the colony. Indeed, only the previous year a cabal of arms dealers had marched on Chapon-Baissac's residence, threatening to storm the gates if he refused to cease his efforts to exert increased influence over customs officials and assert the independence of French Somaliland's judiciary to the detriment of arms dealers.[81]

The substance of de Monfreid's argument against reforming the colony was revealing. His case was, in essence, strategic, drawing on what was increasingly an orthodoxy in international politics in the region. In turning their back on him, de Monfreid claimed that the French government abandoned French interests in the Arabian Peninsula at large – interests he had promoted so keenly for more than a decade. Indeed, de Monfreid used menaces of his own in making his case, threatening the French government in Paris with a public exposé in the press for its lack of patriotism if they refused to support de Monfreid and France's complementary goal of establishing an outpost on the Arabian Peninsula.[82] In support of his cause de Monfreid requested two of his friends, one a professor at the *École nationale de la France d'outre-mer* in Paris and the other a former President of the French Geological Society, write to French ministers to state that, far from being an 'outlaw', de Monfreid was a proven patriot.[83] In a letter to the French prime minister, the former president of the French Geological Society claimed that de Monfreid's enemies styled him as a 'dangerous bandit in the mould of individuals who appear in books and films ... [and] claimed they had unmasked [de Monfreid] through their detective work'.[84] De Monfreid's lawyer in Addis Ababa also sent a letter to the government in France and Djibouti to the same effect.[85]

---

[81] AOM FM 1/AFFPOL/697, Letter, Léon Perrier, Minister for the Colonies, Paris, to Pierre-Amable Chapon-Baissac, Governor, French Somaliland, ??/05/26.

[82] ADC 63 CPCOM 9 – dossier 2, Note, Léon Perrier, Ministry of Foreign Affairs, Paris, 14/11/1927.

[83] AOM FM 1/AFFPOL/ 698 – dossier P8/1, Letter, Pierre Teilhard de Chardin, Professor at the Catholic University, Paris and Pierre Lamare, Professor at the École nationale de la France d'Outre-Mer to Ministry for the Colonies, 6/2/1928.

[84] AOM FM 1/AFFPOL/ 698 – dossier P8/1, Letter M. Lamare, 16 Rue Ernest Cresson, Paris, to Léon Perrier, Minister for the Colonies, Paris, 8/2/1928; Letter, Docteur St. Germain, ex-chief medical officer of the hospital at the University of Montpellier, France, to Pierre Teilhard de Chardin, 29/12/1927.

[85] ADC 63 CPCOM 9 – dossier 2, Statement, M. Chanoit, Lawyer, Addis Ababa, on behalf of M. de Monfreid, 1927.

But the atmosphere in the region was by now one of high geopolit-ical tension and suspicion. With Imam Yahya and Ibn Saud in the ascendancy along the Tihamat Yemen, the case for French control over the southern exit to the Red Sea – and thus over the whole of the international maritime traffic travelling between the Indian Ocean and the Mediterranean – was weaker. The Zaraniq and other potential French allies on the coast had, as we saw in Chapter 3, overextended themselves and collapsed into obscurity. De Monfreid's efforts to persuade the establishment to rekindle France's geopolitical aims in the Arabian Peninsula and their alliance with de Monfreid were in vain. Faced with hostility in French Somaliland and mistrust among the imperial community in the region, in 1928 de Monfreid found himself in a very similar position to that of Ahmad Fatini and his Zaraniq followers earlier in the decade. Having become successful by exploiting the opportunities for cultivating wealth and status amid colonial chaos in the region, the same culture of disorder and upheaval now threatened to destroy him. Such was the nature of international relations in the region by the late 1920s: a stormy, transient arena, in which fortunes were made and lost, alliances forged and ruined, the seeds of the next crisis sown continuously.

Quitting the confines of French Somaliland for good, de Monfreid moved to Abyssinia, to the bustling railway town of Dire Dawa, a stop on the route between Djibouti and Addis Ababa, and not far from where he had begun his career in the region, almost two decades earlier. Yet by now de Monfreid was much more deeply connected in the region, as well as an astute navigator of the chaotic international political realm. It was rumoured that Emperor Haile Selassie himself, then still under the regency of Empress Zewditu, had granted de Monfreid a license to provide Harar with electricity. By July 1928, more rumours circulated in Djibouti that de Monfreid was conspiring with the Emperor to conquer a tract of French Somaliland extending from the salt flats of Lake Assal to the port of Tadjoura.[86]

In the process, de Monfreid marshalled his disruptive energies into the service of older regional geopolitical rivalries. Wittingly or not, de

---

[86] AOM FM 1/AFFPOL/696, Letter, Pierre-Amable Chapon-Baissac, Governor, French Somaliland, to André Maginot, Minister for the Colonies, February, 1929, enclosing letter, dated 28/7/28. See also, AOM FM 1/AFFPOL/700 – dossier 1, Letter, Pierre-Amable Chapon-Baissac, Governor, French Somaliland, to Paul Reynaud, Minister for the Colonies, Paris, 13/2/1929.

Monfreid had become an instrument of Abyssinia and the Afar Sultans, who sought to revive earlier iterations of their empires – such as Aksum and the Adal Sultanate – which once governed large tracts of northeastern Africa stretching all the way from the Gulf of Tadjoura to the Shoan highlands. In the competitive, chaotic colonial realm, the Abyssinian state struck an alliance with its Muslim former rivals, harnessing de Monfreid's ambitions and the disgruntlement of the Afar Sultans, who rose to power after the break-up of the Adal Sultanate but had been marginalised by the French government, which strongly favoured the Sultan of Tadjoura. The coalition planning to dislodge the Sultan of Tadjoura and wrest the northern coast of the Gulf of Tadjoura from the French included representatives of the post-Adal sultanates, including Aussa and Rohayto, notably the ruling Shaykh Issa and Tiklat Ayal. These two joined with the Abyssinian government and de Monfreid to revive their power and give Abyssinia independent access to the sea.[87]

In pursuit of the goal to oust the Sultan of Tadjoura, the professor and the former president of the French Royal Geographical Society who had acted as de Monfreid's supporters in his petition to the French prime minister now travelled to Djibouti under the guise of undertaking a geological survey to the west of French Somaliland. The mission served as an official pretext to visit the interior and carry supplies towards the Abyssinian border. Soon after landing, the Frenchmen met with a caravan of camels that de Monfreid had hired through representatives of the Sultan of Aussa. The pair planned to strike for the region around Lake Assal, close to the border with Abyssinia, where they would distribute gifts of arms purchased in Djibouti to an assembly of Afar chiefs. But Governor Chapon-Baissac was immediately suspicious of their intentions and blocked their initial application for a visa to visit the interior of French Somaliland and promulgated a law compelling all Europeans visiting the hinterland to apply for permission from the Governor and take a military escort. Yet by the time it came into force the men had already crossed the border into Abyssinia, to the town of Dessie, where in early 1929 de Monfreid and

---

[87] ADC 63 CPCOM 9 – dossier 2, Letter, Pierre-Amable Chapon Baissac, Governor, French Somaliland, to Léon Perrier, Minister for the Colonies, Paris, 13/10/1927.

an Italian contingent joined them.[88] The party now consisted of the Frenchmen, several Abyssinians, two Russians and an Italian guard of twenty-eight askaris accompanying representatives of the Sultan of Rohayto, a fact suggesting the Italian government also backed the plan. Having set up camp on the outskirts of Dessie, they met a delegation of five Afar and Abyssinians chiefs, all widely known as opponents of the current, French-allied Sultan of Tadjoura.[89]

While the proceedings of the conference remain tantalisingly obscure – neither official intelligence channels nor de Monfreid himself left any record of the events – subsequent events suggest the conference succeeded in assuring local support to oust the reigning Sultan of Tadjoura and establishing an independent province in Tadjoura. In the spring of 1929, de Monfreid returned to France to seek support for the project in Europe. At his house in the Parisian suburbs, de Monfreid courted a circle of journalists, including the writer and journalist Joseph Kessel, with whom he produced articles denouncing French colonial rule in Somaliland, partly using Bolshevik anti-colonial propaganda. Indeed, de Monfreid and Kessel contacted the Soviet Ambassador in Hodeida to canvass revolutionary support for their mission to give Abyssinia access to the sea.[90] By the end of the year, de Monfreid and Kessel formulated a plan to return to French Somaliland, meet with the rebel chiefs, and expose the corrupt conditions in the colony to the French public.

Already a well-established writer, Kessel found a sponsor in the French daily *Le Matin*, for whom he was commissioned to write an investigation into the persistence of slave trading in French Somaliland. Kessel's motivations in taking up the commission are unclear, but he planned to join de Monfreid on a fresh trip to the border region between French Somaliland and Absyssinia in early 1930. In late 1929, de Monfreid himself returned to Djibouti, bound for his farm

---

[88] AOM FM 1/AFFPOL/696, Telegraph, Pierre-Ambale Chapon-Baisac, Governor, French Somaliland, to Léon Perrier, Minister for the Colonies, Paris, 22/11/1928, and Letter, Pierre-Amable Chapon-Baissac, Governor, French Somaliland, to Léon Perrier, Minister for the Colonies, Paris, 25/12/1928.

[89] AOM FM 1/AFFPOL/696, Letter, Pierre-Amable Chapon-Baissac, Governor, French Somaliland, to André Maginot, Minister for the Colonies, Paris, February 1929, 28/7/28.

[90] AOM FM 1/AFFPOL/700 – dossier 1, Letter, Pierre-Amable Chapon-Baissac, Governor, French Somaliland, to François Piétri, Minister for the Colonies, Paris, 2/10/1930 and 13/2/1929.

near Dire Dawa. With Chapon-Baissac still in power, de Monfreid remained the subject of considerable official suspicion; it is testament to his belief in his own influence that de Monfreid continued to defy the law, carrying with him some 1,500 unlicensed rounds of Gras rifle ammunition in his luggage. Customs caught de Monfreid, however, impounded the ammunition, and demanded a 50,000-Franc surety, repayable on the arms' disposal by legal means. De Monfreid protested the penalty, claiming – with a half-truth – that the arms were destined for a hunting trip sponsored by the Abyssinian government, and that the French Ministry in Abyssinia had ordered the shipment.[91] To avoid further trouble, de Monfreid abandoned the ammunition, advanced Kessel the money to pay the customs surety and set off hastily for Abyssinia.

Kessel arrived in Djibouti in early 1930. On arrival, Kessel attempted to pay the surety on de Monfreid's behalf, making himself the subject of suspicion. In an effort to keep Kessel from leaving Djibouti, the Governor banned all Europeans from leaving the colony's urban areas without his permission – on pain of a prison sentence – and summoned Kessel to his office.[92] The meeting, as Chapon-Baissac put it, ended 'stormily'.[93] Shortly after his meeting with Chapon-Baissac, Kessel dispatched copy for *Le Matin*'s front page to the effect that French Somaliland's governor Chapon-Baissac had a 'blind hatred' of de Monfreid and was bent on blocking the journalist's investigations into the slave trade in the colony. Whether intended or not, the implication was clear to Chapon-Baissac: the Governor was himself complicit in the slave trade.[94]

---

[91] AOM FM 1/AFFPOL/696, M. Roue, head of division, customs department, Djibouti, to M Hugonnier, head of customs, Djibouti, 14/1/1930, and Letter, M. Hugonnier, head of customs, Djibouti, to Pierre-Amable Chapon-Baissac, Governor, French Somaliland, 16/1/1930 and 19/1/1930. See also, Letter, Henri de Monfreid to Pierre-Amable Chapon-Baissac, Governor, French Somaliland, 14/1/1930.

[92] AOM FM 1/AFFPOL/696, Letter, Pierre-Amable Chapon-Baissac, Governor, French Somaliland, to François Piétri, Minister for Colonies, Paris, 23/1/1930.

[93] IOR/L/PS/12/4090, Extract of Report of Proceedings of HMS Dahlia, period ending 31/7/1930.

[94] AOM FM 1/AFFPOL/696, J. Kessel. 'Marchés des esclaves: enquête de Joseph Kessel – Le Rôle du Gouverneur', *Le Matin*, 4/6/1930; Letter, Pierre-Amable Chapon-Baissac, Governor, French Somaliland, to François Piétri, Minister for the Colonies, Paris, 1/7/1930; Letter, Pierre-Amable Chapon-Baissac, Governor, French Somaliland, to François Piétri, Minister for the Colonies, Paris, 21/1/

If de Monfreid and Kessel's purpose had been to discredit or even cause the dismissal of Chapon-Baissac, the plan misfired. Chapon-Baissac responded with a raft of dismissals, including the colony's highest-ranking judges on charges of taking bribes from de Monfreid or his associates. Chapon-Baissac also ordered de Monfreid's deportation to Paris to face trial for the non-payment of court fines in relation to drugs smuggling charges brought against him by the Djibouti courts in response to the League of Nations memorandum in early 1927. Finally, Chapon-Baissac ordered the seizure of de Monfreid's assets in Djibouti, including a hotel, boats and property in Obock.[95] In May 1931 a Parisian court reaffirmed Djibouti's judgement against de Monfreid and increased the fine to 371,000 francs, delegating the task of raising the money to the French Legation in Abyssinia, where de Monfreid by now owned various assets, including a farm near Harar, as well as an electric factory, a mechanic's shop and a bakery, all in Dire Dawa.[96] De Monfreid's role in efforts to redraw the map of northeast Africa, along with his career in French Somaliland, lay in ruin. The fate of the plot to oust the Sultan of Tadjoura, by contrast, remains a mystery. However, in 1930 the Empress Zewditu died, leaving Haile Selassie as Emperor in his own right. Perhaps he lost sight of the project during the transition; or perhaps he had become suspicious of the Italians' involvement – in 1934 they would use Dessie as a base to invade Ethiopia. In the absence of external support, the Afar chiefs' chances of success against the French-backed Sultan of Tadjoura dwindled; the plan faded; the alliance fell apart.

Conclusion

Following the failure of his plot to install new leadership in Tadjoura, de Monfreid himself went into semi-retirement. Inspired by his exploits, several journalistic investigations into gunrunning and slave

---

1930, and Extract of Report of Proceedings of HMS Dahlia, period ending 31/7/1930.

[95] AOM FM 1/AFFPOL/ 698 – dossier P8/1, Letter, Interim Governor, French Somaliland, to Albert Sarraut, Minister for the Colonies, Paris, 9/7/1932.

[96] AOM FM 1/AFFPOL/ 698 – dossier P8/1, Letter, André Tardieu, President of the Council, Ministry for Foreign Affairs, Paris, to Louis de Chappedelaine the Minister for the Colonies, Paris, 19/3/1932.

trading followed in the early 1930s,[97] and also led de Monfreid himself to pursue a writing career, starting with a collaboration with Ida Treat, a journalist and (later) Francophile American college professor.[98] Yet even in retirement he continued to attract influential support for his strategic vision for France in the Red Sea arena. Ironically, one of his most assertive supporters was Aristide Briand, of Kellogg–Briand pact fame, the 1928 treaty purporting to outlaw war between some sixty-two international signatories. Then France's minister for foreign affairs, Briand seemed to champion de Monfreid's reinstatement in French Somaliland in a letter to the minister for the colonies in 1931, stating that de Monfreid was like the 'famous Colonel Lawrence', who had skills which 'in exchange for certain protections' would make him an asset among France's 'diverse representatives in the Red Sea and Gulf of Aden region'.[99]

There was indeed something rare, even Lawrence-like about de Monfreid, whose contribution to the region's history was the pursuit of French interests on the Arabian Peninsula during and after World War I. Like Lawrence, de Monfreid's interests were split between the populations whose allegiance he sought to cultivate and those of his imperial masters. Similarly, it was against the backdrop of war, covert espionage operations and geopolitical competition that Lawrence and de Monfreid both operated.[100] In de Monfreid's career, we see the culmination of the anarchic approach to international relations, and a nadir for the permissive, aristocratic, gift-based and reciprocal forms of diplomacy indigenous to the region. Indeed, de Monfreid did not act in a local vacuum: he depended on the existence of willing local allies in the Tihamat Yemen and in the Gulf of Tadjoura to support him. Like the Zaraniq or the followers of Yusuf 'Ali, these allies were groups

---

[97] For example, IOR/L/PS/12/4090, 'The "middle passage": Slavery to-day', by George Percival-Kaye, Formerly Second in Command of HMS Sussetta of Red Sea and Persian Gulf Patrol, 1917–19, in *The Slave Market News Quarterly* – October, 1934. See also, Waterhouse, *Gun Running*.

[98] The first being Henry de Monfreid and Ida Treat, *Pearls, Arms and Hashish: Pages from the Life of a Red Sea Navigator* (London: Victor Gollancz Ltd., 1930).

[99] AOM FM 1/AFFPOL 698 – dossier P8/1, Letter, Aristide Briand, Ministry for Foreign Affairs, to François Piétri, Minister for the Colonies, Paris, 16/4/1931.

[100] Priya Satia, *Spies in Arabia: The Great War and the Cultural Foundations of Britain's Covert Empire in the Middle East* (Oxford: Oxford University Press, 2008).

primed to respond to de Monfreid's combative, confrontational form of diplomacy.

Cut off from these local networks, and having lost much of his influence in French Somaliland, de Monfreid turned for support to the Italians, who had their own designs on Abyssinia following the election of the fascist nationalist Mussolini. In the early 1930s, de Monfreid continued to reside in the countryside around Dire Dawa, working on various infrastructure development schemes. Yet de Monfreid's outspoken support for Italy's colonial ambitions brought him into conflict with the Abyssinian government, however, and in 1933 Haile Selassie expelled de Monfreid for writing seditious newspaper articles championing Italian colonialism and criticising Selassie's Emperorship.[101] On his return to Europe, de Monfreid instead wrote colonial adventure novels alongside pro-Italian propaganda throughout the 1930s, appearing at political rallies and conferences advocating Italian rule in what was by now increasingly known as Ethiopia.[102]

As we have seen, de Monfreid was more powerful than an adventurer: he played an important role in the region's international relations. A local saying exaggerated the situation only slightly by claiming de Monfreid, 'has conquered all men, [even] from the white-man's country'. As the saying continued, de Monfreid and his colonial allies were 'like the sea, immense and menacing'.[103] The southern Red Sea indeed became a violent, chaotic place at the hands of men such as de Monfreid, Ahmad Fatini and Yusuf 'Ali during the colonial era. Many Europeans, Africans and Arabs profited from and perpetuated the culture of competition and chaos among different power-brokers in the region, and profited from the decline of local conventions of diplomacy and the waning of the regional aristocracy's hold over international politics. As well as men such as Yusuf 'Ali, Shaykh Ambari, Ahmad Fatini and de Monfreid, the list of beneficiaries was considerable, and included several extant British arms companies such

---

[101] FM/ 1AFFPOL/ 698 – dossier P8/1, Telegram, Pierre-Amable Chapon-Baissac, Governor, French Somaliland, to Albert Sarraut, Ministry for the Colonies, Paris, 15/5/1933.

[102] AS Ministero Interno – Divizione Polizia Politica – Fascicoli Personali – 1927. Pacco 418. De Monfreid, Enrico – Scrittore. See also Mickaël Bethe-Selassié, *La jeune Ethiopie: Un haut-fonctionnaire éthiopien Berhanä-Marqos Wäldä-Tsadeq (1892–1943)* (Paris: L'Harmattan, 2009).

[103] Cited in de Monfreid and Treat, *Pearls, Arms and Hashish*, p. 9.

as Francis, Times and Co., Carling and Co., Bucknall and the Persia Line.[104] But like Yusuf 'Ali, Ahmad Fatini and others before him, de Monfreid was both the architect and the victim of international chaos. They were all part of the creation of colonial chaos. In the Conclusion of this study, we see that the legacy of this culture of anarchy endures to the present day.

---

[104] For other examples, see IOR R/20/A/1214, 'Memorandum' and 'High treason – British firm supplies arms to Mullah', *Daily Express*, 1/09/1903, and Note, signed Angus Hamilton, Agent for Reuters. See also, NA FO 2/970, Letter, William Carling to Colonel Harrington, Somaliland Field Force, Berbera, 1/10/1901.

Conclusion

The truth is, sir, that men do what their power permits them to do.

Captain Chillingworth, in *Sea of Poppies*

They turned on themselves ... as if they were out to prove that they could be better at cruelty than their elders.

Ahl, in *Crossbones*

As Captain Chillingworth observed in Amitav Ghosh's novel *Sea of Poppies*,[1] men will do what their power permits them to do. Chillingworth, a European sea captain during the Opium Wars, was a law unto himself. For Chillingworth, there was no law at sea – colonial officials made, arbitrated and enforced the law in their seaborne fiefdoms. The rugged, individualistic approach to maritime law which Ghosh conjures is strongly reminiscent of the EIC officials in Aden's approach to their relations with their neighbours in the southern Red Sea. Chillingworth could easily have been a Playfair, or a Goodfellow, or a Filonardi. The ramifications of this new regional relationship with power, particularly military power, have been far-reaching. The character Ahl in Nuruddin Farah's novel *Crossbones*,[2] which explores contemporary piracy in Somalia, observed that Somalis have sought to outdo their forebears in their practice of violence. Ahl's observation is a grim and strange contemporary echo of the colonial culture evoked by Ghosh's Chillingworth character. We have traced some of the real historical characters who fill the space between these two creative evocations. The characters in Ghosh's and Farah's novels, like the real characters in this study, shine a light on the dark side of liberal internationalism and competitive pluralism – that is, on the prevailing global mode of international relations that persists to this

[1] Amitav Ghosh, *Sea of Poppies* (London: Penguin Books, 2009), p. 262.
[2] Nuruddin Farah, *Crossbones* (London: Penguin Books, 2011), p. 41.

day in the southern Red Sea region. We have seen that imperial voices –
including colonial officials and some later observers – attributed the
chaos, bloodshed, extreme geopolitical competitiveness and the ever-
worsening cycles of violence in the region witnessed during the colonial
period to the inherent tribalism and backwardness of Somali and
Yemeni society. Even to this day, commentators speak about the
'pre-modern formlessness' of African politics, African warfare and
ultimately of African society. But as authors like Ghosh and Farah
indicate, such a view is anachronistic. Chaos was a colonial creation.

To borrow the words of the historian Markus Vink, a 'life-cycle of
the Indian Ocean ended' in the early nineteenth century.[3] New political
imperatives shaped the map of the region. Chaos replaced the logic of
cooperation at the level of international relations. This shift was the
product of colonialism. It was the result of the export of a particular
approach to maritime law and international relations that, to use
Hobbes' language, showed a preference 'for going down to defeat
fighting rather than consenting to unresisted subjugation'.[4] This study
has sought to show that not only was chaos a product of colonialism,
but also that chaos had its own logic. I have argued that chaos was the
consequence of colonial Europeans and ambitious Africans and Arabs
undermining traditional royals who dominated the region's foreign
relations, severing the connections between the region's royal lineages
and fragmenting the region's political map. By reading the colonial
archives through the lens of international relations and as a clash of
maritime legal traditions, I have sketched the new, competitive and
adversarial logic of international politics that emerged in the southern
Red Sea in the colonial era.

The stories in this study point to a layer of international relations, a
sea-level reality, in which conflict and violence became increasingly
normal. Bernard Cohn, a historian of South Asia, argues that colonialism operated on and through law – but that the law could have
profoundly paradoxical and even contrary effects on society.[5] As we
saw in the Majerteen case in Chapter 1, the negotiation of treaties
invariably followed military defeat. Treaties became both projections
of power and instruments of a new form of international

---

[3] See Vink, 'Indian Ocean studies', p. 57.
[4] Wight, 'Why is there no international relations theory?', p. 43.
[5] Bernard S. Cohn, *Colonialism and Its Forms of Knowledge: The British in India*
(Princeton: Princeton University Press, 1996).

governmentality that emphasised competition.[6] In other words, the disordering of indigenous networks and diplomatic procedures unfolded in the course of the negotiations following the wreck of steamships along the coast. As the historians Lauren Benton and Lisa Ford recently argued in their book *Rage for Order*, 'some of the most important conversations about global order' occurred not in the metropolis but rather 'in the course of mundane jurisdictional disputes arising in and on the boundaries of empires'.[7]

Shipwrecks, attacks against shipping, arms trading and alliance making were all catalysts for debate about coastal sovereignty in the southern Red Sea; they created opportunities for discursive exchange around coastal rulers' rights to claim salvage. They were ways in which sub-imperial actors not only 'used' the colonial system but also helped shape it, albeit along destructive lines. In the course of these interactions between coastal rulers and colonial interlopers, two different views of sovereignty and maritime law accommodated one another. As the nineteenth century progressed, the accommodation became increasingly one-sided. A new logic of competition and opposition alienated actors such as Sultan Uthman, who had grown up in an era when the Ottomans, Hadramis, Omanis, Zanzibaris and Gujaratis were still powerful and influential independent actors in the regional arena of international relations. For these indigenous protagonists, gift giving, reciprocity, plurality and sharing was key. Rather than competing at one another's expense, the rulers of these empires coexisted, respecting one another's sovereignty and jurisdictions. The new colonial landscape made no room for those who believed in plurality or held deep-rooted convictions about the possibility of collaboration between the rulers of different coastal regions of the southern Red Sea.

Reflections

By paying attention to these sea-level activities and exchanges, a new picture of diplomacy and international relations emerges. As the story

---

[6] Compare Robert Travers, 'A British Empire by treaty in eighteenth-century India', in Saliha Belmessous (ed.), *Empire by Treaty: Negotiating European Expansion, 1600–1900* (Oxford: Oxford University Press, 2014), p. 134.

[7] Lauren Benton and Lisa Ford, *Rage for Order: The British Empire and the Origins of International Law, 1800–1850* (Cambridge, MA: Harvard University Press, 2016), pp. 4–5.

of the incident in which a British colonial official compelled the Majerteen Sultan to inflict bloody and summary punishment on his own people or face bombardment of his coastline by British warships (see the Introduction and Chapter 1) shows, the culture of diplomacy that Europeans exported to the southern Red Sea region was violent and calculating. The focus was on destruction, on subordination, even humiliation. Uthman was forced to behead his own subjects. Ahmad Fatini continually threatened violence, even collecting unexploded shells when he was ostracised from the arms markets.

On the one hand, littoral populations experienced the change in the nature of international politics, the upsurge in colonial chaos, as alienation. As the international relations scholar Amr Sadet has argued '[a]s far as the Muslim world is concerned, globalisation seeks to deconstruct their state structures ... [so] as to re-inscribe them' in Western colonial powers' own image.[8] Indeed, leaders of the non-Western world faced a grim choice during the colonial era – participate in the international political economy of violence, or face destruction themselves. There was no escape. Leaders such as Uthman, Yusuf 'Ali and Shaykh Ambari also played the game of military patronage, of geopolitics and international competition. As a consequence, they found their leadership hollowed out, eroded from the sides. They co-created a culture of international relations that was highly unstable.

The way in which colonial diplomacy was conducted was both democratising and divisive. At the same time as regional diplomacy became less aristocratic, rule-bound and lineage-dependent and more accessible to all, it also became more open to disruptors, upstarts and outsiders such as the Yusuf 'Alis, the Ahmad Fatinis and the de Monfreids, and in the process became more unstable and competitive. Colonial rule divided and disordered regional networks of diplomacy and aristocratic links that had bound coastal aristocracies in the southern Red Sea region, but it did not replace these indigenous inter-governmental links, diplomatic codes and legal idiom with anything equally as comprehensive or harmonious. The colonial treaty regime was one in which contractual clarity and certainty was achieved at the cost of fundamental values such as reciprocity, stability, peace and mutual recognition. Colonial international relations was a void that sucked in concepts such as *aman*, the *dar al-'ahd* and *aban*, devalued

---

[8] Sabet, 'The Islamic Paradigm of Nations', pp. 187, 185–188.

them and transformed them into shadow of their precolonial practice. The concepts endured in name, but were transformed in content – *aban* became more a form of gatekeeping rather than a way of ingratiating outsiders, the abode of treaties became a highly contested domain fraught with competition for recognition, and the notion of protection took on a new air of menace. The legacy of this transformation of the colonial state into a gatekeeper, an intermediary with external military patronage, can be seen throughout Africa and indeed across the colonial Middle East.[9]

In the process of undermining indigenous modes of diplomacy and styles of international relations, colonial conquest created a chaotic, highly fragmented landscape of mutually antagonistic groups, all competing for military patronage, treaties, better terms and renewed membership in the international community. Competition, retaliation and one-upmanship replaced mutual recognition as the dominant style of diplomacy. Violence became the normal way in which subregions of the coast interacted with one another. As Chabal and Daloz argued, modernity in Africa was inextricably linked to increased disorder, patrimonialism and instability.[10] This was no less the case in the international realm than the domestic one. The politics of survival is the international, as well as national, politics of colonial modernity.

Scholars have parsed this messiness that colonialism created within and between African and Middle Eastern states as a form of hybridity. Colonial states became 'a palimpsest of contested sovereignties, codes, and jurisdictions'.[11] Indeed it is almost a commonplace in international relations scholarship that there has never been uniformity in the international state system, either across place or over time.[12] As early as the 1980s, Richard Ashley hypothesised that multiple distinctive regions

[9] William Reno, *War in Independent Africa* (Cambridge: Cambridge University Press, 2011), p. 20; Frederick Cooper, *Africa Since 1940: The Past of the Present* (Cambridge: Cambridge University Press, 2002), esp. pp. 156–190; Ariel Ahram and Charles King, 'The warlord as arbitrageur', *Theory and Society*, 41(2) (2012), p. 173.

[10] Chabal and Daloz, *Africa Works*. See also Jean-François Bayart, 'Africa in the world: A history of extraversion', *African Affairs*, 99(395) (2000), esp. p. 260.

[11] John L. Comaroff and Jean Comaroff, 'Law and disorder in the postcolony: An introduction', in Jean Comaroff and John L. Comaroff (eds), *Law and Disorder in the Postcolony* (University of Chicago Press, 2006), p. 9.

[12] Grovogui, 'Regimes of Sovereignty', pp. 317–318. See also Mbembe, 'At the edge of the world', pp. 259–284.

made up the international state system, each encrusted with its own diplomatic and political cultures, agreements, histories and power relations.[13] The result was a legal system that reflected a 'chaotic mess of competing, overlapping, constantly fluid groups, more or less inclusive, with entirely heterogeneous principles of membership', in which rival conceptions of order competed for influence, 'whilst discrete sovereignties tend to resist encroachment on autonomy previously enjoyed'.[14]

The pluralism of the colonial era took on a distinctly adversarial and competitive complexion in the southern Red Sea. Colonial international law and diplomatic relations integrated some indigenous concepts, but whitewashed many others. While the diplomatic vestiges of older connections linking the politics and economies of the Red Sea and the wider Indian Ocean realm have remained in the form of lateral connections between littoral rulers, the nature of those connections, the dominant legal and diplomatic culture of the region, has become increasingly violent and fractured. Yusuf 'Ali, Ahmad Fatini and Henry de Monfreid are good examples of men who believed they had a right to all things, even the state. European diplomacy was of the type in which negotiation – for example, over the terms of salvage agreements – was frequently conducted using the guns of the Royal Navy as a bargaining tool. Britain included clauses to exclude coastal rulers entering agreements with other European powers. The Ottomans, Italy and France retaliated by seeking to undermine Britain with gifts of firearms to lure coastal rulers into agreements with them. It was a diplomacy that played neighbours off against one another and admitted upstarts and outsiders to the fold where this served colonial geopolitical aims. It was a diplomacy of firearms dealing and coups d'états, of threats and retaliation, rather than gift giving and mutual recognition.

Kenneth Waltz described the persistence of anarchy, competition and chaos in the modern international realm as 'dismaying'.[15] Only by delving into the nineteenth century can we plumb the depths of the

---

[13] See Richard K. Ashley, 'The poverty of neo-realism', *International Organisation*, 38(2) (1984), pp. 238–242, 272–273. See also Benton, *A Search for Sovereignty*; Thomas Blom Hansen and Finn Stepputat, 'Sovereignty revisited', *Annual Review of Anthropology*, 35 (2006), pp. 297.

[14] Griffiths, 'What is legal pluralism', p. 36.

[15] Kenneth N. Waltz, *Theory of International Politics* (Reading: Addison-Wesley Publishing, 1979), p. 66.

international chaos that enveloped – and envelops – the Red Sea. The region was never cleanly cosmopolitan; it was never a frictionless, interconnected idyll devoid of geopolitical rivalries. Nor did it suddenly become a conflict-ridden frontier during the colonial period. The sea was always simultaneously an arena of connection and division.[16] However, the nineteenth century saw the region become more split than united. The reasons the Red Sea proved a site of intense division during the colonial period – and has continued to harbour extraordinary levels of conflict to this day – have been the subject of this study. The roots of conflict, we have seen, were in the transactional, adversarial and competitive approach to maritime law and international politics that Europeans brought with them and imposed on the region. Colonialism was a form of rule that fostered interregional competition, whose aim was geopolitical aggrandisement, which instrumentalised violence as a way of achieving political goals by means other than – or in addition to – diplomacy.

The reasons underlying Europeans' aggressive approach to the maritime realm lie in Europe's own history of international relations as well as in the colonial setting itself. On the one hand, the peculiar fractiousness of European attitudes must lie in Europe, in the battlefields of the seventeenth century and the jurisprudence of thinkers such as Grotius. On the other hand, reasons might be found in the fact that Europeans were outsiders who sought to make the region their own, to throw off their long-lived dependence on regional rulers and commercial networks and stamp their own culture, their own version of order and their own commercial rules onto the region. In turn, European colonists promulgated an approach to maritime law and international diplomacy which they thought of as freedom, but which in practice meant entitlements to acquire, powers to subvert regional rulers' authority and circumnavigate local convention. Europeans' approach made the system of international relations in the southern Red Sea more competitive in nature, more transactional in style, and its protagonists quicker to turn to violence in the pursuit of strategic aims than ever before.

This notion of maritime freedom and law owed a debt to jurists like Grotius. Grotius rationalised Dutch traders' Indian Ocean prize-taking, arguing they were at war with the Portuguese. Similar

---

[16] Cf. David Abulafia, *The Boundless Sea: A Human History of the Oceans* (Oxford: Oxford University Press, 2019).

rationalisations of colonial chaos-making could be seen in the colonial Red Sea, and across the Indian Ocean, including the Persian Gulf,[17] and notably the Sulu Sultanate in southeast Asia in the eighteenth and early nineteenth century. Whereas in the Red Sea the British interfered in northeastern Somalia because they wanted to safeguard shipping and ensure supplies for Aden, in southeast Asia the EIC sought to break into the Chinese tea market by strong-arming China's regional trading partners – such as in Sulu Sultanate in contemporary northern Borneo and the southern Philipines – to their cause. As a result of the EIC's actions, the Sulu Sultanate became unstable and split apart. Across the world, the aims and consequences of European colonial diplomacy were very similar: Europeans sought to gain access to markets or security for their commercial shipping and the manner in which they achieved it resulted in division and conflict in the affected regions.[18] A current of disorder swept through the whole Indian Ocean realm, beginning in the seventeenth century with commercial contests between the Portuguese, the Dutch and others. It culminated in episodes such as the ones we have seen in this study, when gunboats replaced gifts as the medium of diplomacy.

British imperialists in the eighteenth and nineteenth centuries left their imprint on the diplomatic and international legal cultures across the global maritime realm. The legal historians Benton and Ford argue that through a diverse set of actors and interactions, the British nineteenth-century 'rage for order' was a universal project to fold all states doing business with the British Empire into a single legal order that left its mark from the Strait of Magellan to the Strait of Malacca.[19] The rage for a new global and imperial legal order, as we have seen in the southern Red Sea context, was an even more invasive species of imperialism, perhaps, than even Benton and Ford's argument allows. The British initiated a chain reaction of change, coercing established

---

[17] See James Onley, *Britain and the Gulf Shaikhdoms, 1820-1971: The Politics of Protection* (Doha: Georgetown University School of Foreign Service in Qatar, 2009).

[18] James Francis Warren, *The Sulu Zone: The Dynamics of External Trade, Slavery and Ethnicity in the Transformation of a Southeast Asian Maritime State, 1768–1898* (Singapore: National University of Singapore, 1981), p. 15, esp. pp. 38–67. See also Eric Tagliacozzo, *Secret Trades, Porous Borders: Smuggling and States along a Southeast Asian Frontier, 1865–1915* (New Haven & London: Yale University Press, 2005).

[19] Benton and Ford, *Rage for Order*.

regional rulers to engage in an entirely different way of conducting international relations, and inciting obliging upstarts to enter the fray on the new terms of violence and competition with shipments of firearms and promises of recognition.

Colonial chaos in international relations generated its own destructive energy in the early twentieth century. By the 1920s, many indigenous and other imperial powers participated in this new system and its culture of international relations: French, Italians and Germans, Yemenis, Abyssinians, private foreign citizens, coastal chiefs and local military strong-men all took part, all embroiled in the same new adversarial, competitive system of international relations. The imperial rage for order was as much about a cultural, systemic shift as it was about recrafted statutes, harmonised constitutions and a global common law. In fact, the creation of a new global "order" was far more chaotic, more fragmented and more inherently disorderly than it was consolidated, rational and universal. Imperial modernity pulled painfully in opposing directions: one towards standardisation and globalisation, and another towards fragmentation, division and war.

We saw in Chapters 1 and 2 of this study that by interceding in regional networks of diplomacy and international relations in the course of negotiations over incidents of shipwreck along the northeastern Somali coast, British colonial officials from Aden cleaved apart existing webs of treaty relations and obligation between regional sovereigns. At first the British met the Majerteen as they found them, on the Majerteen Sultanate's own terms, which was one of shared sovereignty, mutual recognition, permissiveness, gift giving and international cooperation in the maritime arena. The British entered alliances that echoed the terms of earlier agreements between the Majerteen rulers and their royal allies in Mukalla, Muscat and Egypt. But as the century wore on, the British became increasingly imperious and forceful in their dealings with Majerteenia's rulers, reneging on agreements and seeking out new allies from outside the Majerteen royal family who offered more in exchange for less, but at the cost of dishonouring treaties. The consequences of this shift for the conduct of international politics in northeast Africa were profound. For Uthman, the change diminished and hollowed out his historic position and reduced him to the status of a gatekeeper, forced to engage in a logic of violence in exchange for military patronage; to trade arms and attack ships in an effort to maintain his position as a European military client. Similarly, British officials' enthusiasm for forging allegiances with self-styled rulers opened the international arena to a host of military strongmen.

There was a moment in African history during the nineteenth century when Europeans ceased to recognize regional monarchies and their practice of diplomacy as 'functionally equivalent to their own'.[20] As the historian of West Africa Rebecca Shumway remarked of the relations between the British and the Fante on the Gold Coast of West Africa, the shift followed a relatively long period 'when treaty making between African political authorities and Europeans was a legitimate and mutually understood mechanism of diplomacy'.[21] In Chapter 3 we saw that in the southern Tihama, the British and Ottomans bypassed established rulers entirely, fashioning a novel model of international relations based on the distribution of firearms. In response, local coastal upstarts jockeyed to secure patronage. One ruler, Shaykh Nasr Ambari, used this military patronage from the British and Ottomans to establish a quasi-independent chiefdom which at its peak mobilised a following of some 10,000 fighting men and their families.

In Chapter 4, we saw the international arena open to a host of ambitious upstarts who traded on the region's instability, exploiting inter-imperial rivalries for patronage. For much of the decade following his arrival in the region in 1911, Henry de Monfreid existed symbiotically with the French colonial state based in Djibouti. He terrorised merchant shipping in the Gulf of Tadjoura in exchange for payments of protection, ran a multimillion-franc illicit arms business, and channelled arms to French military allies in the Arabian Peninsula to lay the ground for a French colony on the Shaykh Said peninsula. The French colonial state and de Monfreid collaborated to perpetuate the adversarial, chaotic culture of international relations. But de Monfreid fell prey to the very chaos from which he profited. In the mid-1920s de Monfreid clashed with the French Somaliland government under the leadership of Pierre-Amable Chapon-Baissac. In an effort to restore his position, but abandoning the pillar of French strategy in the Red Sea built on expansion into the Arabian Peninsula, de Monfreid sought support from

---

[20] Grovogui, 'Regimes of Sovereignty', pp. 330–331.

[21] Rebecca Shumway, 'Palavers and treaty making in the British acquisition of the Gold Coast Colony (West Africa)', in Saliha Belmessous (ed.), *Empire by Treaty: Negotiating European Expansion, 1600–1900* (Oxford: Oxford University Press, 2014), p. 163.

various international patrons – including Haile Selassie – to oust the Sultan of Tadjoura and install an Abyssinian-Afar government along the northern lip of the Gulf of Tadjoura. In the process, de Monfreid helped create a violent, adversarial and transactional culture of international relations in the region, one in which the participants either won or lost. Some, like Uthman, simply lost. Others, like de Monfreid, won and lost.

Aftershocks

De Monfreid's plan failed, but the chaotic, violent and competitive culture of international relations in the region endured. In spite of the proliferation of cooperative international organisations in the twentieth century, the international regime in the southern Red Sea struggled to shed the violent, retaliatory and contentious culture initiated by colonial conquest in the nineteenth century. Local diplomacy retains a distinctly competitive and militaristic flavour. Organisations promoting international and military cooperation, such as the United Nations, the European Union and NATO, combined with the rise of Chinese and Indian naval strength, checked any single international actor's efforts to dominate the region by strength. But the spirit in which international relations are conducted has changed remarkably little in the last century.

In the 2000s and 2010s, for example, Somali leaders from Puntland – historical Majerteenia – sponsored attacks against international shipping in a pattern reminiscent of events described in Chapters 1 and 2 of this study. On the one hand, the recent Somali upsurge in maritime violence in the region arose because the Puntland government did not have the resources or the access to international bodies such as the International Maritime Organisation to tackle overfishing and toxic waste-dumping in their seas following the collapse of the central Somali state in Mogadishu in the early 1990s. By the early 2000s, a grassroots Somali 'coastguard' emerged to fight off foreign trawlers; in the early 2010s, organised gangs infiltrated the coastguard operations.[22] The gangs took foreign trawlers as prizes; shortly

---

[22] For example, Stefan Eklöf Amirell, 'Maritime piracy in contemporary Africa global and local explanations', *Politique africaine*, 116 (2009), pp. 97–119; Stig Jarle Hansen, 'Debunking the piracy myth: How illegal fishing really interacts with piracy in East Africa', *RUSI Journal*, 156(6) (2011), esp. pp. 26–30; Gary

thereafter they set their sights on larger targets including container ships, which they hijacked for ransom.[23] On the other hand, the speed and scale of the deterioration of security in the northwestern Indian Ocean in the late 2000s can only be fully explained with reference to the divided political landscape which had been established in the colonial period. Rival groups clamoured for a share of ransoms, with hostages often transferred and traded between mutually antagonistic militias in control of different ports along the coast.[24]

De-escalating the situation and re-establishing habits of cooperation and diplomacy have presented a formidable task. Countries with the most to lose in terms of additional cost to trade as well as their military reputations from insecurity in the southern Red Sea – namely the USA and the European nations, alongside China and India – have concentrated on military rather than diplomatic solutions. The main solution to the piracy crisis was the creation of a naval corridor, enforced by international coalitions of navies to protect merchant shipping. Western nations have also pursued tactics that undermine Somalia's sovereignty. United Nations Security Council Resolution 1846, which was passed in 2008 and authorised UN member states to use 'all necessary means' to combat piracy off the coast of Somalia, including by allowing their navies to operate in Somalia's territorial waters, is only the most famous legal example of this.[25]

Moreover, the international legal framework around piracy supports intervention and brinkmanship. Piracy is marginally more tightly

E. Weir, 2009. 'Fish, family, and profit: Piracy and the Horn of Africa', *Naval War College Review*, 62(3), pp. 15–29.

[23] There is a very large literature on contemporary Somali piracy. For example, Jay Bahadur, *The Pirates of Somalia: Inside Their Hidden World* (New York: Pantheon Books, 2011); Jatin Dua, *Captured at Sea: Piracy and Protection in the Indian Ocean* (Berkley: University of California Press, 2019); Awet Tewelde Weldemichael, *Piracy in Somalia: Violence and Development in the Horn of Africa* (Cambridge: Cambridge University Press, 2019).

[24] See Jatin Dua, 'After piracy? Mapping the means and ends of maritime predation in the Western Indian Ocean', *Journal of Eastern African Studies*, 9(3) (2015), pp. 506–507; Stig Jarle Hansen, 'Piracy, security and state formation in the early twenty-first century', in Stefan Amirell and Leos Müller (eds.), *Persistent Piracy: Maritime Violence and State Formation in Global Historical Perspective* (London: Macmillan, 2014), pp. 181–182.

[25] United Nations Security Council Resolution 1846 (2/12/2008). Available at: www.un.org/press/en/2008/sc9514.doc.htm, accessed 05/06/18.

defined today than it was in the nineteenth century: the contemporary legal definition of piracy is 'An illegal act of violence, detention or any act of depredation, committed for private ends ... On the high seas ... in a place outside the jurisdiction of any State.'[26] Yet the concept still offers a considerable margin of discretion to international navies to police the seas, with or without United Nations support. Moreover, since the turn of the millennium, the exigencies of combatting terrorism have provided even more latitude for militarism and realpolitik over diplomatic engagement in Somalia. Similarly, international anti–arms proliferation efforts have failed to achieve their aims in such a chaotic environment. While the UN imposed an arms embargo on Somalia in 1992, requiring all UN member states to limit the sale of arms and ammunition to Somalia, the 2018 Report of the UN Monitoring Group on Somalia documented various types of firearms continuing to enter Somalia via official as well as illicit channels. Indeed, the SEMG estimated that some 75 million rounds of ammunition had entered the country through official channels since 2013.[27]

That both piracy and terrorism offer wide scope to states for Western powers to stage legal interventions against foreign ships and states is clear. By contrast, efforts to bring the region into the diplomatic fold have absorbed far fewer resources than have military efforts. The Somalia conferences in London in 2012 and 2017 were much touted, and in part a diplomatic response to the Somali piracy crisis. But efforts to involve the region have fixated on a modern Western diplomatic style focused on strongarming countries into organising procedurally democratic elections. The approach continues to fail; at the time of writing elections scheduled for 2020 in Somalia looked set for another delay. Moreover, the result of any election is unlikely to legitimate Somalia's politics on either the domestic or the international stage. Rather, the entrenched culture of international relations is of increasingly unappetising-looking carrots and ever-larger sticks.

[26] United Nations Conventions on the High Seas (1958), Art. 15. Available at: http://treaties.un.org/doc/Publication/UNTS/Volume%20450/volume-450-I-6465-English.pdf, accessed 05/06/18.

[27] James Smith, Jay Bahadur, Charles Cater et al., 'Report on Somalia of the Monitoring Group on Somalia and Eritrea', Report No. S/2018/1002 (9/11/2018). Available at: http://undocs.org/Home/Mobile?FinalSymbol=S%2F2018%2F1002&Language=E&DeviceType=Desktop (accessed 13/1/2020).

The same ambivalent relationship between the domestic and international communities continues to bedevil international relations in Yemen. In the 1960s and 1970s, the Saudi Kingdom and the Soviets competed for influence along the southern Red Sea region in a way reminiscent of Anglo-French competition in the nineteenth century, recruiting and then abandoning a range of mutually antagonistic allies across Somalia and Yemen with the sole purpose of undermining each other's local allies.[28] When Cold War tensions dissipated in the mid-1980s, North Yemen's powerful ruler, Ali Abdullah Saleh, replaced one form of foreign patronage with another, signing various natural resource concessions and military contracts with international conglomerates and governments, eventually becoming a stalwart ally of the West in the War on Terror until his overthrow during the Arab Spring in 2011–2012. In the name of defeating international terror – a threat not altogether different to piracy – Saleh channelled military patronage to his allies, spinning a web of political clients who were all ultimately dependent on Saleh personally, in one sense, but also, in a more profound way, on the existence of competitive international interests in the instability of Yemen.[29] The civil war that unfolded following Saleh's overthrow has pitted these local militias against one another in a fight eerily reminiscent of the competition for international patronage in the nineteenth century.

International competition and realpolitik in the southern Red Sea has, if anything, intensified in the post–Cold War era. The international patronage system has created what Alex de Waal describes as a 'political marketplace' for proxies in the region which has proven highly resistant to peace initiatives.[30] This is perhaps most evident in Djibouti, what was French Somaliland. As one journalist reported in 2016, the capital city of Djibouti, Djibouti Port, 'resembles a sprawling garrison'.[31] China, India, North America and Europe all jostle for

---

[28] Roberto Aliboni, *The Red Sea Region: Local Actors and the Superpowers* (London: Routledge, 1985), esp. p. 116; Fred Halliday, *Arabia Without Sultans* (London: Penguin Books Ltd., 1974), pp. 135–136.

[29] Isa Blumi, *Destroying Yemen: What Chaos in Arabia Tells Us about the World* (Berkley: University of California Press, 2018), esp. pp. 142–169.

[30] Alex de Waal, *The Real Politics of the Horn of Africa: Money, War and the Business of Power* (Cambridge: Polity Press, 2015). See also Ginny Hill, 'Yemen: Fear of Failure', Briefing Paper, Chatham House (2010), pp. 3–4.

[31] Katrina Manson, 'Jostling for Djibouti: Why are the world's superpowers jostling for influence in this tiny, impoverished African state?', *Financial Times*

space in the tiny nation and the government derives much of its revenue from military patronage and the leasing of domestic land to foreign militaries. Djibouti was notably the base for thousands of naval personnel during the anti-piracy operations in the late 2000s and early 2010s. For example, Operation Atalanta, the EU Naval Force set up to counter Somali hostage-taking and attacks against ships, involved hundreds of personnel and billions of euros. But Atalanta, like other naval coalitions based in the country, will undoubtedly leave numerous national and private military operations in its wake. The country plays host to an even more fertile mix of competing geopolitical interests today than during the colonial era. It is tempting, therefore, to agree with Martin Wight when he observes that, '[i]nternational anarchy is the one manifestation of the state of nature that is not intolerable.'[32]

But the conclusion is premature. As we have seen, the southern Red Sea has not always been locked in a vicious cycle of inter-state competition, as though in the barrel of a wave; it has not always been, to borrow Acharya and Buzan's phrasing, trapped 'in the realm of survival'.[33] In fact, amid the most recent conflicts in the region, regional links and alliances have resurfaced. As Joseph Kechichian has observed, Oman's Sultan Qaboos – distantly related to the rulers who left Muscat for Zanzibar in the 1840s and who allied with the Majerteen Sultans – approached the country's foreign policy in resolutely independent fashion, often resisting being drawn into regional factions on key Middle Eastern issues, such as over the Iraqi invasion of Kuwait, and even conciliating in the country's approach to Israel. Similarly, Sultan Qaboos was an early advocate of a non-military solution to the collapse of the Somali government in Mogadishu.[34]

A number of regional initiatives involving the contemporary states of the northwestern Indian Ocean littoral have operated along similar lines. For example, the Hormuz Peace Endeavour under the UN Mandate of 1987 was based on commitment to sovereignty, the

---

(1/4/2016). Available at: www.ft.com/content/8c33eefc-f6c1-11e5-803c-d27c7117d132.

[32] Wight, 'Why is there no international relations theory?', p. 45.

[33] Amitav Acharya and Barry Buzan, 'Why is there no non-Western international relations theory? An introduction', in Amitav Acharya and Barry Buzan (eds.), *Non-Western International Relations Theory: Perspectives on and beyond Asia* (Abingdon: Routledge, 2009), pp. 1–25.

[34] Joseph Kechichian, *Oman and the World: The Emergence of an Independent Foreign Policy* (Santa Monica: Rand, 1995), pp. 246, 252–254.

inviolability of international borders and the peaceful resolution of international disputes. In short, it rejected adversarial international relations and led to the Hormuz Community Non-Intervention and Non-Aggression Pact between a number of the northwestern Indian Ocean region's states. In a similar vein in 2001, the Cooperation Council for the Arab States of the Gulf (GCC) set as its goal the creation of a common market, military, currency and customs union between the monarchical states of the Arabian Peninsula.[35] Hormuz and the GCC are only one of a number of regional cooperation organisations.[36] But regional cooperation has proven equally susceptible to the culture of competition and retaliation in the region. Since 2017, the UAE and Saudi Arabia have been in dispute with Qatar, which has driven renewed competition for influence in the southern Red Sea region. Old alliances have furnished new lines of finance in the shipping and port development sector, with the Turkish group al-Bayrak operating the port of Mogadishu since 2014 on the basis of a 55 per cent–45 per cent revenue split between the Turkish company and the Somali national government.[37] Similarly, Dubai's DP World runs Berbera port; P&O Ports, owned by the government of Dubai, runs Bossaso port.[38] Such financial exposure has naturally led GCC countries to take a proactive stance against combatting threats to regional shipping, including Somali piracy.[39]

For every instance of cooperation, a darker side may be found; a counterexample imagined. Financial investment marketed as evidence of cooperation disguises intense geopolitical competition among Middle Eastern states; the rise of capitalism in the Gulf States has created a host of new ethno-economic hierarchies and gender

---

[35] See the Charter of the Gulf Cooperative Council, signed 25/5/1981. Available at: www.gcc-sg.org/en-us/AboutGCC/Pages/Primarylaw.aspx, accessed 11/1/2020.

[36] Others include the Community of Sahel-Saharan States (CEN-SAD); the Indian Ocean Rim Association (IORA); the Inter-Governmental Authority on Development (IGAD); the League of Arab States (LAS); the Nile Basin Initiative (NBI); The Organisation of the Islamic Conference (OIC)

[37] See www.albayrak.com.tr/en/case-studies/port-management/, accessed, 11/1/2020.

[38] See www.dpworld.com/what-we-do/our-locations/Middle-East-Africa/Berbera/somaliland and http://poports.com/media/po-ports-wins-30-year-concession-for-port-of-bosasso-in-puntland, accessed 11/1/2020.

[39] See Afyare Elmi and Said Mohammed, 'Research Paper: The Role of the GCC Countries in Ending Piracy in the Horn of Africa', Arab Center for Research and Policy Studies Doha (2016), pp. 1–16.

inequalities in the region. The issues of piracy and terrorism have compelled foreign states – including states from the Middle East, Europe, America and Asia – to compete for political allies and military proxies in the region, bestowing military patronage that feeds further conflicts. The region remains, in many ways, stuck in the barrel of the colonial wave of international chaos and competition. But as regional governments reassume the independence they lost when British and other imperial forces marginalised them from the international stage a century and a half ago, and the influence of Europe and North America recedes, an increasingly multipolar world presents the possibility for a new kind of international relations. The possibility of greater cohesiveness, of a cooperative rather than a competitive mode of international relations, lies deeply submerged in the history of the region. But whether it can be rediscovered is uncertain.

Appendix

Majerteen-Mukalla Treaty 1875

A treaty concluded in Mukalla on 9 December 1875 between two parties, the naqib of Mukalla, Sultan Uthman Mahmud and Nur Uthman.

There were present the two lordly and honorable [parties], namely, the Naqib Umar b. Salah b. Muhammad b. Abd al-Habib al-Kasadi and the sultans of Mijirtin. The [aforementioned have] settled and acquitted [themselves] in regard to the killing of the Somali who was killed in bandar al-Mukalla, Sacid b. Ibrahim Fahiya from [the] Wabunayya.

Consequently, the said Mijirtin, having [received] satisfaction and a gift, cut themselves off from [the case of] the killing. The aforesaid no longer have a rightful case against the naqib Umar bin Salah, neither a claim nor a petition. Likewise, the naqib Umar b. Salah has dropped charges against [the] Mijirtin in regard to the one whom Rami killed. The naqib Umar b. Salah has cut [himself] off from his claim; he no longer has a claim in [this case]. After that the aforesaid, the naqib Umar b. Salah and the sultans, concluded among themselves obligations, agreements and bonds, to the effect that their condition should be one, and their port cities should be as one. Each of the two parties will have authority [literally, 'his seal'] in [his own] ports over [his own] subjects and others. Whenever a Somali brings a complaint to the sultans, the sultans will bring this to the attention of the naqib Umar b. Salah. If one of the Arabs, or anyone who is subject to the naqib Umar b. Salah, brings a complaint against Somalis to him, the naqib Umar will bring this to the attention of the sultans. Whosoever is an adversary to the naqib Umar will have neither aid nor assistance nor advantage from the Somalis. Whosoever brings an offence to the naqib Umar b. Salah, and comes to their [the sultans'] land, will not be allowed to sell in their land, nor to stay with them. If anyone brings offence to Somalis in the land of the naqib Umar, he will not be allowed to sell, or to stay with him. This took place among the aforesaid, and God is the Guardian, the Guarantor. God is the Best of Witnesses. Umar b. Muhammad witnessed to this. Hamid al-Dhayani witnessed to it.[1]

Playfair Treaty 1866

ENGAGEMENT concluded between LIEUTENANT-COLONEL W. L. MEREWETHER, C. B., POLITICAL RESIDENT, ADEN, and SOOLTAN MAHMOOD BIN-YOOSOOF, CHIEF of the MIJJERTEYN TRIBE of SOMALI and ELDERS of the said TRIBE, 1866.

Influenced by motives of humanity and by a desire to conform to the principles on which the Great English Government is conducted, we lend a willing ear to the proposals of our friend Lieutenant-Colonel William Lockyer Merewether, C. B., Political Resident at Aden, that we should covenant with him and each other to abolish and prohibit the exportation of slaves from any one part of Africa to any other place in Africa or Asia or elsewhere under our authority. We, whose names and seals are set to this bond, do therefore, in the sight of God and of men, solemnly proclaim our intention to prohibit the exportation of slaves from Africa by every means in our power; we will export none ourselves, nor permit our subjects to do so; and any vessel found carrying slaves shall be seized and confiscated, and the slaves shall be released.

20/2/1866 (4th of the month Shawal 1282) at Bunder Muraya.

(Sd.) SOOLTAN MAHMOOD YOOSOOF.

Witnesses to the above :

(Sd.) MOOSA-BIN-YOOSOOF OTHMAN.

([His seal]) SAMUNTAR OTHMAN.

([His seal]) ADREES MAHMOOD.

([His seal]) W. L. MEREWETHER, Lieut.-Col.*

Political Resident, Aden.

(True copy.)

---

[1] The above is Lidwien Kapteijns and Jay Spaulding's translation in, 'Indian Ocean diplomacy: Two documents relating to the nineteenth-century Mijertein coast', *Sudanic Africa*, 13 (2002), pp. 25–26. The original (Arabic, and French translation) may be found in Révoil, *Voyages*, p. 207.

(Sd.) W. L. MEREWETHER, Lieut.-Col., Political Resident, Aden.
Confirmed by order of the Governor-General in Council, dated the
16th May 1866.[2]

Rejected Goodfellow Treaty 1879

Thus Goodfellow returned to Aden with the following agreement,
signed in the name of Uthman Mahmud, 'Sultan of the Mijjertain
tribe'.

1. To provide protection to any ship and any crew of any foreign
   power wrecked on Majerteen shores
2. To transport such wrecked crews to Aden if they will it
3. To guard any abandoned ship and give speedy notice of such a
   wreck to the Governor of Aden
4. To wait for instructions before relinquishing guard of the ship
5. To allow 'the Great Government' [i.e. the British] to erect a light
   house or beacon and to protect any such structure
6. For the above to receive a yearly stipend of 360 [MT] dollars as well
   as any salvage to which they are entitled according to British law,
   adjudicated by a British representative or the Governor of Aden
   who will determine what is customary.[3]

Draft Captain King Treaty 1884

'Influenced by motives of friendship and with a desire to conform to
the principles on which the great British Government is conducted, and
wishing to preserve peace and to foster security on our shores, we, the
Chiefs of the Mijerteyn Somal, Othman Mahmood, Sultan of the
Mijerteyn Tribe, ... etc... Yousuf Ali Yousuf, Gulaid Yousuf ...
[agree that]

---

[2] Aitchison (ed.), *A Collection of Treaties, Vol. XIII*, p. 222. The treaty can also be
found in an earlier volume (VII) of Aitchison's collection, when it was placed in
the Persian-Omani volume. See Sir Charles Aitchison (ed.), *A Collection of
Treaties, Engagements, and Sunnuds, Relating to India and Neighbouring
Countries, Vol. VII, the Treaties Relating to the Bombay Presidency* (Calcutta:
Military Orphan Press, 1865), p. 323.

[3] IOR R/20/A/512, Vol. 810 Africa, Mijjertain – Draft of agreement concluded
between the sultan and family and Major Goodfellow on behalf of Government
for protection of ships wrecked – also extent of territorial jurisdiction.

1) Protection shall be afforded to all victims of shipwreck on their shores and the crew shall receive good treatment. This applies to British vessels, subjects and the subjects and vessels of other powers.
2) Should the master or crew of any wreck wish to continue to Aden we will aid them.
3) If a wreck on their shores is abandoned, they will protect the wreck and notify Aden.
4) The wreck will be protected until they receive instructions from Aden.
5) In exchange for 'good behaviour' and observance of the treaty, the Elders shall receive a stipend of $360 per year as well as any salvage from the wreck in accordance with the decision of the Resident of Aden.[4]

ENGAGEMENT *entered into by the* MIJJERTEYN SOMALIS, 1884. [The Captain King Treaty]

ARTICLE 1.

That in the event of any steamer, or ship, or other vessel belonging to the British Government, or to a British subject, or to any other power, or to the subjects of any other power, being wrecked upon our shores or in distress, protection shall be accorded to her and to all on board, and the latter shall receive good treatment.

ARTICLE 2.

That should the master, crew, or passengers of any wreck or casualty wish to proceed to Aden, we will protect them and conduct them thither, or give them the best means in our power of proceeding there.

ARTICLE 3.

That should any steamer, ship, or vessel be wrecked, suffer casualty, or be abandoned, we will not only protect and guard such steamer, ship, or vessel from plunder and wilful damage to our utmost ability, but we will give speedy notice of such wreck to the Political Resident of Aden.

---

[4] IOR R/20/E/123, Treaty, signed J. S. King, Anthony Gwyn, J. W. Yerbury and Ripon, Viceroy and Governor General of India, 29/7/1884.

ARTICLE 4.

That such steamer, ship, or vessel will be protected by us as aforesaid until instructions in reply to our said notice are given and received from the Political Resident of Aden.

ARTICLE 5.

That for such acts of good-will and friendship, and as imposing on us, our heirs and successors, the obligation aforementioned, we shall receive from the British Government, conditionally on our good behaviour and so long as we act strictly up to our obligation, a yearly stipend of 360 $ (three hundred and sixty dollars). And we shall also expect to receive such salvage as by any right according to British law we may be entitled to; and according as the Great British Government, through their representative, the Political Resident of Aden for the time being, may on the merits of each case determine by the custom in such cases.

In token of the conclusion of this lawful and honourable bond, Othman Mahmood, Sultan of the Mijjerteyn tribe, Noor Othman, Ismail Othman, Samuntar Othman, Ahmed Mahmood, Hajji Idrees Mahmood, Mahammad Shirwa Noor, Yousuf Mahmood, Yousuf Ali Yousuf, Gulaid Yousuf and Hajji Mahammad Fahiya, Elders, on behalf of themselves, their heirs and successors.

1/5/1884, equivalent to the 5th day of the month Rajab 1301 A H., at Bunder Muraya.[5]

German East Africa Company Treaty with Yusuf 'Ali 1886

Jusef Ali Jusef, Sultan of the Somali of Hobga, whose dominion extends from the sea-coast twenty-five days' journey inland, and from Hobga to the port of Warscheich, near Makdischo [has concluded the following Treaty with] Claus von Andersen, the employé of Mr. Charles Peters and the German East African Company, on the 26th November 1885.

Henceforth the Sultan Jusef Ali will be the friend of Charles Peters and his Company, and gives him permission to bring his countrymen if there should be anywhere here tracts devoid (of inhabitants) and

---

[5] C. U. Aitchison, *A Collection of Treaties, Engagements and Sandads Relating to India and Neighbouring Countries, Vol. XIII* (Calcutta: Superintendent Government Printing, 1909), pp. 223-224.

provided with water. Should he desire to cultivate the land, he is allowed to do so; should there be water in any given place, and he may desire to conduct it to the sea, he is permitted to do so; should he desire to fish in the rivers, or to travel about or to cut wood, or shoot and hunt, or to excavate iron or other material, or to search for coal, he is allowed to do all these things and everything thereto appertaining; if his people desire to trade in the country they may do so; and should any one seek to do them injury, or to kill them, they may defend themselves; and if people who are charged with a mission of the Sultan should be travelling anywhere, and some one attempts to inter- fere with them by force in that case Charles Peters, and similarly the Sultan of the Germans, shall come forward as the opponent of such a person. And should Charles Peters desire to send ships to the harbour to Hobga, he may do so. In consideration of the above the Sultan Jusef is to be paid yearly, in Alula or Hobga, 2,000 reals.

Approved.

Signed Jusef Ali Jusef.[6]

German East Africa Company Treaty with Sultan Uthman 1886

The dominion of Sultan Otman Mahmud Jusef, Ruler over the whole Medschertin people, extends from East Cape along the sea-coast to the port of Ziada, and twenty days' journey inland, further in the direction of Cape Hafun, which lies midway in the line.

The architect Horneche, in the name of his Prinipal, Duk Dekta Kartal Biles, who is our Associate;

We undertake to protect from injury the maritime trade and the ships of the Sultan against all Christians, Arabs, and others. He accepts this, and in return undertakes to support the crews of vessels stranded on the coasts of his country, to renounce his rights appertaining to the foreshores, and to forward the rescued crews to Aden. His Highness the Sultan shall receive therefore 1,900 reals (Maria Theresa dollars) which we shall pay to him, if they are not paid by the English. Upon this subject an understanding has come between us.

---

[6] IOR R/20/A/1171, Red Sea and Somali Coast – Confidential – [Section 288], Appendix FF. Translation of the German Translation of the Arabic Text of Treaty between the Representative of the East African Company and the Somali Sultan Jusef.

If Duk's ships desire to enter the ports of the Sultan for the purposes of trade they shall be allowed to do so.

Should our Principal come in order to enter upon the land in any chosen districts within the territories of the Sultan, the Sultan shall permit him to so. Should he desire to shoot birds, or to cut firewood, or to dig in a mountain in order to search for iron, or to erect shops for the purpose of selling and buying, or to make a garden and to plant it, he shall be allowed to do so.

If it please God to call the Sultan from this life, and he leaves children, and should one of the Christian [?] Chiefs come with the intention of robbing the children of the Sultan of their property, we will render assistance against such a proceeding.

The Sultan Otman has confirmed this Treaty, which was drawn up on Sunday, the 26th Dul Kada (des Jahres) 1323.

Signed Sultan Otman Mahummad Hasan.[7]

Filonardi's Treaty with Sultan Uthman Mahmud Yusuf 1889

Treaty of Protection between Italy and the Sultan of the Migertini (Mijjertayn Somalis). Signed at Bender Alula, 7th April 1889.

We, Sultan Osman Mahmud Jusuf, Sultan of all the Migertini, have of our own free will put to this Act our hand and seal.

We have placed our country and all our possessions, from Ras Auad to Ras-el-Kyle (Uadi Nogal being the farthest limit), under the protection and government of His Majesty Umberto I, King of Italy; and this we have done through the Representatives of His Majesty the King, viz:

V. Filonardi, Italian Consul at Zanzibar; Captain Amoretti, commanding his Majesty's ship *Rapido*; and Captain Porcelli, commanding His Majesty's ship *Staffeta*.

We have agreed that the Italian flag shall be hoisted in the countries above mentioned.

We declare that we will not make Treaties or Contracts with any other Governments or persons.

---

[7] IOR R/20/A/1171, Red Sea and Somali Coast – Confidential – [Section 288], Appendix GG. Translation of the German Translation of the Arabic Text of Treaty concluded with the Sultan of Medschertin Somali.

We declare besides, that we will prevent as far as we are able, all unjust acts directed against Italian subjects and their friends in all our possessions.

We have signed this Act of our own free will and full understanding, and this which we have signed will remain binding upon us, our heirs, brothers, subjects, and their descendants.

We append our signatures and seals to this Act in the full possession of our faculties of mind and body ...

Osman Mahmud Jusuf, Sultan of the Migertini
Jusuf Ali Jusuf, Sultan of Oppia.[8]

Pestalozza Treaty with Sultan Uthman Mahmud Yusuf 1902

Further to the former Convention between Italians and Sultan Uthman Mahmoud of 7/4/1889, as well as Sultan Uthman Mahmoud's declaration to the Italian Government dated 16/11/1894, Sultan Uthman confirms that he has contravened the terms of these agreements, as a result of misunderstanding. Thus, Cav. Giulio Pestalozza and Sultan Uthman Mahmoud, on behalf of his sons and successors, sign a new agreement to the effect that:

1) He places himself, his sultanate and territory under the Protection of the Italian govt. He hoists the Italian flag at all ports of call along his shores.
2) All Majerteen Sambuks should register with the Italian govt and fly the Italian flag.
3) The Sultan agrees to protect all Italians in his territory, although the Italian govt reserves jurisdiction over them.
4) The Sultan and his subjects should afford all assistance to shipwrecks on their shores. The Sultan will have for himself and subjects adequate recompense for all aid, per the decision of the Italian Consul at Aden.
5) The Sultan forbids the import of arms and ammunition to his territory. All imports must first have the authorisation of the Italian govt – on pain of a fine not less than 200 Rs per gun. The

---

[8] MAESS ASMAI Posizione 59/ Numero 1 – Somalia Settentrionale, 1886–1889, Fasciolo 5, Trattato col Sultano di Obbia.

Sultan shall be personally responsible for payment of this fine in cases where the culprits flee.

6) The Italians may build a light house at Cape Guardafui. The rights and agreements signed with Bunder Felah and Bunder Alula remain in force.[9]

[9] IOR R/20/E/236, Letter, British Ambassador, Rome, to the Foreign Office, London, 23/11/1901, forwards Italian Convention between the Italian Government and the Sultan of the Mijjertines on 18/8/1901.

Bibliography

A New Map of Arabia, Including Egypt, Abyssinia, the Red Sea, from the Latest Authorities [F-1–1] (1/1), Qatar National Library, 12886, in Qatar Digital Library. Available at: www.qdl.qa/archive/qnlhc/12886.1. (Accessed 29 July 2020).

Abir, Mordichai, 'The Ethiopian slave trade and its relation to the Islamic world', in John R. Willis (ed.), *Slaves and Slavery in Muslim Africa* (London: Frank Cass, 1985), pp. 123–136.

Abulafia, David, *The Boundless Sea: A Human History of the Oceans* (Oxford: Oxford University Press, 2019).

Acharya, Amitav and Barry Buzan, *Non-Western International Relations Theory: Perspectives on and beyond Asia* (Abingdon: Routledge, 2016).

'Why is there no non-Western international relations theory? An introduction', in Amitav Acharya and Barry Buzan (eds.), *Non-Western International Relations Theory: Perspectives on and beyond Asia* (Abingdon: Routledge, 2016), pp. 1–25.

Ahmad, Abdussamad H., 'Ethiopian slave exports at Matamma, Massawa and Tajura, c. 1830–1885', in William Gervase Clarence-Smith (ed.), *The Economics of the Indian Ocean Slave Trade* (London: Frank Cass, 1989), pp. 93–102.

Ahram, Ariel and Charles King, 'The warlord as arbitrageur', *Theory and Society*, 41(2) (2012), pp. 169–186.

Alexandrowicz, C. H., *An Introduction to the History of the Law of Nations in the East Indies: 16th, 17th and 18th Centuries* (Oxford: Clarendon Press, 1967).

Aliboni, Roberto, *The Red Sea Region: Local Actors and the Superpowers* (London: Routledge, 1985).

Allen, James de Vere, 'Habash, Habshi, Sidi, Sayyid', in Jeffrey C. Stone (ed.), *Africa and the Sea: Proceedings of a Colloquium at the University of Aberdeen, March 1984* (Aberdeen: Aberdeen University African Studies Group, 1985), pp. 131–151.

Alpers, Edward, 'Piracy and the Indian Ocean', *Journal of African Development*, 13(1 & 2) (2011), pp. 17–38.

Amirell, Stefan Eklöf, 'Maritime piracy in contemporary Africa global and local explanations', *Politique africaine*, 116 (2009), pp. 97–119.

Anand, Ram Prakash, *Origin and Development of the Law of the Sea: History of International Law Revisited* (The Hague: Martinus Nijhoff, 1983).

Anderson, Clare, *Subaltern Lives: Biographies of Colonialism in the Indian Ocean, 1790–1920* (Cambridge: Cambridge University Press, 2012).

Anghie, Antony, *Imperialism, Sovereignty and the Making of International Law* (Cambridge: Cambridge University Press, 2005).

Anon., *The Somali Peninsula: A New Light on Imperial Motives* (Mogadishu and London: Information Services of the Somali Government, 1962).

Armitage, David, 'The elephant and the whale: Empires of land and sea', *Journal for Maritime Research*, 9(1) (2007), pp. 23–36.

Ashley, Richard K., 'The poverty of neo-realism', *International Organisation*, 38(2) (1984), pp. 225–286.

Austen, Ralph, 'The Islamic Red Sea slave trade: An effort at quantification', in Robert L. Hess (ed.), *Proceedings of the Fifth International Conference on Ethiopian Studies* (Chicago: University of Illinois Press, 1979), pp. 443–467.

Bahadur, Jay, *The Pirates of Somalia: Inside Their Hidden World* (New York: Pantheon Books, 2011).

Baldry, John, 'al-Yaman and the Turkish occupation 1849–1914', *Arabica*, 23(2) (1976), pp. 156–196.

'Anglo-Italian rivalry in Yemen and 'Asīr 1900–1934', *Die Welt des Islams*, 17(1/4) (1976–1977), pp. 155–193.

'British naval operations against Turkish Yaman 1914–1919', *Arabica*, 25 (2) (1978), pp. 148–197.

'The French claim to Sayh [Shaykh] Sa'id (Yaman) and its international repercussions, 1868–1939', *Zeitschrift der Deutschen Morgenlandischen Gesellschaft*, 133(1) (1983), pp. 93–133.

'The Yamani island of Kamaran during the Napoleonic Wars', *Middle Eastern Studies*, 16(3) (1980), pp. 246–266.

Bang, Anne K., *The Idrissi State in 'Asir, 1906–1934: Politics, Religion and Personal Prestige as Statebuilding Factors in Early Twentieth-Century Arabia* (Bergen: Centre for Middle Eastern and Islamic Studies, 1996).

Barendse, Rene J., *The Arabian Seas: The Indian Ocean World of the Seventeenth Century* (Abingdon: Routledge, 2015, first published 2002).

'Trade and state in the Arabian Seas: A survey from the fifteenth to the eighteenth century', *Journal of World History*, 11(2) (2000), pp. 173–225.

Battera, Francesco, *Della tribù allo Stato nella Somalia nord-orientale: il caso dei Sultani di Hobiyo e Majerteen, 1880–1930* (Trieste: University of Trieste, 2004).

Bayart, Jean-François, 'Africa in the world: A history of extraversion', *African Affairs*, 99(395) (2000), pp. 217–267.

Bayart, Jean-François, Stephen Ellis and Béatrice Hibou, 'From kleptocracy to the felonious state?', in Jean-François Bayart, Stephen Ellis and Béatrice Hibou (eds.), *The Criminalization of the State in Africa* (Bloomington: Indiana University Press, 1999), pp. 1–31.

Bayly, Christopher A., *Imperial Meridian: The British Empire and the World, 1780–1830* (Harlow: Pearson, 1989).

The New Cambridge History of India: Indian Society and the Making of the British Empire (Cambridge: Cambridge University Press, 1988).

Beachey, Ray W., 'The arms trade in East Africa in the late nineteenth century', *Journal of African History*, 3(3) (1962), pp. 451–467.

Beehler, W. H., *The History of the Italian Turkish War: September 29, 1911 to October 18, 1912* (Annapolis: Proceedings of the United States Naval Institute, 1913).

Bemath, Abdul S., 'The Sayyid and Saalihiya Tariga reformist, anticolonial hero in Somalia', in Said S. Samatar (ed.), *In the Shadow of Conquest: Islam in Colonial Northeast Africa* (Trenton: Red Sea Press, 1992), pp. 33–47.

Benton, Lauren, 'Abolition and imperial law, 1790–1820', *The Journal of Imperial and Commonwealth History*, 39(3) (2011), pp. 355–374.

A Search for Sovereignty: Law and Geography in European Empires, 1400–1900 (Cambridge: Cambridge University Press, 2010).

Law and Colonial Cultures: Legal Regimes in World History, 1400–1900 (Cambridge: Cambridge University Press, 2001).

'Legal spaces of empire: Piracy and the origins of ocean regionalism', *Comparative Studies in Society and History*, 47 (4) (2005), pp. 700–724.

Benton, Lauren and Lisa Ford, *Rage for Order: The British Empire and the Origins of International Law, 1800–1850* (Cambridge, MA: Harvard University Press, 2016).

Bethe-Selassié, Mickaël, *La jeune Ethiopie: Un haut-fonctionnaire éthiopien Berhanä-Marqos Wäldä-Tsadeq (1892–1943)* (Paris: L'Harmattan, 2009).

Bischoff, Paul-Henri, Kwesi Aning and Amitav Acharya, *Africa in Global International Relations: Emerging Approaches to Theory and Practice* (Abingdon: Routledge, 2016).

Bishara, Fahad, *A Sea of Debt: Law and Economic Life in the Western Indian Ocean, 1780–1950* (Cambridge: Cambridge University Press, 2017).

'"No country but the ocean": Reading international law from the deck of an Indian Ocean dhow, ca. 1900', *Comparative Studies in Society and History*, 60(2) (2018), pp. 338–366.

'Paper routes: Inscribing Islamic law across the nineteenth-century western Indian Ocean', *Law and History Review*, 32(4) (2014), pp. 797–820.

Blumi, Isa, *Destroying Yemen: What Chaos in Arabia Tells Us about the World* (Berkley: University of California Press, 2018).

Foundations of Modernity: Human Agency and the Imperial State (New York: Routledge, 2011).

Rethinking the Late Ottoman Empire: A Comparative Social and Political History of Albania and Yemen, 1878–1918 (Istanbul: The Isis Press, 2003).

Blyth, Robert J., 'Aden, British India and the development of steam power in the Red Sea, 1825–1839', in David Killingray, Margarette Lincoln and Nigel Rigby (eds.), *Maritime Empires: British Imperial Maritime Trade in the Nineteenth Century* (Woodbridge: The Boydell Press, 2004), pp. 68–83.

Bois, Paul, *Le grand siècle des Messageries Maritimes* (Marseilles: Chambre de Commerce et de l'Industrie Marseille-Provence, 1992).

Bose, Sugata, *A Hundred Horizons: The Indian Ocean in the Age of Global Empire* (Cambridge, MA: Harvard University Press, 2006).

Braudel, Fernand, Siân Reynolds (trans.), *The Mediterranean and the Mediterranean World in the Age of Philip II, Volume 1* (London: University of California Press, 1995).

Bridges, Roy, 'The visit of Frederick Forbes to the Somali Coast in 1833', *The International Journal of African Historical Studies*, 19(4) (1986), pp. 679–691.

Brunschwig, Henri, 'Une colonie inutile: Obock, 1862–1888', *Cahiers d'études africaines*, 8(29) (1968), pp. 32–47.

Buckler, F. W., 'India and the Far East 1848–1858', in Adolphus W. Ward and George P. Gooch (ed.), *The Cambridge History of British Foreign Policy 1783–1919, Vol. 2* (Cambridge: Cambridge University Press, 1923), pp. 199–219.

Bull, Hedley, *The Anarchical Society of States: A Study of Order in World Politics Fourth Edition* (London: Palgrave Macmillan, 2011, first published 1977).

Cable, Boyd, *A Hundred Year History of the P & O: Peninsular and Oriental Steam Navigation Company, 1837–1937* (London: Ivor Nicholson and Watson Limited, 1937).

Cahen, Claude, 'Himaya', in *The Encyclopaedia of Islam, Vol. 3* (Leiden: Brill, 1971), p. 394.

'Himaya: Notes pour l'histoire de la himaya', in Louis Massignon (ed.), *Mélanges Louis Massignon, Vol. 1* (Damascus: Institut Français, 1961), pp. 287–293.

Cairoli, Aldo, *Le origini dei protettorati italiani sulla Somalia settentrionale, 1884–1891* (Trieste: University of Trieste, 1987).

Camelin, Sylvanie, 'Reflections on the system of social stratification in Hadhramaut', in Ulrike Freitag and William Gervase Clarence-Smith (eds.), *Hadhrami Traders, Scholars and Statesmen in the Indian Ocean, 1750–1960* (Leiden: Brill, 1997), pp. 147–156.

Casale, Giancarlo, 'Global politics in the 1580s: One canal, twenty thousand cannibals, and an Ottoman plot to rule the world', *Journal of World History*, 18(3) (2007), pp. 267–296.

Cassenelli, Lee V., *The Shaping of Somali Society: Reconstructing the Past of a Pastoral People, 1600–1900* (Philadelphia: University of Pennsylvania Press, 1982).

Chabal, Patrick and Jean-Pascal Daloz, *Africa Works: Disorder as Political Instrument* (Oxford: James Currey, 1999).

Chaudhuri, Kitri N., *The Trading World of Asia and the English East India Company* (Cambridge: Cambridge University Press, 1978).

Trade and Civilization in the Indian Ocean: An Economic History from the Rise of Islam to 1750 (Cambridge: Cambridge University Press, 1985).

Chew, Emrys, *Arming the Periphery: The Arms Trade in the Indian Ocean during the Age of Global Empire* (London: Palgrave Macmillan, 2012).

Chittick, H. Neville, 'An archaeological reconnaissance in the Horn: The British Somali expedition, 1975', *Azania*, 11 (1976), pp. 117–133.

Clapham, Christopher, *Africa and the International System: The Politics of State Survival* (Cambridge: Cambridge University Press, 2005).

Clausewitz, Carl von, J. J. Graham (trans.), *On War* (Ware, Herts: Wordsworth Editions, 1997).

Cohn, Bernard S., *Colonialism and Its Forms of Knowledge: The British in India* (Princeton: Princeton University Press, 1996).

Comaroff, John L. and Jean Comaroff, 'Law and disorder in the postcolony: An introduction', in Jean Comaroff and John L. Comaroff (eds.), *Law and Disorder in the Postcolony* (Chicago: University of Chicago Press, 2006), pp. 1–56.

Cooley, Alexander and Hendrik Spruyt, *Contracting States: Sovereign Transfers in International Relations* (Princeton: Princeton University Press, 2009).

Cooper, Frederick, *Africa Since 1940: The Past of the Present* (Cambridge: Cambridge University Press, 2002).

Plantation Slavery on the East Coast of Africa (New Haven: Yale University Press, 1977).

Dalrymple, William, *The Anarchy: The Relentless Rise of the East India Company* (London: Bloomsbury, 2019).

Darwin, John, 'Imperialism and the Victorians: The dynamics of territorial expansion', *The English Historical Review*, 112(447) (1997), pp. 614–642.

Deringil, Selim, "They live in a state of nomadism and savagery': The Late Ottoman Empire and the post-colonial debate', *Comparative Studies in Society and History*, 45(2) (2003), pp. 311–342.

Dirks, Nicholas B., *The Scandal of Empire: India and the Creation of Imperial Britain* (Cambridge, MA: Harvard University Press, 2006).

Dixon, Jeffrey S. and Meredith Reid Sarkees, *A Guide to Intra-State Wars: An Examination of Civil Wars, 1816–2014.* Correlates of War Series (Thousand Oaks: SAGE Publications, 2016).

Dresch, Paul, *A History of Modern Yemen* (Cambridge: Cambridge University Press, 2002).

Dua, Jatin, 'After piracy? Mapping the means and ends of maritime predation in the Western Indian Ocean', *Journal of Eastern African Studies*, 9 (3) (2015), pp. 505–521.

'A sea of trade and a sea of fish: Piracy and protection in the western Indian Ocean', *Journal of Eastern African Studies*, 7(2) (2013), pp. 353–370.

Captured at Sea: Piracy and Protection in the Indian Ocean (Berkley: University of California Press, 2019).

Dubois, Colette, 'The Red Sea ports during the revolution in transportation, 1800–1914', in Leila Tarazi Fawaz and C. A. Bayly (eds.), *Modernity and Culture: From the Mediterranean to the Indian Ocean* (New York: Columbia University Press, 2002), pp. 58–74.

'Une traite tardive en Mer Rouge méridioniale: la route des esclaves du golfe de Tadjoura, 1880–1936', in Henri Medard, Marie-Laure Derat, Thomas Vernet, Marie Pierre Ballarin (eds.), *Traites et esclavages en Afrique orientale et dans l'océan Indien* (Paris: Karthala, 2013), pp. 197–222.

Dunn, Kevin C. and Timothy M. Shaw, *Africa's Challenge to International Relations Theory* (Basingstoke: Palgrave Macmillan, 2001).

Durrill, Wayne K., 'Atrocious misery: The African origins of famine in northern Somalia, 1839–1884', *American Historical Review*, 91(2) (1986), pp. 287–306.

Ehret, Christopher, *History and the Testimony of Language* (Berkley: University of California Press, 2011).

Elmi, Afyare and Said Mohammed, 'Research paper: The role of the GCC Countries in ending piracy in the Horn of Africa', Arab Center for Research and Policy Studies Doha (2016), pp. 1–16.

Ewald, Janet, 'Crossers of the sea: Slaves, freedmen, and other migrants in the northwestern Indian Ocean, c. 1750–1914', *The American Historical Review*, 105(1) (February, 2000), pp. 75–89.

'The Nile Valley system and the Red Sea slave trade, 1820–1880', in William Gervase Clarence-Smith (ed.), *The Economics of the Indian Ocean Slave Trade* (London: Frank Cass, 1989), pp. 71–91.

Farah, Caesar E., *The Sultan's Yemen: Nineteenth-Century Challenges to Ottoman Rule* (London: I. B. Tauris, 2002).

Farah, Nuruddin, *Crossbones* (London: Penguin Books, 2011).

Fattovich, Radolfo, 'The contacts between southern Arabia and the Horn of Africa in Late Prehistoric and Early Historical Times: A view from Africa', in A. Avanzini (ed.), *Profumi d'Arabia* (Rome: 'L'Erma' di Bretschneider, 1997), pp. 273–286.

'The development of ancient states in the northern Horn of Africa, c. 3000 BC–AD 1000: An archaeological outline', *Journal of World Prehistory*, 23(3) (2010), pp. 145–175.

Feierman, Steven, 'A century of ironies in East Africa, 1780–1890', in Philip Curtin, Steven Feierman, Leonard Thompson, et al., *African History: From Earliest Times to Independence* (New York: Longmann, 1995), pp. 352–376.

Fisher, Michael H., 'Diplomacy in India, 1526–1858', in H. V. Bowen, Elizabeth Mancke and John G. Reid (eds.), *Britain's Oceanic Empire: Atlantic and Indian Ocean Worlds, c. 1550–1850* (Cambridge: Cambridge University Press, 2012), pp. 249–281.

Fleisher, Jeffrey, Paul J. Lane, Adria LaViolette et al., 'When did the Swahili become maritime?', *American Anthropologist*, 117(1) (2015), pp. 100–115.

Fletcher, Pascal and Louise Ireland (eds.), 'Somali pirate kingpins enjoy "Impunity": UN expert', *Reuters* (18/7/2012). Available at: www .reuters.com/article/uk-somalia-un-piracy-idUKBRE86G0ZF20120718?edition-redirect=uk

Fontrier, Marc, *Abou-Bakr Ibrahim: Pacha de Zeila, Marchand d'esclaves; Commerce et diplomatie dans le Golfe de Tadjoura, 1840–1885* (Paris: Harmattan, 2003).

Gallagher, John and Ronald Robinson, 'The imperialism of free trade', *The Economic History Review*, 6(1) (1953), pp. 1–15.

Gardiner, Alan H., 'New literary works from ancient Egypt', *The Journal of Egyptian Archaeology*, 1(1) (1914), pp. 20–36.

Gavin, R. J., *Aden under British Rule 1839–1967* (London: C. Hurst & Company, 1975).

Gellner, Ernest, 'Tribalism and the state in the Middle East', in Philip S. Khoury and Joseph Kostiner (eds.), *Tribes and State Formation in the Middle East* (Berkley: California University Press, 1990), pp. 109–126.

Ghanem, Isam, 'The legal history of 'Asir (al-Mikhlaf al-Sulaymani)', *The Arab Law Quarterly*, 5(3) (1990), pp. 211–214.

Ghosh, Amitav, *Sea of Poppies* (London: Penguin Books, 2009).

Gilbert, Erik, *Dhows and the Colonial Economy of Zanzibar, 1860–1970* (Oxford: James Currey, 2004).

'Review: Abdul Sheriff, dhow cultures and the Indian Ocean: Cosmopolitanism, commerce and Islam', *Journal of the Economic and Social History of the Orient*, 54(2) (2011), pp. 278–280.

Gjersø, Jonas Fossli, 'The scramble for East Africa: British motives reconsidered, 1884–95', *Journal of Imperial and Commonwealth History*, 43 (5) (2015), pp. 831–860.

Glassman, Jonathon, *Feasts and Riot: Revelry, Rebellion and Popular Consciousness on the Swahili Coast, 1856–1888* (Portsmouth, NH: Heinemann, 1995).

War of Words, War of Stones: Racial Thought and Violence in Colonial Zanzibar (Bloomington: Indiana University Press, 2011).

Goitien, Shlomo, 'Portrait of a medieval India trader: Three letters from the Cairo Geniza', *Bulletin of the School of Oriental and African Studies*, 50 (1987), pp. 449–464.

Gommans, Jos, *Mughal Warfare: Indian Frontiers and High Roads to Empire, 1500–1700* (London: Routledge, 2002).

González-Ruibal, Alfredo, Jorge de Torres, Manuel Antonio Franco et al., 'Exploring long distance trade in Somaliland (AD 1000–1900): Preliminary results from the 2015–2016 field seasons', *Azania*, 52(2) (2017), pp. 135–172.

Graham, Gerald S., *Britain in the Indian Ocean: A Study of Maritime Enterprise, 1810–1850* (Oxford: The Clarendon Press, 1967).

Grandclément, Daniel, *L'incroyable Henry de Monfreid* (Paris: Grasset, 1998).

Grant, Jonathan A., *Rulers, Guns and Money: The Global Arms Trade in the Age of Imperialism* (Cambridge, MA: Harvard University Press, 2007).

Green, Molly, *Catholic Pirates and Greek Merchants: A Maritime History of the Mediterranean* (Princeton: Princeton University Press, 2010).

Griffiths, John, 'What is legal pluralism', *The Journal of Legal Pluralism and Unofficial Law*, 18(24) (1986), pp. 1–55.

Grovogui, Siba N., *Beyond Eurocentrism and Anarchy: Memories of International Order and Institutions* (New York: Palgrave Macmillan, 2006).

Grovogui, Siba, 'Regimes of sovereignty: International morality and the African condition', *European Journal of International Relations*, 8(3) (2002), pp. 315–338.

Guilfoyle, Douglas, 'Somali Pirate Skiff', in Jessie Hohmann and Daniel Joyce (eds.), *International Law's Objects* (Oxford: Oxford University Press, 2018), pp. 443–452.

Gunder Frank, Andre, *ReORIENT: Global Economy in the Asian Age* (Berkley: University of California Press, 1998).

Gupta, Ashin Das, *Indian Merchants and the Decline of Surat, c. 1700–1750* (Wiesbaden: Franz Steiner Verlag, 1979).

Merchants of Maritime India, 1500–1800 (London: Routledge, 1994).

'Trade and politics in eighteenth century India', in Muzaffar Alam and Sanjay Subrahmanyam (eds.), *The Mughal State, 1526–1750* (Delhi: Oxford University Press, 1998), pp. 181–214.

Hall, Richard, *Empires of The Monsoon: A History of the Indian Ocean and Its Invaders* (London: HarperCollins, 1996).

Halliday, Fred, *Arabia Without Sultans* (London: Penguin Books, 1974).

Hamilton, David, 'Imperialism ancient and modern: A study of British attitudes to the claims to sovereignty to the northern Somali coastline', *Journal of Ethiopian Studies*, 5(11) (1967), pp. 9–35.

Hamilton, H. C. and W. Falconer (trans.), *The Geography of Strabo: In Three Volumes* (London: Henry G. Bohn, 1857).

Hansen, Stig Jarle, 'Debunking the piracy myth: How illegal fishing really interacts with piracy in East Africa', *RUSI Journal*, 156(6) (2011), pp. 26–31.

'Piracy, security and state formation in the early twenty-first century', in Stefan Amirell and Leos Müller (eds.), *Persistent Piracy: Maritime Violence and State Formation in Global Historical Perspective* (London: Macmillan, 2014), pp. 175–188.

Hansen, Thomas Blom and Finn Stepputat, 'Sovereignty revisited', *Annual Review of Anthropology*, 35 (2006), pp. 295–315.

Hathaway, Jane and Karl K. Barbir (contrb.), *The Arab Lands under Ottoman Rule, 1516–1800* (Harlow: Pearson, 2008).

Healy, D. C. S., 'British perceptions of treaties with the Somalis, 1884–1897', in Hussein M. Adam and Charles L. Geshekter (eds.), *Proceedings of the First International Conference of Somali Studies* (Atlanta: Scholars Press, 1992), pp. 167–205.

Healy, Sally and Ginny Hill, 'Yemen and Somalia: Terrorism, Shadow Networks and the Limitations of Statebuilding', Briefing Paper, Chatham House (2010).

Hébié, Mamadou, *Souveraineté territoriale par traité: une étude des accords entre puissances coloniales et entités politiques locales* (Paris: Presses Universitaires de France, 2015).

Heeren, Arnold Hermann Ludwig, *Handbuch der Geschichte des europäischen Staatensystems und seiner Kolonien* (Göttingen: Johann Friedrich Bower, 1830).

Hess, Robert, *Italian Colonialism in Somalia* (Chicago: University of Chicago Press, 1966).

Hess, Robert L., 'Italy and Africa: Colonial ambitions in the First World War', *Journal of African History*, 4(1) (1963), pp. 105–126.

Hill, Christopher, 'Radical pirates?', in *The Collected Essays of Christopher Hill: Volume Three: People and Ideas in 17th Century England* (Brighton: Harvester Press Limited, 1986), pp. 161–187.

Hill, Ginny, 'Yemen: Fear of Failure', Briefing Paper, Chatham House (2010), pp. 1–12.

Hill, S. C., 'Episodes of piracy in the eastern seas', *Indian Antiquary*, 48 (1919), pp. 1–159.

Ho, Enseng, *The Graves of Tarim: Genealogy and Mobility across the Indian Ocean* (Berkley: University of California Press, 2006).

Höhne, Markus V., 'Traditional authorities in northern Somalia: Transformation of positions and powers', *Max Planck Institute for Social Anthropology Working Papers*, 82 (2006), pp. 1–28.

Holden, Peregrine and Nicholas Purcell, *The Corrupting Sea: A Study of Mediterranean History* (Oxford: Blackwell, 2000).

Huber, Valeska, *Channelling Mobilities: Migration and Globalisation in the Suez Canal Region and Beyond, 1869–1914* (Cambridge: Cambridge University Press, 2015).

Hubert, Jean-François, *The Art of Champa* (New York: Parkstone Press, 2005).

Hurd, Ian, 'Law and the practice of diplomacy', *International Journal*, 66(3) (2011), pp. 581–596.

Hussain, Nasser, *The Jurisprudence of Emergency: Colonialism and the Rule of Law* (Ann Arbor: University of Michigan Press, 2003).

Hyde, Lewis, *The Gift: Imagination and the Erotic Life of Property* (New York: Random House, 1979).

Imbert-Vier, Simon, 'Afars, Issas ... and Djiboutians: Toward a history of denominations', *Northeast African Studies*, 13(2) (2013), pp. 123–150.
Tracer des frontières à Djibouti: des territoires et des hommes au XIXe et XXe siècles (Paris: Karthala, 2011).

Ingham, Kenneth (ed.), *The Foreign Relations of African States: Proceedings of the Twenty-fifth Symposium of the Colston Research Society Held in the University of Bristol, 1973* (London: Butterworths, 1974).

Ingiriis, Mohamed Haji, 'The history of Somali piracy: From classical piracy to contemporary piracy, c. 1801–2011', *Le Marin du Nord*, 23(3, 4) (July, 2013), pp. 239–266.

Ingram, Edward, 'A preview of the great game in Asia: 1: The British of Perim and Aden in 1799', *Middle Eastern Studies*, 9(1) (1973), pp. 3–18.

Insoll, Timothy, *The Archaeology of Islam in Sub-Saharan Africa* (Cambridge: Cambridge University Press, 2003).

Jones, Jeremy and Nicholas Ridout, *A History of Modern Oman* (Cambridge: Cambridge University Press, 2015).

Oman, Culture and Diplomacy (Edinburgh: Edinburgh University Press, 2012).

Kaplan, Robert D., 'The coming anarchy: How scarcity, crime, overpopulation, tribalism, and disease are rapidly destroying the social fabric of the planet', *The Atlantic* (February, 1994). Available at: www.theatlantic.com/magazine/archive/1994/02/the-coming-anarchy/304670/.

Kapteijns, Lidwien and Jay Spaulding, 'Indian Ocean diplomacy: Two documents relating to the nineteenth-century Mijertein coast', *Sudanic Africa*, 13 (2002), pp. 21–28.

Kechichian, Joseph, *Oman and the World: The Emergence of an Independent Foreign Policy* (Santa Monica: Rand, 1995).

Keene, Edward, 'A case study of the construction of international hierarchy: British treaty-making against the slave trade in the early nineteenth century', *International Organization*, 61(2) (2007), pp. 311–339.

Kemény, Anna Milanini, *La Società d'esplorazione commerciale in Africa e la politica coloniale, 1879–1914* (Florence: University of Milan Press, 1973).

Kempe, Michael, '"Even in the remotest corners of the world": Globalized piracy and international law, 1500–1900', *Journal of Global History*, 5 (3) (2010), pp. 353–372.

Kennedy, David, *Of War and Law* (Princeton: Princeton University Press, 2007).

Khadiagala, Gilbert M. and Terrence Lyons (eds.), *African Foreign Policies: Power and Process* (Boulder: Lynne Rienner, 2001).

Khadduri, Majid, *The Islamic Law of Nations* (Baltimore: The Johns Hopkins Press, 1966).

War and Peace in the Law of Islam (Baltimore: The Johns Hopkins Press, 1955).

Khalileh, Hassan S., *Islamic Maritime Law: An Introduction* (Leiden: Koninklijke Brill, 1998).

Khoury, P. S. and J. Kostiner (eds.), *Tribes and State Formation in the Middle East* (London: I. B. Taurus, 1991).

King, Gillian, *Imperial Outpost – Aden: Its Place in British Strategic Policy* (London: Oxford University Press, 1964).

Kitchen, Kenneth A., 'The elusive land of Punt revisited', in Paul Lunde and Alexandra Porter (eds.), *Trade and Travel in the Red Sea Region: Proceedings of Red Sea Project I 2002* (Oxford: British Archaeological Report International, 2004), pp. 25–31.

Krämer, Gudrun, Denis Matringe, John Abdallah Nawas and Everett K. Rowson (eds.), *The Encylopaedia of Islam, Third Edition* (Leiden: Brill, 2007).

Krasner, Stephen, *Sovereignty: Organised Hypocrisy* (Princeton: Princeton University Press, 1999).

Kuehn, Thomas, *Empire, Islam, and Politics of Difference: Ottoman Rule in Yemen, 1849–1919* (Leiden: Brill, 2011).

Kühn, Thomas, 'Shaping and reshaping colonial Ottomanism: Contesting boundaries of difference and integration in Ottoman Yemen, 1872–1919', *Comparative Studies of South Asia, Africa and the Middle East*, 27(2) (2007), pp. 315–331.

Laitin, David D., *Politics, Language, and Thought: The Somali Experience* (Chicago: Chicago University Press, 1977).

Layton, Simon, 'Discourses of piracy in an age of revolutions', *Itinerario*, 35 (2) (2011), pp. 81–97.

'Hydras and Leviathans in the Indian Ocean world', *International Journal of Maritime History*, 25(3) (2013), pp. 213–225.

Lewis, A., 'Maritime skills in the Indian Ocean', *Journal of the Economic and Social History of the Orient*, 16(2–3) (1973), pp. 238–264.

Lewis, Ioan M., *A Pastoral Democracy: A Study of Pastoralism and Politics among the Northern Somali of the Horn of Africa* (Oxford: James Currey, 1999).

'Dualism in Somali notions of power', *Journal of the Royal Anthropological Institute of Great Britain and Ireland*, 93(1) (1963), pp. 109–116.

Peoples of the Horn of Africa: Somali, Afar and Saho (London: Haan, 1998, first published 1955).

Saints and Somalis: Popular Islam in a Clan-Based Society (Lawrenceville: The Red Sea Press, 1998).

Low, D. A., *Fabrication of Empire: The British and the Uganda Kingdoms 1890–1902* (Cambridge: Cambridge University Press, 2009).

Manawi, Mostafa, *The Ottoman Scramble for Africa: Empire and Diplomacy in the Sahara and the Hijaz* (Stanford: Stanford University Press, 2016).

Mancke, Elizabeth, 'Early modern expansion and the politicization of oceanic space', *Geographic Review*, 89(2) (1999), pp. 225–236.

Manson, Katrina, 'Jostling for Djibouti: Why are the world's superpowers jostling for influence in this tiny, impoverished African state?', *Financial Times* (01/04/2016). Available at: www.ft.com/content/8c33eefc-f6c1-11e5-803c-d27c7117d132.

Margariti, Roxani Eleni, *Aden and the Indian Ocean Trade: 150 Years in the Life of a Medieval Arabian Port* (Chapel Hill: University of North Carolina Press, 2007).

Margariti, Roxani Eleni, 'Mercantile networks, port cities, and "pirate" states: Conflict and competition in the Indian Ocean world of trade before the sixteenth century', *Journal of Economic and Social History of the Orient*, 51 (2008), pp. 543–577.

Marston, Thomas E., *Britain's Imperial Role in the Red Sea Area, 1800–1878* (Hamden: The Shoe String Press, Inc., 1961).

Martin, B. G., *Muslim Brotherhoods in Nineteenth Century Africa* (Cambridge: Cambridge University Press, 1976).

Masters, Bruce, *The Arabs of the Ottoman Empire, 1516–1918: A Social and Cultural History* (Cambridge: Cambridge University Press, 2013).

Mathew, Johan, *Margins of the Market: Trafficking and Capitalism across the Arabian Sea* (Berkley: University of California Press, 2016).

'Smoke on the water: Cannabis smuggling, corruption and the Janus-faced colonial state', *History Workshop Journal*, 86 (2018), pp. 67–89.

Mawani, Renisa and Iza Hussin, 'The travels of law: Indian Ocean itineraries', *Law and History Review*, 32(4) (2014), pp. 733–747.

Mazrui, Ali A., 'Towards abolishing the Red Sea and re-Africanizing the Arabian Peninsula', in Jeffrey Stone (ed.), *Africa and the Sea: Proceedings of a Colloquium at the University of Aberdeen* (Aberdeen: Aberdeen University African Studies Group, 1985), pp. 97–103.

Mbembe, Achille, 'At the edge of the world: Boundaries, territoriality, and sovereignty in Africa', *Public Culture*, 12(1) (2000), pp. 259–284.

McDougall, James, 'The British and French empires in the Arab World: Some problems of colonial state-formation and its legacy', in Sally Cummings and Raymond Hinnebusch (eds.), *Sovereignty After Empire: Comparing the Middle East and Central Asia* (Edinburgh: Edinburgh University Press, 2011), pp. 44–65.

Meeson, Nigel and John A. Kimbell, *Admiralty Jurisdiction and Practice Fifth Edition* (Abingdon: Routledge, 2018).

Meloy, John, 'Imperial strategy and political exigency: The Red Sea spice trade and the Mamluk Sultanate in the fifteenth century', *Journal of the American Oriental Society*, 123(1) (2003), pp. 1–19.

'The privatisation of protection: Extortion and the state in the Circassian Mamluk period', *Journal of the Economic and Social History of the Orient*, 47(2) (2004), pp. 195–212.

Menkhaus, Ken, 'State collapse in Somalia: Second thoughts', *Review of African Political Economy*, 30(97) (2003), pp. 405–422.

Messick, Brinkley, *The Calligraphic State: Textual Domination and History in a Muslim Society* (Berkley: University of California Press, 1996).

Middleton, Roger, 'Piracy in Somalia: Threatening Global Trade, Feeding Local Wars', Briefing Paper, Chatham House (2008).

Miller, Michael B., *Shanghai on the Metro: Spies, Intrigue and France between the Wars* (Berkley: University of California Press, 1994).

Mills, James H., *Cannabis Britannica: Empire, Trade, and Prohibition, 1800–1928* (Oxford: Oxford University Press, 2003).

Miran, Jonathan, 'Mapping space and mobility in the Red Sea region, c. 1500–1950', *History Compass*, 12(2) (2014), pp. 197–216.

Red Sea Citizens: Cosmopolitan Society and Cultural Change in Massawa (Indianapolis: Indiana University Press, 2009). (I)

'"Stealing the Way" to Mecca: West African pilgrims and illicit Red Sea passages, 1920s–50s', *Journal of African History*, 56(3) (2015), pp. 389–408.

Morin, Didier, *Dictionnaire historique Afar (1288–1982)* (Paris: Karthala, 2004).

Munro-Hays, Stuart, 'The foreign trade of the Aksumite port of Adulis', *Azania*, 17 (1982), pp. 107–125.

Newbury, Colin, *Patrons, Clients and Empire: Chieftaincy and Over-rule in Asia, Africa and the Pacific* (Oxford: Oxford University Press, 2003).

Omerod, G. W. Bowersock, *The Throne of Adulis: Red Sea Wars on the Eve of Islam* (Oxford: Oxford University Press, 2013).

Onley, James, *Britain and the Gulf Shaikhdoms, 1820–1971: The Politics of Protection* (Doha: Georgetown University School of Foreign Service in Qatar, 2009).

Panikkar, Kavalam M., *India and the Indian Ocean: An Essay on the Influence of Sea Power on Indian History* (London: George Allen and Unwin, 1946).

Pankhurst, Richard, 'Indian trade with Ethiopia, the Gulf of Aden and the Horn of Africa in the nineteenth and early twentieth centuries', *Cahiers d'Études Africaines*, 14(55) (1974), pp. 453–497.

'The Ethiopian slave trade in the nineteenth and early twentieth centuries: A statistical inquiry', *Journal of Semitic Studies*, 9(1) (1964), pp. 220–228.

'The trade of the Gulf of Aden ports of Africa in the nineteenth and early twentieth centuries', *Journal of Ethiopian Studies*, 3 (1965), pp. 36–81.

Parker, Geoffrey, *The Military Revolution: Military Innovation and the Rise of the West, 1500–1800* (Cambridge: Cambridge University Press, 1988).

Pearson, Michael, *Before Colonialism: Theories on Asian-European Relations 1500–1750* (Delhi: Oxford University Press, 1988).

Pérotin-Dumon, Anne, 'The pirate and the emperor: Power and the law on the seas, 1450–1850', in C. Richard Pennell (ed.), *Bandits at Sea: A Pirates Reader* (London: New York University Press, 2001), pp. 25–54.

Peterson, J. E., *Yemen: The Search for a Modern State* (Abingdon: Routledge, 2016, first published 1982).

Picquart, Agnès, 'Le commerce des armes à Djibouti de 1888 à 1914', *Revue française d'histoire d'outre mer*, 58(213) (1971), pp. 407–432.

Pietsch, Tamson, 'A British sea: Making sense of global space in the late nineteenth century', *Journal of Global History*, 5 (2010), pp. 423–446.

Pogge, Thomas W., 'Sovereignty and cosmopolitanism', *Ethics*, 103(1) (1992), pp. 48–75.

Prange, Sebastian R., 'A trade of no dishonor: Piracy, commerce, and community in the western Indian Ocean, twelfth to sixteenth century', *The American Historical Review*, 116(5) (2011), pp. 1269–1272.

'The contested sea: Regimes of maritime violence in the pre-modern Indian Ocean', *Journal of Early Modern History*, 17(1) (2013), pp. 9–33.

Press, Steven, *Rogue Empires: Contracts and Conmen in Europe's Scramble for Africa* (Cambridge, MA: Harvard University Press, 2017).

Prijac, Lukian, 'Aperçus sur la franc-maçonnerie française à Djibouti de 1911 à 1940', *Pount: cahiers d'etudes: Corne de l'Afrique – Arabie du Sud*, (1) (2007), pp. 101–130.

Ranganathan, Surabhi, *Strategically Created Treaty Conflicts and the Politics of International Law* (Cambridge: Cambridge University Press, 2014).

Reese, Scott, *Imperial Muslims: Islam, Community and Authority in the Indian Ocean, 1839–1937* (Edinburgh: Edinburgh University Press, 2018).

Renewers of the Age: Holy Men and Social Discourses in Colonial Benaadir (Leiden: Brill, 2008).

Reid, Richard, *Frontiers of Violence in North-East Africa: Genealogies of Conflict since c.1800* (Oxford: Oxford University Press, 2011).

Reno, William, 'Redefining statehood in the global periphery', in Eric Wilson and Tim Lindsey (eds.), *Government of the Shadows: Parapolitics and Criminal Sovereignty* (London: Pluto Press, 2009), pp. 130–150.

War in Independent Africa (Cambridge: Cambridge University Press, 2011).

Richards, J. F., 'The Formulation of imperial authority under Akbar and Jahangir', in Muzaffar Alam and Sanjay Subrahmanyam (eds.), *The Mughal State, 1526–1750* (Delhi: Oxford University Press, 1998), pp. 126–167.

Risso, Patricia, 'Cross-cultural perceptions of piracy: Maritime violence in the western Indian Ocean and the Persian Gulf region during a long eighteenth century', *Journal of World History*, 12(2) (2001), pp. 293–319.

Roberts, Richard, 'Law, crime, and punishment in colonial Africa', in John Parker and Richard Reid (eds.), *The Oxford Handbook of Modern African History* (Oxford: Oxford University Press, 2013), pp. 171–188.

Roberts, Richard and Benjamin Lawrence (eds.), *Trafficking in Slavery's Wake: Law and the Experience of Women and Children* (Athens: Ohio University Press, 2012).

Ross, Carne, *Independent Diplomat: Dispatches from an Unaccountable Elite* (Ithaca: Cornell University Press, 2007).

Rubin, Alfred, *The Law of Piracy* (Newport: Naval War College Press, 1988).

Sabet, Amr G. E., 'The Islamic paradigm of nations: Toward a neoclassical approach', *Religion, State & Society*, 31(2) (2003), pp. 179–202.

Samatar, Ahmed I., 'Review of Lewis, I. M., A *Modern History of the Somali: Nation and State in the Horn of Africa*', H-Africa, H-Net Reviews (December, 2003). Available at: www/h-net.org/reviews/showrev.php?id=8552.

Samatar, Said S., *Oral Poetry and Somali Nationalism: The Case of Sayyid Mahammad 'Abdille Hasan* (Cambridge: Cambridge University Press, 1982).

Satia, Priya, *Spies in Arabia: The Great War and the Cultural Foundations of Britain's Covert Empire in the Middle East* (Oxford: Oxford University Press, 2008).

Schoenbrun, David, 'Violence and vulnerability in East Africa before 1800 CE: An agenda for research', *History Compass*, 4(5) (2006), pp. 741–760.

Schuman, Lein Oebele, *Political History of the Yemen at the Beginning of the 16th Century: Abu Makhrama's Account of the Years 906–927 (1500–1521 A.D.)* (Groningen: Druk V. R. B. Kleine, 1960).

Searight, Sarah, 'The charting of the Red Sea', *History Today*, 53(3) (2003), pp. 33–40.

Serjeant, R. B., 'Hadramawt to Zanzibar: the Pilot Poem of the Nakhudha Sa'id Ba Tayi' of al-Hami', in R. B. Serjeant and G. Rex Smith (eds.), *Farmers and Fishermen in Arabia* (Aldershot: Variorum, 1995), pp. 287–306.

   'Maritime customary law off the Arabian coasts', in M. Mollat (ed.), *Sociétés et compagnies de commerce en Orient et dans l'Océan Indien,* Actes du VIIIième colloque international maritime (Beyrouth, 1966) (Paris: Armand Colin, 1970), pp. 195–207.

Sheikh-Abdi, Abdi A., *Divine Madness: Muhammad Abdulle Hassan, 1856–1920* (London: Zed Books, 1992).

   Tales of Punt: Somali Folktales (Macomb: Dr. Leisure, 1993).

Sheriff, Abdul, *Dhow Culture of the Indian Ocean: Cosmopolitanism, Commerce and Islam* (New York: Columbia University Press, 2010).

Shumway, Rebecca, 'Palavers and treaty making in the British acquisition of the Gold Coast colony (West Africa)', in Saliha Belmessous (ed.), *Empire by Treaty: Negotiating European Expansion, 1600–1900* (Oxford: Oxford University Press, 2014), pp., 161–185.

Sicherman, Harvey, *Aden and British Strategy, 1839–1968* (Philadelphia: Foreign Policy Research Institute, 1972).

Smith, Matthew C. and Henry T. Wright, 'The ceramics from Ras Hafun in Somalia: Notes on a classical maritime site', *Azania*, 23 (1988), pp. 15–41.

Smith, Tim Mackintosh, *Yemen: Travels in Dictionary Land* (London: John Murray, 1997).

Spruyt, Hendrick, *The Sovereign State and its Competitors* (Princeton: Princeton University Press, 1994).

Steensgards, Niels, *Carracks, Caravans and Companies: The Structural Crisis in the European-Asian Trade in the Early Seventeenth Century* (Lund: Studentlitteratur, 1973).

Stern, Philip J., *The Company-State: Corporate Sovereignty and the Early Modern Foundations of the British Empire in India* (Oxford: Oxford University Press, 2011).

Stoler, Ann L., 'Colonial archives and the arts of governance: On the content in the form', in Carolyn Hamilton, V. Harris, M. Pickover, G. Reid, R. Saleh and J. Taylor (eds.), *Refiguring the Archive* (Cape Town: David Philip, 2002), pp. 83–102.

Stone, Francine, 'The Ma'azibah and the Zaraniq of Tihama', *New Arabian Studies*, 6 (2004), pp. 132–155.

Subramaniam, Lakshmi, *The Sovereign and the Pirate: Ordering Maritime Subjects in India's Western Littoral* (Oxford: Oxford University Press, 2016).

Subrahmanyam, Sanjay, 'Connected histories: Notes toward a reconfiguration of early modern Eurasia', *Modern Asian Studies*, 31(3) (1997), pp. 735–762.

  Courtly Encounters: Translating Courtliness and Violence in Early Modern Eurasia (Cambridge, MA: Harvard University Press, 2012).

  'Of Imarat and Tijarat: Asian merchants and state power in the western Indian Ocean, 1400 to 1750', *Comparative Studies in Society and History*, 37(4) (1995), pp. 756–763.

  The Mughal State, 1526–1750 (Delhi: Oxford University Press, 1998).

  The Political Economy of Commerce: Southern India, 1500–1650 (Cambridge: Cambridge University Press, 1990).

Tagliacozzo, Eric, *Secret Trades, Porous Borders: Smuggling and States along a Southeast Asian Frontier, 1865–1915* (New Haven and London: Yale University Press, 2005).

Tambiah, Stanley, *World Conqueror and World Renouncer* (Cambridge: Cambridge University Press, 1976).

Thomson, Janice E., *Mercenaries, Pirates and Sovereigns: State Building and Extra-Territorial Violence in Europe* (Princeton: Princeton University Press, 1994).

Tibbetts, G. R., 'Arab navigation in the Red Sea', *The Geographical Journal*, 127(3) (1961), pp. 322–334.

Tilly, Charles, 'War making and state making as organised crime', in Peter Evans, Dietrich Rueschemeyer and Theda Skocpol (eds.), *Bringing the State Back In* (Cambridge: Cambridge University Press, 1985), pp. 169–191.

Touval, Saadia, 'Treaties, borders, and the partition of Africa', *The Journal of African History*, 7(2) (1966), pp. 279–293.

Travers, Robert, 'A British Empire by treaty in eighteenth-century India', in Saliha Belmessous (ed.), *Empire by Treaty: Negotiating European Expansion, 1600–1900* (Oxford: Oxford University Press, 2014), pp. 132–160.

Trüper, Henning, 'Save their souls: Historical telelogy goes to sea in nineteenth-century Europe', in Henning Trüper, Dipesh Chakrabarty and Sanjay Subrahmanyam (eds.), *Historical Teleologies in The Modern World* (London: Bloomsbury, 2015), pp. 117–141.

Tuck, Richard, *The Rights of War and Peace: Political Thought and the International Order from Grotius to Kant* (Oxford: Oxford University Press, 2009).

Um, Nancy, 'Spatial negotiations in a commercial city: The Red Sea port of Mocha, Yemen, during the first half of the eighteenth century', *Journal of the Society of Architectural Historians*, 62(2) (2003), pp. 178–193.

Urbina, Ian, *The Outlaw Ocean: Crime and Survival in the Last Untamed Frontier* (London: Vintage, 2019).

Vink, Markus, 'From port-city to world-system: Spatial constructs of Dutch Indian Ocean studies, 1500–1800', *Itinerario*, 28(2) (2004), pp. 45–116.

'Indian Ocean studies and the "new thalassology"', *Journal of Global History*, 2 (2007), pp. 41–62.

Waal, Alex de, *The Real Politics of the Horn of Africa: Money, War and the Business of Power* (Cambridge: Polity Press, 2015).

Waller, Richard, 'Ecology, migration, and expansion in East Africa', *African Affairs*, 84(336) (1985, pp. 347–370.

Waltz, Kenneth N., *Theory of International Politics* (Reading: Addison-Wesley Publishing, 1979).

Warren, James Francis, *Iranun and Balangingi: Globalization, Maritime Raiding and the Birth of Ethnicity* (Singapore: National University of Singapore, 2003).

The Sulu Zone: The Dynamics of External Trade, Slavery and Ethnicity in the Transformation of a Southeast Asian Maritime State, 1768–1898 (Singapore: National University of Singapore, 1981).

Washbrook, David, 'South Asia, the world system and world capitalism', *Journal of Asian Studies*, 49(3) (1990), pp. 479–508.

Waterfield, Gordon, *Sultans of Aden* (London: John Murray, 1968).

Waterhouse, Francis A., *Gun Running in the Red Sea* (London: Sampson Low, 1936).

Weir, Gary E., 'Fish, family, and profit: Piracy and the Horn of Africa', *Naval War College Review*, 62(3) (2009), pp. 15–29.

Weir, Shelagh, *A Tribal Order: Politics and Law in the Mountains of Yemen* (Austin: University of Texas Press, 2007).

Weldemichael, Awet Tewelde, *Piracy in Somalia: Violence and Development in the Horn of Africa* (Cambridge: Cambridge University Press, 2019).

Wendt, Alexander, 'Anarchy is what states make of it: The social construction of power politics', *International Organisation*, 46(2) (1992), pp. 391–425.

   Social Theory of International Politics (Cambridge: Cambridge University Press, 2012).

Werner, Michael and Bénédicte Zimmermann, 'Beyond comparison: Histoire croisée and the challenge of reflexivity', *History and Theory*, 45(1) (2006), pp. 30–50.

Wesson, Robert G., *The Imperial Order* (Berkley: University of California Press, 1967).

Wick, Alexis, 'Self-portrait of the Ottoman Red Sea, 20th of July 1777', *The Journal of Ottoman Studies*, XL (2012), pp. 399–434.

   The Red Sea: In Search of Lost Space (Berkley: University of California Press, 2016).

Wight, Martin, 'Why is there no international relations theory?', *International Relations*, 2(1) (1960), pp. 35–48.

Wilkinson, John, *Arabia's Frontiers: The Story of Britain's Boundary Drawing in the Desert* (London: I. B. Tauris, 1991).

Willis, John M., 'Making Yemen Indian: Rewriting the boundaries of imperial Arabia', *International Journal of Middle East Studies*, 41 (2009), pp. 23–38.

   Unmaking North and South: Cartographies of the Yemeni Past (New York: Columbia University Press, 2012).

Wills, Jr., John E., 'Review: *Maritime Asia, 1500–1800: The Interactive Emergence of European Domination*', *The American Historical Review*, 98(1) (1993), pp. 83–105.

Wolf, Eric R., *Europe and the People Without History* (Berkley: University of California Press, 1997).

Young, William C., 'From many, one: The social construction of the Rashayida tribe in eastern Sudan', *Northeast African Studies*, 4(1) (1997), pp. 71–108.

Published Primary Sources

Agatharchides, 'On the Erythraean Sea', in Karl Müller (ed. and trans.), *Geographi Graeci Minore: Vol. 1* (Paris: The French Institute of Typography, 1882), pp. 111–195.

Aitchison, Sir Charles (ed.), *A Collection of Treaties, Engagements, and Sunnuds, Relating to India and Neighbouring Countries, Vol. VII, the Treaties Relating to the Bombay Presidency* (Calcutta: Military Orphan Press, 1865).

(ed.), *A Collection of Treaties, Engagements and Sandads Relating to India and Neighbouring Countries, Vol. XIII, the Treaties &c Relating to Turkish Arabia, Aden and South Coast of Arabia, Somaliland, R. Shoa, and Zanzibar* (Calcutta: Superintendent Government Printing, 1909).

d'Albertis, Enrico Alberto, *In Africa: Victoria Nyanza e Benadir* (Bergamo: Istituto Italiano d'Arti Grafiche, 1906).

d'Angremont, 'Le naufrage du «Mei Kong»', *Le Monde Illustré* (28/7/1877). Available at: http://gallica.bnf.fr/ark:/12148/bpt6k6384381v/f7.item (Accessed 12 November 2015).

Anon, 'Suez Canal Traffic', *The Montreal Gazette* (July 2, 1903).

'Sultan of Obbia a Prisoner', *New York Times* (1903). Available at: http://query.nytimes.com/mem/archive-free/pdf?res=FB0B12FF3A5412738DDDAC0894DA405B838CF1D3

The Red Sea and Gulf of Aden Pilot: Eighteenth Edition (London: The Hydrographic Department, Admiralty, 2015).

Baldacci, Giulio, 'The promontory of Cape Guardafui', *African Affairs*, 9, (33) (1909), pp. 59–72.

Bird, James, 'Observations on the manners of the inhabitants who occupy the southern coast of Arabia and shores of the Red Sea; with remarks on the ancient and modern geography of that quarter, and the route, through the desert, from Kosir to Keneh', *Journal of the Royal Geographical Society of London*, 4 (1834), pp. 192–194.

Burckhardt, Johann Ludwig, *Travels in Arabia an Account of those Territories in Hedjaz which the Mohammedans Regard as Sacred* (London: Henry Colburn, 1829).

Cornwallis, Sir Kinahan, *Asir Before World War One: A Handbook* (Oleander, 1916).

Crossland, Cyril, *Desert and Water Gardens of the Red Sea: Being an Account of the Natives and the Shore Formations of the Coast* (Cambridge: Cambridge University Press, 1913).

Cruttenden, Charles J., 'Memoir on the Western or Edoor tribes, inhabiting the Somali coast of N.-E. Africa, with the southern branches of the family of Darrood, resident on the banks of the Webbe Shebeyli, commonly called the River Webbe', *The Journal of the Royal Geographical Society of London*, 19 (1849), pp. 49–76.

'Report on the Mijjertheyn tribe of Somallies, inhabiting the district forming the north-east point of Africa', *Transactions of the Bombay Geographical Society*, 7 (1844–1846), pp. 111–126.

Douin, G., *L'Histoire du règne du Khédive Ismaïl: L'Empire Africain, Vol III, Deuxième Partie: 1869–1873* (Cairo: L'Imprimerie de l'Institut Française d'Archéologie Orientale de Caire, 1938).

Ferrand, Gabriel, *Les Çomalis* (Paris: Ernest Leroux, 1902).

Graves, Lt.-Col. Charles, 'Le Cap Guardafui. Rapport à S. E. Général Stone-Pacha', *Société khédiviale de géographie* 9 (August 1880), pp. 29–45.

Grotius, Hugo, Gwladys L. Williams (trans.), *Commentary on the Law of Prize and Booty* (Oxford: Clarendon Press, 1950, first published, 1608).

Guillain, Charles, *Documents sur l'histoire, géographie et le commerce de l'Afrique Orientale, Deuxième Partie* (Paris: Arthus Bertrand, 1849).

Haines, Captain S. B., 'Memoir to accompany a chart of the south coast of Arabia, from the entrance of the Red Sea to Misenat', *Journal of the Royal Geographical Society*, 9 (1839), pp. 125–156.

d'Héricourt, Charles-Xavier Rocher, *Second voyage sur les deux Rives de la Mer Rouge dans le pays des Adels et le royaume de Choa* (Paris: Arthus Bertrand, 1846).

Hertslet, Sir Edward, *The Map of Africa by Treaty. Vols I–III* (London: Harrison and Sons, 1909).

Hunter, Captain F. M., *An Account of the British Settlement of Aden in Arabia* (London: Trübner, 1877).

Hobbes, Thomas, J. C. A. Gaskin (ed.), *Leviathan, or The Matter, Forme, & Power of a Common-Wealth Ecclesiasticall and Civill* (Oxford: Oxford University Press, 1996, first edition, 1651).

Irwin, Eyles, *A Series of Adventures in the Course of a Voyage up the Red Sea, on the Coasts of Arabia and Egypt... in the Years 1780 and 1781* (London: J. Dodsley, 1787).

J. M., 'L'Affaire de l'«Aveyron»', *Bulletin - Société de géographie commerciale de Bordeaux*, Série II, Annèe VII (1884), pp. 654–658.

Jomard, Edme-François, *Études géographiques et historiques sur l'Arabie, accompagnées d'une carte de l'Asyr et d'une carte générale de L'Arabie* (Paris: Didot Frères, 1839).

Kempthorne, G. W., 'Narrative of a hasty trip to the frankincense country', in George Buist (ed.), *Proceedings of the Bombay Geographical Society, from September 1841 to May 1844* (Bombay: The Times Press, 1844), pp. xxx–xxxii.

Kessel, Joseph, *Fortune Carrée* (Paris: Julliard, 1955).

Kirk, R., 'Report on the route from Tadjoura to Ankobar, travelled by the mission to Shwá, under charge of Captain W. C. Harris, Engineers, 1841 (close of the dry season)', *Journal of the Royal Geographical Society of London*, 12 (1842), pp. 221–238.

Low, Charles Rathbone, *History of the Indian Navy, 1613–1863, Vol. II* (London: Richard Bentley, 1877).

Makin, William J., *Red Sea Nights* (London: Jarrolds Publishers, 1932).

Malécot, Georges, 'Quelques aspects de la vie maritime en Mer Rouge dans la premiere moitié du XIXe siècle', *L'Afrique et l'Asie Modernes*, 164 (1990), pp. 22–43.

Miles, Captain S.B., 'On the neighbourhood of Bunder Marayah', *Journal of the Royal Geographical Society of London*, 42 (1872), pp. 61–76.

Monfreid, Henry de, Guillaume de Monfreid (ed.), *Aventures extraordinaires (1911–1921). Lettres d'Abyssinie. Lettres de la Mer Rouge. Lettres d'Egypte, Arabie, Erythrée, Inde et autres lieux* (Paris: Arthaud, 2007).

Monfreid, Henry de, *Hashish: A Smuggler's Tale* (London: Penguin Books, 2007, first published 1935).

Journal de bord, 1913–1923 (Paris: Arthaud, 1983).

L'escalade: l'envers de l'aventure (Paris: Grasset, 1970).

La Poursuite du Kaïpan (Paris: Grasset, 1934).

Secrets of the Red Sea (London: Faber and Faber, 1934).

Monfreid, Henry de, Helen Buchanan Bell (trans.), *Sea Adventures* (Harmondsworth, England: Penguin Books, 1946, first translated 1937).

Monfreid, Henry de and Ida Treat, *Pearls, Arms and Hashish: Pages from the Life of a Red Sea Navigator* (London: Victor Gollancz Ltd., 1930).

Niebuhr, Carsten, Robert Heron (trans.), *Travels Through Arabia and Other Countries in the East* (Belfast: William Macchie, 1792).

Owen, W. F. W., *Narrative of Voyages to Explore the Shores of Africa, Arabia, and Madagascar, Vol. 1* (New York: J. & J. Harper, 1833).

Parkinson, R. B., (ed. and trans.), *The Tale of Sinuhe and Other Ancient Egyptian Poems, 1940–1640 BC* (Oxford: Oxford University Press, 1997).

Pliny the Elder, Philemon Holland (trans.), *Pliny's Natural History: in Thirty-Seven Books* (London: George Barclay, 1847–1848).

Portenger, Hendrick, R. D. May (ed.), *A Narrative of the Sufferings and Adventures of Hendrick Portenger: A Soldier of the Late Swiss Regiment de Mueron, who was wrecked on the shore of Abyssinia in the Red Sea* (London: Sir Richard Philips and Co., 1819).

Rawson, Sir Rawson W., 'European territorial claims on the coasts of the Red Sea, and its southern approaches, in 1885', *Proceedings of the Royal Geographical Society*, 7.2 (1885), pp. 93–112.

Reclus, Élisée, A. H. Keane (ed.), *Earth and Its Inhabitants: Africa, Vol. IV: South and East Africa* (New York: D. Appleton and Company, 1890).

Révoil, Georges, *La vallée du Darror: Voyage au pays Çomalis* (Paris: Challamel Aîné, 1882).

Voyages au Cap des Aromates (Afrique Orientale) (Paris: Librarie de la société des gens de lettres, 1880).

Rigby, C. P., 'On the origin of the Somali race, which inhabits the north-eastern portion of Africa', *Transactions of the Ethnological Society of London*, 5 (1867), pp. 91–95.

Robecchi-Brichetti, Luigi, *Somalia e Benaadir; viaggio de esplorazione nell'Africa Orientale* (Milan: Carlo Aliprandi, 1899).

Roscoe, Edmund S., *Reports of Prize Cases Determined in the High Court of Admiralty from 1745 to 1859, Vol. 1* (London: Stevens and Sons, 1905).

Salt, Henry, *A Voyage to Abyssinia, and Travels into the Interior of that Country, Executed under the Orders of The British Government, in the Years 1809 and 1810* (London: W. Bulmer and Co., 1814).

Schoff, Wilfred H., (trans.), *The Periplus Erythraen Sea: Travel and Trade in the Indian Ocean by a Merchant of the First Century* (New York: Longmans, Green, and Co., 1912).

Sinclair, Reginald (ed.), *Documents of the History of Southwest Arabia: Tribal Warfare and Foreign Policy in Yemen, Aden and Adjacent Tribal Kingdoms, 1920–1929, Vol. 1* (Salisbury, NC: Documenting Publications, 1976).

Smith, James, Jay Bahadur, Charles Cater et al., 'Report on Somalia of the Monitoring Group on Somalia and Eritrea', Report No. S/2018/1002 (9/11/2018). Available at: http://undocs.org/Home/Mobile? FinalSymbol=S%2F2018%2F1002&Language=E&DeviceType= Desktop. (Accessed 13 January 2020).

Stanton, Col. E. A., 'Secret letters from the Khedive Ismail in connection with an occupation of the east coast of Africa', *Journal of the Royal African Society* 34(136) (1935), pp. 269–282.

Thesiger, Wilfred, 'A Journey Through the Tihama, the 'Asir, and the Hijaz Mountains', *The Geographical Journal*, 110(4/6) (1947), pp. 188–200. *The Life of My Choice* (London: Collins, 1987).

Villiers, Alan, *Sons of Sinbab* (New York: C. Scribner's Sons, 1940).

Wellsted, Lieut. J. R., *Travels in Arabia; In Two Volumes; Vol. 2: Sinai; Survey of the Gulf of Akabah; Coasts of Arabia and Nubia* (London: John Murray, 1838).

Published Treaties, United Nations Resolutions and Case Law

Actes de la Conférence de Bruxelles (1889–1890) (Bruxelles: F. Hayez, 1890).

Charter of the Gulf Cooperative Council (signed 25/5/1981).

United Nations Convention on the Law of the Sea (1982). Available at: www .un.org/Depts/los/convention_agreements/texts/unclos/unclos_e.pdf. (Accessed 18 February 2020).

United Nations Conventions on the High Seas (1958). Available at: http://
    treaties.un.org/doc/Publication/UNTS/Volume%20450/volume-450-I-
    6465-English.pdf. (Accessed 5 June 2018).
United Nations Security Council Resolution 1846 (2/12/2008). Available at:
    www.un.org/press/en/2008/sc9514.doc.htm. (Accessed 5 June 2018).
Masefield AG v. *Amlin Corporate Member Ltd* [2011] 1 Lloyd's Rep 630
    (Court of Appeal, Civil Division).
Owners of the Glengyle v. *Neptune Salvage Co Ltd* [1898] A.C. 519 (HL).
The 'William Beckford' [1800] 165 E. R. 492 (Adm).
Suez Fortune Investments Ltd, Piraeus Bank AE v. *Talbot Underwriting Ltd
    and others* [2018] EWHC 2929 (Comm).

Unpublished Primary Sources

India Office Records, British Library – London, U.K.

IOR R/20/E/2, Minutes of Secret Council, Bombay Government, 4/04/
    1838.
IOR R/20/E/23, File 131, Charles John Cruttenden, 1844, Aden: Report on
    the Myjerthyn Tribe of Somalia.
IOR R/20/E/32, Lt. Cruttenden's Memoir of the Somali tribes. 20/9/1848.
IOR R/20/E/57, Relative to the forcible seizure of the Brig *Telegraph* and the
    expulsion of Master and Crew of that Vessel by the Somalis of the Coast
    near Cape Felix, 1858.
IOR R/20/E/64, Affairs at Berbera, re. wreck of Cruttenden and request for
    thanks to be sent to the Majerteyn Sultan for his hospitality, date
    unknown & Relative to the treaty concluded with the Somali tribes,
    May 1860.
IOR R/20/E/67, Acquisition by France of the Port of Obokh near Aden,
    1862.
IOR R/20/E/69, Engagement with the Sultan of the Mijertain tribe of Somalis
    for the suppression of the slave trade on that coast & Treaties with the
    Naqibs of the ports of Shihr and Mukalla, 1863.
IOR R/20/E/69, Mocha and Obokh: recent visit of Brigadier Coghlan.
IOR R/20/E/83, Purchase of Shaikh Saeed, Bunder, Bab-el-Mandeb, by a
    French-man, 1869.
IOR R/20/E/86, Report by Captain S. B. Miles describing that portion of the
    African coast in the vicinity of Bunder Muryah, the chief port of the
    Mijjerteyn tribe of Somalies, 17/4/1871.
IOR R/20/E/102, Précis of correspondence that has taken place between
    1840 and 1874 on British relations with the African ports in the Gulf of
    Aden, compiled from the Aden Residency records. 1874.

IOR R/20/E/107, Negotiations with H. H. the Khedive of Egypt relative to the Somali coast, 1878.

IOR R/20/E/121, Ratification of Major Goodfellow's Convention with the Majertain Somalis.

IOR R/20/E/123, Political Department, Aden, Notes, Vol. IV, No. 5 of 1884: Mijertteyn Chiefs: Agreement.

IOR R/20/E/122, Somali Coast: Relative to the alleged intention of the Italian Government to annex some port on the African coast.

IOR R/20/E/123, Political Department, Aden, Notes, Vol. IV, No. 5 of 1884.

IOR R/20/E/133, Reported French designs on connection with Sheikh Sa'id on the Arabian Coast, 1882.

IOR R/20/E/134, Regarding the establishment of French Settlement at Sheikh Syed at the entrance of the strait of Bab-el-Mandeb, 1882.

IOR R/20/E/137, Intention of the Political Resident to send his Acting First Assistant to Mukalla and the Somali coast in order to deliver the copy of the Treaty to the Jemadar of Shihr as well as the 500 dollars to the Sultan of Mijertain and to deliver to Sultan 'Uthman Muhammad the copy of the treaty, 1883.

IOR R/20/E/142, The Subjection of the Subaihi Country to the authority of the Sultan of Lahej. Memo. No. 6518, Resident, Aden.

IOR R/20/E/143, Offer made by M. Sautereau to sell the site of a coaling station at Shaikh Sa'id to Her Majesty's Government.

IOR R/20/E/143, Mussa and Aussa Islands – Assertion of British rights to – Regarding Tajoura Affairs.

IOR R/20/E/152, Somali Coast: Ras Hafun: Annexation of Hobbia, a small port some 200 miles south of Ras Hafun by Yusuf Ali Chief of Alula.

IOR R/20/E/159, The Red Sea and Somali Coast – Confidential Printed Papers, 1886.

IOR R/20/E/167, Regarding the establishment of a French penal settlement at Obock.

IOR R/20/E/170, Somali Coast: Restrictions on the trade in arms and ammunition in the Red Sea and on the Somali coasts.

IOR R/20/E/173, Proposed Italian Protectorates over the territories from the Eastern limits of the British Protectorate on the Somali Coast as far as the borders of Zanzibar territories, 1889.

IOR R/20/E/176, Question of a Protectorate Treaty over the Subaihi, 1889.

IOR R/20/A/196, Slave Trade, 1905–1923; Slave Trade between the French and Turkish territories.

IOR R/20/E/236, Aden, Djibouti and Assab: Alleged trade in arms between Djibouti and the ports on the African coast of the Gulf of Aden, 1902.

IOR R/20/E/245, Subaihi attack on Hakim.

IOR R/20/E/297, Salvage Agreements entered into by the Aden Residency with the Attifi and Barhemi Sheikhs, 1911.

IOR R/20/A/512, Vol. 810 Africa, Mijjertain – Agreement concluded between the Sultan and family and Major Goodfellow on behalf of Government for protection of ships wrecked – also extent of territorial jurisdiction.

IOR R/20/A/512, Vol. 810 Africa, Details Respecting Steamer *Vortigern* In Compliance with The Request of The Political Resident, H.M.S. *Daphne* at Aden, February, 1879.

IOR R/20/A/1171, Printed Papers Relating to the Red Sea and Somali Coasts. Red Sea and Somali Coast – Confidential – [section 288] & German Proceedings on the Somali (Mijjerteyn) Coast.

IOR R/20/A/1214, Illicit arms trade,1903–1904.

IOR R/20/A/1221, Illicit Traffic in Arms and Ammunition, 1905. Somaliland Intelligence Report, 5/12/1905.

IOR R/20/A/1280, Somaliland: Restrictions imposed at Aden on dhows belonging to Somalis disloyal to the Somaliland authorities, 1905–1908.

IOR R/20/A/1288, Copies of important correspondence on the subject of arms and ammunition and the political situation, furnished by the commissioner, Somaliland, 1906–1907.

IOR R/20/A/1559, Slave Trade: Slave traffic between Midi and Jeddah.

IOR R/20/A/1300, File No. 11/7, 1905, Subject: Arms and Ammunition – Piracy – Intelligence of Italy Obtained by Britain.

IOR R/20/A/1300, Re the request of the Idrissi to send a British man-of-war to Hodeida to suppress the acts of piracy, 1921.

IOR 20/I/1301, Piracy, Recrudescence of piracy in the Red Sea, Wartime discussions about the Red Sea patrol.

IOR R/20/A/1301, Arms and Ammunition: Piracy in the Red Sea, recrudescence of piracy in the Red Sea, 1920.

IOR R/20/A/2716, Piracy – Re. an act of – committed on the Sambuk al Alawi by the Zaranik tribesmen between Mokha and Taif.

IOR R/20/A/2716, Piracy – re. dhows *Mobashir*, nacouda Mabrook Bakobaira, belonging to Syed Omer bin Jaha Assafi by certain pirates from Sheikh Said.

IOR R/20/A/2716, Complaint of Sheikh Ahmed Fetini Gunaid to the effect that his sambook was attacked and looted by the Imamic soldiers at Salif, 5/12/1925.

IOR R/20/A/2716, Piracy committed by a Zaranik armed dhow on 11th February 1926 North of Loheiya in an Aden dhow owned by Obeid and carrying goods of certain Aden merchants.

IOR R/20/A/2716, Piracy Re. An act of piracy committed on the Sambuk *al Alawi* by the Zaranik tribesmen between Mocha and Taif, 25/09/1922.

IOR R/20/A/2716, Complaint of Mr. Hassan Mohammed Saleh Jaffer, a merchant of Aden, against the Hakhami tribe at Dubab and their chief Sheikh Nasr al Ambari for plundering the Sambuk *Fath al Khair*.

IOR R/20/A/2716, Complaint of Mr. Hassan Mohammed Saleh Jaffer, a merchant of Aden, against the Hakhami tribe at Dubab and their chief Sheikh Nasr al Ambari for plundering the Sambuk *Fath al Khair*.

IOR R/20/A/2716, Mr Antone Chan – Regarding the Commandering of goods of Mr Antone Chan by the Imamic Authorities at Loheiha.

IOR R/20/A/2716, Regarding Petition of Mohamed Hassan Shanfoo, and inhabitant of Kamaran claiming for the recovery of 21 bags of Jawari which were looted from a Loheiya dhow, 18/9/28.

IOR R/20/A/2759, Slave Trade, 1924–1936. Slaves: Re. Capture of boy in Perim by the Assistant Resident of Perim, and sent to Aden, later repatriated to Abyssinia.

IOR R/20/A/2962, Claim of Sheikh Naser Ambari of Sheikh Said against the Turkish government, 1919.

IOR R/20/A/2921, The Preparations made by the Imam of Sanaa for hostilities with Ibn Saud and the Idrissi, 1926.

IOR R/20/A/2965, Blockade [of the Red Sea].

IOR R/20/A/3022, Regarding the departure to Bombay of Motor dhow *el Tair*, Master Monfreid, a French subject who is suspected on gun running.

IOR R/20/A/3038, Zaraniq: Overtures for friendly relations with HM's Government, 1922.

IOR R/20/A/4077, Red Sea Trade Policy, 1915.

IOR R/20/A/4085, Aden Government, War, Foreign and Suspicious Persons – Mons. de Monfreid.

IOR R/20/A/4554, Circulars; Socotra and Kishn, Somali, Subehi, Turks in Yemen.

IOR R/20/A/4923, Hodeida Reports – News, 1918–1920.

IOR R/20/A/4925, Miscellaneous Reports by Hasan Kanfuni Effendi (Political Clerk, Hodieda), 1926–1929.

IOR R/20/A/4926, News Reports from Hassan Kunfuni – Hodeida, 1929–1930.

IOR L/PS/6/526, coll 53/6 Apr. 1863. Correspondence of the Government of India with the Bombay Government regarding the measures taken to obtain satisfaction from the Mijyrteyn tribe of Arabs in Somaliland for their massacre of fifteen sailors belonging to HMS *Penguin*.

IOR/L/PS/12/4090, Slavery and the Slave Trade – Red Sea and Arabia (attitude of Ibn Saud).

IOR/L/PS/12/4088, Slavery and the Slave Trade – Slave Traffic in the Red Sea (Use of Air Patrols).

National Archives/Colonial Office Records – London, UK

NA CO 323/973/9, Colonies, General: Original Correspondence. Drug Smuggling: activities of Henri de Monfried [sic].

NA CO 530/111, Seychelles Original Correspondence. Mons. de Monfried [sic]. In France.

NA CO 535/ 85/ 17, Governor Harold Kittermaster on Somaliland 'Why do the Somalis occupy to-day their present position in the scale of civilization and development?'

NA DO 35/570/5, Convention of St Germain-en-Laye, 1919.

NA ADM 116/928A, Red Sea – piracy and slave traffic, 1902–1905.

NA ADM 116/929, Admiralty Records – Vol. 1 – Somaliland – Operations, 1902–1905.

NA ADM 116/930, Admiralty Records – Operations in Somaliland – Vol. II, dispatches for parliament, 1902–1905.

NA ADM 116/931, Somaliland, Printed Journal of Principal Events, 10 December 1902–30 June 1904.

NA ADM 116/2291, Situation at Jeddah and Red Sea. 1925.

NA FO 2/970. Arms Traffic, Somaliland: Somaliland, Red Sea. Vol. 4. 1903–1905.

NA FO 78/5484, Piracy in the Red Sea, 1902–1905.

NA FO 367/34/102, Arms and Liquor Traffic, Case 622, and The Illicit Traffic in Arms from Somaliland, 1906.

NA FO 367/35, Africa, Arms and Liquor Traffic. 1906. Arms Traffic in the Red Sea.

NA FO 403/83, Further correspondence respecting the Red Sea and the Somali Coast, January-June 1885.

NA L/PS/11/81, Red Sea: piracies in Yemen waters, 1914.

NA MT 23/160/2, Disembarkation of Somaliland delegation at Obbia. Report of the senior Naval Officer. 1903.

State Archives – Rome, Italy

AS Colonia Eritrea Somalia Italiana, File No. 1/3/262 – Buste 454 – Presidenza del Consiglio dei Ministri, 1913.

AS Ministero Interno – Divisione Polizia Politica – Fascicoli Personali – 1927. Pacco 418.

Foreign Office Archives – Rome, Italy

MAESS ASMAI Posizione 59/ Numero 1 – Somalia Settentrionale – 1886–1889, Fasciolo 7, Prottetorato italiano sui Sultanati di Obbia e Migiurtina, 1890. 'Riforma, 24 June 1890'.

MAESS ASMAI Posizione 59/ Numero 2 – Somalia Settentrionale – 1887–1909, Fasciolo 15 – Vaire, 1897–1900.

MAESS ASMAI Posizione 59/ Numero 2 – Somalia Settentrionale, 1887–1909, Fasciolo 25 – Ostilia tra I dui Sultani, Yusuf Ali di Obbia e Osman Mahmud dei Migiurtini. 1899–1901.

MAESS ASMAI Posizione 59/ Numero 2 – Somalia Settentrionale – 1887–1909, Fasciolo 26 – Atti di pirateria dei migiurtini contre pescatori nelle acque di Socotra. 1900–1901.

MAESS ASMAI Posizione 59/ Numero 2 – Somalia Settentrionale – 1887–1909, Fasciolo 28 e 29 – Mission Pastalozza per indicare il Sultan Osma Mahmud con mezzi pacifica a riconocesa il prottetorato, reprimare il contraband d'armi e riconiscenza la . . . situazione special in Alula. Azione punitive contro il Sultan Osman Mohamed e sequestro d'armi. 1901.

MAESS ASMAI Posizione 59/ Numero 2 – Somalia Settentrionale – 1887–1909, Fasciolo 30, 31, 32 – Tentativi di riforma della trattato col Sultan Osman Mahmud, dopo l'azione punitive.

MAESS ASMAI Posizione 59/ Numero 2 – Somalia Settentrionale, 1887–1909, Fasciolo 33 – Nuova convenzione col Sultan Osman Mahmud, 1901–1902.

MAESS ASMAI Posizione 59/ Numero 3 – Somalia Settentrionale – Azione Italiana su Obbia e Migiurinia, 1902–1904, Fasciolo 33 – Nuova convenzione col Sultan Osman Mahmud, 1901–1902.

MAESS ASMAI Posizione 59/ Numero 3 – Somalia Settentrionale – Azione Italiana su Obbia e Migiurinia, 1902–1904, Fasciolo 48 – Rifuito del Sultan Osman Mahmud, 1903–1904.

MAESS ASMAI Posizione 59/ Numero 4 – Somalia Settentrionale – Azione Italiana su Obbia e Migiurtinia, 1904–1908, Fasciolo 57 – I due Sultani protetti di contendono Durbo.

MAESS ASMAI Posizione 59/ Numero 4 – Somalia Settentrionale – Azione Italiana su Obbia e Migiurtinia, 1904–1908, Fasciolo 59 – Progetti di riordinamento del protettorato Italiano. Suggerimenti per l'assetto. Proposte Capello. (1904–1908).

MAESS ASMAI Posizione 59/ Numero 4 – Somalia Settentrionale – Azione Italiana su Obbia e Migiurtinia, 1904–1908, Fasciolo 64 – Bandiera Nazionale ai sambuchi d'Obbia e della Migiurtinia, 1904–1905.

MAESS ASMAI Posizione 59/ Numero 4 – Somalia Settentrionale – Azione Italiana su Obbia e Migiurtinia, 1904–1908 – Fasciolo 81, Istituzione della residenza di Hafun (Salazar, Citerni, Pantano). (1909).

MAESS ASMAI Posizione 60/ Numero 1 – Somalia Settarionale – Traffico d'armi e repression (1897–1903). Fasciolo 1. Traffico e contrabanndo d'armi sulla coste di Obbia e Miguirtina, 1897–1900.

MAESS ASMAI Posizione 60/Numero 1 – Somalia Settarionale – Traffico d'armi e repression (1897–1903). Fasciolo 2 – Azione repression italiana

per sofefesineze il contraband delle armi mediante anche eventuale occu-
pazione di Alula ed altri parti della costa.

MAESS ASMAI Posizione 60/Numero 1 – Somalia Settarionale – Traffico
d'armi e repression (1897–1903), Fasciolo 3 – Commercio delle Arme a
Giubuti, 1901.

MAESS ASMAI Posizione 60/Numero 1 – Somalia Settarionale – Traffico
d'armi e repression (1897–1903), Fasciolo 7 – Cattura di Sambuchi per
contraband d'armi. 1902–1903.

MAESS ASMAI Posizione 60/ Numero 2 – Somalia Settrionale – Traffico
d'armi e repressione, 1902–1910. Fasciolo 9 – Repressione del contraband
d'armi (aprile–giugno) 1902.

MAESS ASMAI Posizione 62/ Numero 1 – Somalia Settentrionale – Naufragi
sulle coste di Obbia e dei Migiurtini (1898–1909) – Fasciolo 1, Nave
Inglese ad Alula per la protezione di un piroscofo naufragato, 1898–1899.

MAESS ASMAI Posizione 62/ Numero 1 – Somalia Settentrionale – Naufragi
sulle coste di Obbia e dei Migiurtini (1898–1909), Fasciolo 3 – Nostro
consenso per disincaglio del vapore inglese *Indra*, naufragato a Ras
Hafun.

MAESS ASMAI Posizione 62/ Numero 1 – Somalia Settentrionale – Naufragi
sulle coste di Obbia e dei Migiurtini (1898–1909), Fasciolo 6 – Naufragio
del piroscofo Tedesco *Astoria* salvaggio missione dello R. Mare Colombo.
1901–1902.

MAESS ASMAI Posizione 62/ Numero 1 – Somalia Settentrionale – Naufragi
sulle coste di Obbia e dei Migiurtini (1898–1909), Fasciolo 7 – Naufragio
dell *Asturia*, 1902–1907.

MAESS ASMAI Posizione 62/ Numero 1 – Somalia Settentrionale – Naufragi
sulle coste di Obbia e dei Migiurtini (1898–1909). Fasciolo 10 –
Naufragio del piroscofo *Chodoc* compenso e medaglio di salvataggio al
Sultan Osman Mahmud, 1905–1907.

MAESS ASMAI Posizione 91/ Numero 3 – Pirateria e Insurrezione –
Avvenimenti (III Trimestre) & (IV Trimestre) – 1904 & Avvenimenti (I
Trimestre) – 1905 – Yemen.

MAESS ASMAI – Archivio Eritrea – Pacco 614 – 1912, Costa Araba,
Vecchio.

MAESS ASMAI Archivio Eritrea – Pacco 941 – Arabie Varie. Politiche
Statistica. Populazione Europea. 1924–1927.

Diplomatic Archives – Paris, France

ADC 63 CPCOM 9 – dossier 1 – Opposition du Gouvernment Anglais a
l'Admission de Henri de Monfreid a Aden, 1918–1919.

ADC 63 CPCOM 9 – dossier 2 – Agissements de M. de Monfreid, Mars 1923–Mars 1929.

ADP – 1815–1896, Sous-serie: Afrique, Erythree, Somalie Italienne, 1872–1895, Côte: ADP1/ 24. *L'Aveyron*: Naufrage au Cap Guardafui.

Archives d'Outre Mer – Aix-en-Provence, France

AOM FM SG Océan Indien OIND/ 22, dossier 117. Charles Guillain, 'Note sur Abd-al-Gouri et la presqu'ile de Raz-Khafoun', 22/3/1848.

AOM FM SG OIND/10, dossier 43 – Mission confiée à M. Guillain commandant de la Corvette *la Dordogne* – 1839–1841.

AOM FM/SG/CFS 6 – dossier 79 – Situation au point de vue de la traite des esclaves.

AOM Fonds Territoriaux/CFS Yemen 3 – Notice Sur L'Enclave de Cheikh Said, 29 Octobre, 1917.

AOM FM 1/AFFPOL/93 – Sheikh Said – 1907–1938 – Schaik Said – divers.

AOM FM 1/AFFPOL/93 – Sheikh Said – 1907–1938 – Demande de concession formée par M. Corbie.

AOM FM 1/AFFPOL/123 – dossier 2 – Organisation de la garde indigène à Djibouti, 1910–1918.

AOM FM 1/AFFPOL/689 – Affaire de contrebande d'armes et munitions à Tadjourah, 4 Octobre, 1913–1920.

AOM FM 1/AFFPOL/696 – dossier ?? – Monfreid, Kessel & Slave Trade – Dossier Judiciare de Henry de Monfreid.

AOM FM 1/AFFPOL/696 – dossier ?? – Traite des noirs, enquête J. Kessel.

AOM FM 1/AFFPOL/696 – dossier 1 & 3 – Traites des Noirs – sa repression, (1902–1923).

AOM 1/AFFPOL 696 – dossier ?? – Traites des esclaves dans la Mer Rouge, Rapports du commandeur du *Diana*.

AOM FM 1/AFFPOL/697 – Affaire de Djibouti – 1932. 'L'Affaire Chapon-Baissac'.

AOM FM 1/AFFPOL/697 – Affaire de Djibouti – 1932. 'Open letter', Pierre-Amable Chapon-Baissac, *La Dépêche coloniale illustrée* , 17/7/1926.

AOM FM 1/AFFPOL/ 698 – dossier 2 – Affaires concernant M. Henri de Monfreid – contrebande de Hachiche, 1923–1924.

AOM FM 1/AFFPOL/698 – dossier P8/1 – Communication des Affaires Etrangères a.s. M. de Monfreid, 1930–1931.

AOM FM 1/AFFPOL/698 – dossier 2 – Affaires concernant M. Henri de Monfreid – expulsion d'Aden.

AOM FM 1/AFFPOL/698 – dossier P8/1 – Execution d'un jugement contre M. de Monfreid, 1932.

AOM FM 1/AFFPOL/698 – dossier P8/1 – Expulsion de M. H. de Monfreid du Territoire Abyssin.

AOM FM 1/AFFPOL/ 698 – dossier P8/1 – Interventions en faveur de H. de Monfreid.

AOM FM 1/AFFPOL/700 – dossier 1 – dossiers individuels – renseignements concernant M. Larivière et ses affronts avec MM de Monfreid et Lamare.

AOM FM 1/AFFPOL/700 – dossier 1 – dossiers individuels – renseignements sur Gregory Arnaud, beau frere de Repici, Del Valle de Paz, M. Larivière et de Monfreid.

AOM FM 1/AFFPOL/3144, Cession d'armes à la Somalie Italienne, 1901.

League of Nations Archives – Geneva, Switzerland

LN, Social and Opium Sections, 1928–1932, Registry File 773 – 12 A/ 61714/24297 – 'Illicit traffic in drugs by M. Henri de Monfreid'.

LN, Registry Files, 1928–1932, Registry File 3120 – 12/11391/157 – Illicit Traffic in Egypt by an Austrian Organisation – 1929–1938.

LN, Social and Opium Sections – File No. O.C. 1118 – Rapport sur les agissmements d'une bande internationale se livrant au traffic illicite des stupéfiants entres quelques pays d'Europe et l'Egypte.

University of St. Andrews, Special Collections, St. Andrews, Scotland

Msdep14/6/6 – Playfair Collection – Robert Lambert Playfair's Private Papers, 1857–1875.

Index

Lightning Source UK Ltd.
Milton Keynes UK
UKHW022138070722
405557UK00004B/39

9 781108 845663